Occasions of Faith

University of Pennsylvania Press
SERIES IN CONTEMPORARY ETHNOGRAPHY
Dan Rose and Paul Stoller, General Editors

Camille Bacon-Smith. *Enterprising Women: Television Fandom and the Creation of Popular Myth*. 1991

Robert R. Desjarlais. *Body and Emotion: The Aesthetics of Illness and Healing in the Nepal Himalayas*. 1992

John D. Dorst. *The Written Suburb: An American Site, An Ethnographic Dilemma*. 1989

Douglas E. Foley. *Learning Capitalist Culture: Deep in the Heart of Tejas*. 1990

Kirin Narayan. *Storytellers, Saints, and Scoundrels: Folk Narrative in Hindu Religious Teaching*. 1989

Sally Ann Ness. *Body, Movement, and Culture: Kinesthetic and Visual Symbolism in a Philippine Community*. 1992

Dan Rose. *Patterns of American Culture: Ethnography and Estrangement*. 1989

Paul Stoller. *The Taste of Ethnographic Things: The Senses in Anthropology*. 1989

Lawrence J. Taylor. *Occasions of Faith: An Anthropology of Irish Catholics*. 1995

Edith Turner, with William Blodgett, Singleton Kahona, and Fideli Benwa. *Experiencing Ritual: A New Interpretation of African Healing*. 1992

Jim Wafer. *The Taste of Blood: Spirit Possession in Brazilian Candomblé*. 1991

OCCASIONS OF FAITH

An Anthropology of Irish Catholics

Lawrence J. Taylor

University of Pennsylvania Press

Philadelphia

Publications of the American Folklore Society
New Series

Elaine Lawless, General Editor

Cover: Woman at the Well of the Holy Women (photo by the author).

Library of Congress Cataloging-in-Publication Data
Taylor, Lawrence J.
    Occasions of faith : an anthropology of Irish Catholics / Lawrence
J. Taylor.
        p.   cm. — (Series in contemporary ethnography)
    Includes bibliographical references and index.
    ISBN 0–8122–3295–X (cloth). — ISBN 0–8122–1520–6 (pbk.)
    1. Catholic Church — Ireland — Donegal (County) — History — 20th
century.   2. Catholic Church — Ireland — History — 20th century.
3. Donegal (Ireland : County) — Religious life and customs.
4. Ireland — Religious life and customs.   I. Title.   II. Series.
BX1506.2.T39   1995
305.6'2041693 — dc20   95-3032
                                                         CIP

10 9 8 7 6 5 4 3 2

For Maeve and Daria

Contents

Figures

Preface and Acknowledgments

"There are two things that people don't like to read about themselves. One of them is lies, and the other's the truth." So publican and sage John Maloney warned me about the Irish reaction to anthropology. His amusing quip has haunted me for the twenty years I have been working in and writing about Ireland. No doubt the book before you is a mixture of the two, in some measure like all our views of one another and ourselves.

What follows is an anthropological exploration of Irish Catholicism in southwest Donegal, the northwestern county of the Island. The problem with most ethnographies of religion, and indeed with similarly focused studies in other disciplines, is that they begin with a definition of religion and then proceed to describe that domain within a particular cultural context. Having described religion, the authors note its varying relations with other domains of human experience and activity. It may have a social function, a psychological function, a conscious political use in domination or revolution. This seems to me to be backward — an excellent way of keeping ourselves from learning anything really important. Rather than begging the question of a universal definition of religion, an ethnographic inquiry is well positioned to explore the particular and specific ways in which "religion" comes to acquire any number of possible shapes — differing in form as well as in content. The very category "religion," as William Cantwell Smith (1963: 15ff.) eloquently argued, came into being at a particular point in western history, in the context of the enlightenment intellectual agenda.[1] To explore Irish Catholicism is to enter into a world — no matter how "folky" or "traditional" — strongly affected by that discourse, itself framed in the general European confrontation between Catholicism and Protestantism. Beyond revealing something of the particular experience of Irish Catholics, I hope to show how religion in general is better understood as a process than as a thing — a product in continuous formation along personal and historical paths.

The work is informed by an anthropology situated — for me, comfortably — between the extremes to which the discipline is being increasingly driven, at least in theoretical pronouncements. That is to say, while I hope to have profited from contemporary insights of a reflexive and critical nature, I have been loath to enter the hall of mirrors and infinite regress (or worse, navel gazing) in which the anthropologist's self-awareness becomes self-absorption. In short, I think that the Irish themselves are interesting, not just what I have to say about — or around — them. Thus I have tried to allow their voices enough space to be heard, and to accord the same respect to my audience, by avoiding needless jargon wherever possible. Nothing is so ironic as an anthropology that pretends to give voice to its subjects only to surround brief snippets of the enticingly open speech with a swirling, impenetrable sea of postmodernisms. To spend years in Ireland and to write like that is to have learned nothing.

Though I began field and archival research specifically focused on religious issues in 1986, my acquaintance with the region goes back to 1973. The descriptions and interpretations that follow are thus based on a rather , extended familiarity with the place and people. I conducted field research in Teelin for three months in 1973 and nine months in 1976, both forays supported by graduate research grants from the State University of New York at Stony Brook, and the intellectual and personal guidance of William Arens. Over the next nine years I made a number of briefer visits to the area, usually with support from Lafayette College. I returned for an extended period of field and archival research in 1986–87, supported by a grant from the National Endowment for the Humanities. I returned once again for the summer of 1989, again with support from Lafayette College, and had the great good fortune to be a Visiting Fulbright Professor at University College Galway and recipient of a Wenner-Gren Research grant in 1992, during which stint I was able to visit southwest Donegal several times again. I am very happy to acknowledge this generous support for the many research ventures that have contributed to the present volume.

Parts of several of the chapters have previously appeared in other forms. In particular, Chapter Four is derived from an article published in *Comparative Studies in Society and History* (Taylor 1985), Chapter Five appeared in similar form in a book edited by Ellen Badone (Taylor 1990a), most of Chapter Six was published in a volume edited by Chris Curtin and Tom Wilson (Taylor 1989a), and parts of Chapters Seven and Eight appeared previously in *Archives de Sciences Sociales des Religions* (Taylor 1990b). Small portions of an article published in a volume edited by Marilyn Silverman and Philip Gulliver (1992a) are dispersed throughout the book. I thank all of these for permission to reprint those sections. The historical photographs come from the Lawrence Collection of the National Library of Ireland in Dublin, whose permission to use them is here thankfully acknowledged. Photographs so marked were taken by Maeve Hickey. Access to folklore archives was much facilitated by Seamus O Cathain of the National Folklore Archive in Dublin, and my translations of stories taken from that source are published with their permission. I am very thankful to Bishop Seamus Hegarty and archivist Father John Silke for access to, and aid in using, the Diocesan Archives of Raphoe. Similar aid was kindly provided by Father Sweeney for the Archdiocesan Archives in Armagh.

A book that has taken this long to write inevitably owes much to very many. Although I have presented much of the book in the form of papers in various venues, I want to take this opportunity to recognize the uniquely interdisciplinary forum provided by the American Conference for Irish Studies, where I have had the rare and invaluable priviledge of the response of literary and historical scholars so vital to an any interdisciplinary venture. Also vital in this regard was the splendid environment provided by University College Galway—much facilitated by the Vice-President Géaroid O Tuathaigh and Dean Tom Boylan. Lafayette College, and my own department in particular, have always provided generous material support as well as an environment conducive to research and writing.

I have also benefited from the critical commentary of friends and colleagues in several countries. Among academics in Ireland I owe a particular debt to Tom Inglis in Dublin, Gearóid O Crualaoich, Joe Ruane, and Willie Smyth in Cork, Desmond Bell in Coleraine; Tom Wilson in Belfast, and Catherine LaFarge, Lionel Pilkington, Sean Ryder, Tadhg Foley, Nollaig McGonagle, Tomás Ó Madagáin, Thomas Bartlett, Nicholas Canny, Gearóid Ó Tuathaigh, Tony Varley, and Ricca Edmonson in Galway and Seán Ó hEochaidh of Gortahork, Donegal. Elsewhere, Jojada Verrips (Amsterdam), and American academics Patrick Hill (who sent me to Teelin), William Christian, James Fernandez, Ivan Karp, Michael G. Kenny, Dick Taatgen, Dan Bauer, Hervé Varenne, Ray McDermott, Patricia Donahue, Eric Ziolkowski, Jill Dubisch, Susan Rogers, Ellen Badone, Jane Schneider, James Donnelly, and Eugene Hynes. Separate and special thanks are due to those who read and critiqued the manuscript: Chris Curtin (sociology, UCGalway), Niall Ó Ciosáin (history, UCGalway), and George Saunders (anthropology, Lawrence University, Wisconsin), whose extensive suggestions proved invaluable. Patricia Reynolds Smith of the University of Pennsylvania Press has been a wonderfully supportive editor. Jackie Wogotz of Lafayette supplied vital secretarial work.

My wife, Maeve Hickey Taylor, also provided an invaluable critical reading of the manuscript, took many of the photographs, and was a constant source of aid in the field, as well as in the thinking out and writing that followed. More subtly and profoundly, her own work has done much to shape my work and life. She is to be thanked as well for putting up with my manias. So too is my step-daughter, Daria, who has been a great source of joy to me and whom I was proud to bring to this wonderful corner of the world.

As I hope is obvious in the text, I owe everything to the people of Teelin and the surrounding area; they have been unfailingly kind and helpful. I hope they will look upon this book as a small tribute to the richness of their place and lives. The names of contemporary locals — except for such public figures as Father James McDyer and those who explicitly requested their real names be used — have been changed to preserve to whatever extent possible their anonymity. To thank particular individuals by name may compromise that intention, but it must be said that this book could not have been written without the aid and inspiration of the late John Maloney — whose wit and wisdom enliven these pages as they did my stay in his country. I also owe a special debt to Phonsey Ward and the Ward family, Enda Cunningham, the late Mickey and Paddy Gally (Gallagher) and Paddy Chondie (Haughey), Hugh and Rose Byrne, Ellen and Mary Ann Ward, Dr. Conal Cunningham, the Pringle family, Hugh and Mrs. Kathleen O'Donnell, Brigid Cannon, Jerry Breslin, and of course many others. *Is é bunadh an pharoiste a chuir an t-ainm dochtuir orm!*

My view of religion, like that of the people I am writing about, is inevitably a product of my own path, my own encountered texts, my own interpretive community. I am not Irish, nor even Catholic, and of course that has a profound effect on what follows. My ability to "understand," in the German sense of *verstehen* is limited. On the other hand, if I am correct in my judgment that there are markedly different ways of being Irish Catholic, then my lack of rootedness in any particular one of them may be crucial to the description of several. I have also been told by Irish colleagues that it is difficult for an Irish man or woman to write about Catholicism without being pulled inexorably by deeply rooted emotions, encompassing everything from uncritical reverence to blinding resentment. I myself do not feel these things when thinking and writing about the Church in Ireland — although I do not find it difficult to see why those raised and living there do. Through the twenty years I have been going to Ireland I have encountered the institutional Church and its representatives in a wide range of guises; there are positions and practices of the Church with which I disagree, sometimes strongly, there are others that I admire, and there are even those that have influenced me over the years, changing my own beliefs and perceptions. My many Irish friends represent the full range of involvements in, and reactions to, the Church, and I must confess to finding their ways of being Catholic, lapsed Catholic, or angry ex-Catholic all plausible. The difficult task I have set for myself here is to write about the Church in its local guises as an anthropologist interested in power, meaning, and the construction of experience, while retaining respect for the beliefs and truths of my Irish hosts and friends. This task is made easier by the fact that I know I do not possess any greater beliefs or truths myself.

Dijon, France

1. Introduction

It was still light when the bus pulled out of Killybegs and headed east over the last range of rugged, stone-scattered, brown hills of southwest Donegal. Before us, gentler, greener lands rolled softly away from the street villages of Dunkineely, Mountcharles, Inver, and Donegal Town. As we turned north into the broader road that leads through Barnesmore Gap and on toward Derry, the women's chatting began to subside. They had been talking, as they would at any social gathering, of family matters. The sky darkened and Fiona, the young woman who had organized the trip, sent word forward that the rosary would now begin. With the smoothness of habit, young and old fished beads from handbags and launched into the first five decades.[2] "Hail Mary full of grace . . ." rose from the back rows of the bus and then the response "Holy Mary, Mother of God . . ." resounded from the front. Ten decades, glorious and sorrowful, brought us through the more prosperous looking east Donegal market towns of Ballybofey and Stranorlar, across into the diocese of Derry and, finally, through the gates of Castlefinn parish churchyard.

Our destination was a *Healing Mass* — a recent Charismatic Catholic addition to the regional religious scene that had for some time been drawing minibus-loads to its well advertised monthly sessions. It was the first of several such voyages for me. I was the lone stranger and, in fact, the sole male among twenty-odd women, ranging in age from early twenties to mid-sixties. I met the organizer, Fiona, only a few days before. An almost eerily pallid young woman, she had been welcoming enough, but distanced by what seemed a practiced serenity and a self-conscious religiosity. She and her older colleagues, Margaret and Mary — who wore their new faith more lightly than saintly Fiona — had made several pilgrimages to Medjugorje, the Bosnian village where the Virgin Mary was believed to appear nightly to a group of teenagers. By their account, they had been transfigured by the experience and had decided to follow "Our Lady's" request that her followers "pray and fast." Accordingly, they had organized a small prayer group, which had been meeting weekly in Margaret's house for more than a year.

Map of Ireland showing County Donegal

COUNTY DONEGAL
showing diocesan boundaries

Figure 1. Map of Donegal.

There were about a dozen such groups — generally linked to the "Charismatic Renewal" — in the diocese of Raphoe and many more in the neighboring (and more sophisticated) diocese of Derry. Most were located in the small market towns: central places for the various islands, peninsulas, and mountain fastnesses that comprise the greater part of the region. Our bus had originated in one such town, Killybegs; others came from similar points to the north — Dungloe, Ardara — each following its own path through other mountain passes bound for the same destination (see Figure 1).

Yet, in another sense, the women around me were coming from, and hence going to, significantly different places; different religious experiences. There were the born-again charismatics like Fiona, Mary, and Margaret, for whom this monthly voyage was now a regular feature of extraordinarily ample religious lives that included every possible Church devotion along with the weekly prayer meetings. The voyage was different for Kathleen, another middle-aged, middle class woman on the same bus. Although punctilious in her weekly Mass attendance, Kathleen considered prayer meetings and the like "over the top" — emotionally excessive and doctrinally suspicious fanaticism. For her, the excursion to the Healing Mass was the latest in a series of social-religious outings, typically to more established religious shows such as a Vigil at Knock (a Marian shrine in County Mayo, Ireland, and the most popular pilgrimage destination on the Island) or the *parish mission* conducted every other year in her own village by a team of priests of the Redemptorist order. Kathleen might well bring her personal "intentions" (prayers for cures, good luck in upcoming events, forgiveness, etc.) to any such occasion. While possibly seeking a cure for her persistent arthritis, she was not anticipating a reconstruction of self of the sort Fiona and her cohorts were experiencing. Then there was Una — still a young woman though already squat and kerchiefed — who had come down into town from a mountainy farm in the next parish west. For her, the attraction was not the Mass itself, but the presiding priest, Father McLafferty. Raised with stories of the miraculous curing power of certain priests — alcoholic, "silenced" (removed from the pulpit by the bishop), or otherwise peculiar — Una had heard that this strange cleric from the North might be possessed of "the cure." She sought his efficacious touch and prayers.

*   *   *

This book is an exploration of Irish Catholicism through an ethnography of the historical and contemporary shape and texture of that religion in one corner of the Island nation. The opening vignette, a bus ride to which we will return in the penultimate chapter of the book, is offered here as an orientation, conveying an immediate sense of the "feel" of local religion and of the aims and methods of the ethnography before you. Charismatic prayer groups and Healing Masses are not common, and hardly typical of Catholicism in Ireland, not even in this corner of Donegal. Yet in other respects this bus ride is an apt introduction to the character of local life, the nature of religion as both lived experience and institution, and — not least — the ethnographic act.

The bus ride serves as a metaphor for the personal and social construction of experience, and for the changing shape of the terrain and one's life. In another sense, however, it is more than a metaphor, for it is often the bus in its absolute mundane reality that takes individuals and groups from one occasion to another, from one experience to another. Anthropologist or local, in this part of the world one often takes a bus: not only the government run buses, which wend their infrequent and expensive way between towns and villages, but more often and more memorably the independently owned buses of rural entrepreneurs who both respond to and promote a demand for travel to specific events. In the countryside such excursions are more frequent than one might imagine. There are dances, fairs, shopping and hospital trips, and also "religious occasions."

An anthropological account of local religion begins not with a *religion* as definitive, theological texts define it, nor even a list of beliefs, but rather with people — like Fiona, Kathleen, and Una — acting, thinking, and speaking in a real if always contingent world. We will follow them and others, visiting, in the course of our explorations, holy wells, churches, and pilgrimage sites: fixed, or apparently fixed, places. Yet it is appropriate and instructive to start off with a bus ride — with real people, similar and different, in motion across a landscape. For religion — as this book will attempt to argue and illustrate — is not a thing but a process. Or rather a concatenation of processes, personal and historical.

On the personal level, in Ireland, the journey itself matters enormously, not only the movement, the time spent in transit, but the landscape over and through which one passes. That landscape, as we will see, is pregnant with meaning: the anchor of personal and collective history, the material with which local, regional, or national identity is constructed. And then there is the talk — the mantric litany of the rosary so easily conjoined to the constant exchange of social detail and even to the ever-welcome amusing narrative. Like the landscape to which it is frequently attached, talk frames and shapes the character and meaning of experience, the commonality, and occasionally the distance among the people speaking and listening. So the bus ride itself is a religious event which, like all such events, plays a role in the formation of individual and collective experience.

Yet the same bus ride might be part of another process, unfolding in historical rather than personal time. The Charismatic Renewal movement began in the United States in the 1960s, came to Ireland soon after, and, though at first successful, had already started to decline when the Marian apparition at Medjugorje in 1981 began to attract particular attention from charismatics. The Healing Mass is a regional manifestation of a miracle-centered regime that in turn helps sustain the fervor of the local cells — the prayer groups. This too is religion: a set of institutions that exercise power not only on individual belief but in such larger domains as national social and political life. My hope is to make use of a series of historical and contemporary "occasions" — singular and repetitive events, texts, journeys — to reconnect these aspects of religion, to discover a point from which the intimate world of experience and meaning and the broad sweep of historical formations of power are both clearly visible. Such occasions will also serve as points of entry, for the reader as they were for the ethnographer, into this rich and changing world. The aim of these forays is an anthropology of Irish Catholicism that, although mainly "local" in focus, sheds a different sort of light on Irish Catholicism in general than have other disciplines. In so doing, however, I hope also to contribute to the anthropology of religion, using the Irish case study to explore ways in which often divergent theoretical perspectives and disciplinary approaches can be better integrated.

In a book that argues that one's interpretive framework is a product of both historical process and personal experience, the anthropologist cannot himself be exempted. My focus on religious matters, though clearly made possible by a personal interest in this dimension of human life, is to some extent a product of my fieldwork experience. My initial research interest was decidedly different. I came to this part of Ireland first in 1973 in order to study the social and economic aspects of fishing. Perhaps, after all, it is possible to learn something in the course of ethnographic fieldwork, to see something one was not looking for, to hear something one was not listening for. So I believe, which is why I will turn now to a brief account of my experience in the region, before returning at the end of this chapter to a consideration of theory and methods. In addition to enabling readers to understand my own path to the topical focus of this book, it will introduce them — as I was — to the place and people, providing a more general social and cultural context for understanding the more narrowly focused events described and analyzed in the rest of the book.

*   *   *

My entrance into southwest Donegal was also on a bus, in June 1973, fourteen years before the Healing Mass excursion. A first-year graduate student, I had come to Ireland in search of an Irish speaking fishing community in which I might eventually do my dissertation fieldwork. On the basis of my reading, and at the advice of an Irish-American friend, I set my bearings for southwest Donegal and a community called Teelin, a hundred households nestled along the eastern base of the mountain, Slieve League. Although I had successfully hitchhiked from Dublin to Galway, and then up the west coast from there, I waited long enough on the quieter Donegal roads to give in and take the provincial bus. The ride west from Donegal Town was the first lesson in local geography. The main road ran through easy green pasturelands grazed by cattle or left in meadow for hay, until one passed through the little, but busy fishing port of Killybegs. Once west of that town, the ground was immediately steeper and browner and the fields rockier. The cattle gave way to sheep. As I would later discover, this surface pattern corresponded to a change in the underlying rock, from the calcite that runs through the entire middle of the country, making so much of Ireland famously green, to the ancient granitic rocks of much of the wild west coast. In this division between east and west — and in other respects as well — Donegal is a microcosm of the whole island.

The bus let me off in Carrick, a small street town in the parish of Glencolumbkille (see Figure 2) from which I set off on foot along the Teelin road, whose narrow tarmac headed south alongside the Glen river, a fast running rock-strewn stream from which German tourists liked to pull the odd salmon. A two mile walk brought me into the "center" of Teelin: an apparently defunct pub with the faded legend, "Slieve League Bar" above padlocked doors, several tiny cottage-front shops, and a post-office grocery store. By this point the stream had widened into a small river, whose several hundred yard expanse separated Teelin from the parish of Kilcar to the east. On both sides of the river, fields heavy with hay or neatly rowed with white-flowered potato plants swept down to the water. But the houses on the Teelin side were closer to the river, and its people — to judge by the activity along the shore — clearly more interested in it.

Having found the one family who did "bed and breakfast," I left my pack and strolled down the remaining mile of the road toward Teelin pier. The river had opened into a small bay, protected from the sea by massive rock formations jutting out beyond the pier. On the placid bay waters bobbed a dozen or so rowboats, each with five or six men sitting quietly, calmly chatting and staring in various directions across the surrounding waters. A massive concrete pier seemed to belong to another era when more or larger vessels sought shelter in this harbor. Further testament to a more active, recent past were the striking ruins of the British coast guard station

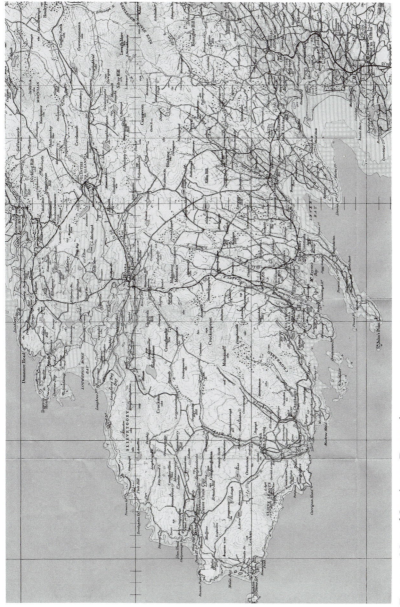

Figure 2. Map of Southwest Donegal.

overlooking the harbor. The waterfront was clearly less productive now; besides the rowboats on the estuary, only three half deckers — fishing boats in the thirty to forty foot range — were moored there. To the west, the land swept up the mountain, with the houses arrayed along the main road or else along the lanes that led up the slopes. The nearly treeless land formed a natural arena; virtually every house commanded a clear view down to the bay. I joined a group of several men positioned in and around an old car poised on the roadside. They mumbled greetings and, while continuing a sporadic *sotto voce* conversation, kept their eyes fixed on the boats below.

At this point I noticed that each boat held not only a crew but a net piled in the stern, from which a line led out of the boat. The other end of this line rested in the hands of another man, sitting or leaning against a rock on the shore. It seemed an odd way to fish. After an hour or so, their patience — and mine — was rewarded with activity. Immediately below us one boat's crew came to life. Oars shot out and two men began to row furiously out and around a stretch of churning water while two others paid out the net. The shore man held his line taut so that the end of the net remained stationary as the rowers traced a large circle in the water, eventually returning to their starting point and closing the net. The fifth man — actually a young teenage boy — stood aft, furiously hurling small rocks into the gradually disappearing opening, herding the fish into net. The net closed and all hands began dragging it and its slithering contents into the boat. Several dozen salmon flashed silver in the sun, to the restrained but still apparent delight of the crew. Up on the bank, the men beside me were hardly less interested themselves. Their riveted eyes counted each flash. So did the men in the other boats. And so, I discovered as I looked up the hills behind me, did many others. Several hundred yards up a mountain lane, a man had put his spade aside and was now emerging from his cottage armed with binoculars. He too would know the count. Back on the river, the successful crew had finished their haul, and another pantomime began. Without word or gesture, they began to row away from the spot they had occupied toward a place just vacated by another crew. All over the bay, boats were criss-crossing, taking each other's spots, and all without comment or conflict. The rotation completed, the opening scene was re-established: a dozen boats with nets aboard, watchful crews, and waiting spectators. It seemed like a good place to do anthropology.

I spent that summer in Teelin and in the course of the following weeks I met many of the locals, particularly the fishermen. However, staying at a

"B&B," even for the whole summer, made me a tourist, if an especially inquisitive one. I haunted the riverside and the pubs — up the road in Carrick as well as the Slieve League bar in Teelin, which, I eventually discovered, was in fact open to those who knew how to get in. Thus it was the public, and predominantly male, face of the community I knew first.

*   *   *

> "I hear you'll be stayin' with us for a while. Maybe you'd want to put down some potatoes. . . . I'll show you how to lay them down."

The offer came from my neighbor, a seventy-year-old man called Francie Gallagher, and was of course a delight to the anthropologist's ear. It was early March 1976, nearly three years after my first summer in Teelin and we stood in the field before my cottage in Rinnakilla — "the division of the church" — the seamost townland (a kind of rural neighborhood within the larger settlement) in Teelin. I had returned to Ireland that January, spending two months in a Dublin "bed-sit": days in the archives, evenings in an intensive Irish language class (which would continue informally into the small hours in the Gaelic Club basement bar). Returning finally to Teelin, I had stayed for a few weeks a couple of miles up the road in a henhouse quasi-adapted for summer guests while waiting for this cottage to become available. Perhaps the henhouse was all right in the summer, but it had been early March and a battering hailstorm shook me from my first night's sleep.

It was with relief and excitement that I took up occupancy in what I was to think of as "mildew haven," though to all locals it was still named for its last proper inhabitant *toighe* (house) Jimmy Phaddy." (see Figure 3) The house was the standard local cottage, a stone rectangle with a central kitchen, and a bedroom to each side. An outshot bathroom had been added, as had electricity, probably in the late 1950s or soon after, when such modern luxuries reached this corner of Ireland. Like most older cottages — as distinct from the modern cinder-block "bungalows" that were then just beginning to be built in the area — Jimmy Phaddy's house was sited for shelter rather than a view. The back of the house nestled deeply into the steep hillside, squatting beneath the winds that howled down the mountainside like freight trains in the autumn and winter. If it evaded the wind by being built into the earth, the cottage was permanently wet. A constant fire in an open hearth or castiron range would have fought back the damp, but

Figure 3. *Toigh* Jimmy Phaddy, Rinnakilla (photo by the author).

it was a long time since Jimmy had lived in the house. The damp was overpowering, and no amount of fuel burnt in the tiny fireplace, even aided by electric space heaters, made much headway against the mildew.

But such inconvenience now seemed unimportant in the face of Francie's visit and his offer to help with my garden. We were standing in the only bit of land before the cottage that was not in meadow for hay. I was of course thrilled at the visit of a neighbor and more so at the prospect of instruction. Francie fetched a spade, put the implement into my hand, and directed my clumsy attempts until I had finished several wiggly, roughly parallel lines of mounded earth — "lazy beds" — into which I would later entrust my measly crop of potatoes and some carrots and onions. My small garden took little of my time, and I watched with awe as my neighbors dug row after beautiful row, perfectly spaced lines following the contours of the land to allow the superabundant waters to drain off. The arable land was only inches deep, a thin carpet of peaty, acidic soil laid down by the last glacier on granitic bedrock that let no water in. The annual two to three meters of rainfall had nowhere to go, and with no drainage the earth was like a damp sponge in which the potatoes, if not properly drained, would rot. The beds — so straight as to look machine made though every one was done by hand with a spade — began sprouting green plants that leafed and then flowered, but only with constant tending: fertilizing and spraying against blights. The potatoes took up only one of the five to seven acres that comprised most farms in the townland. Other fields were left in meadow, which would be allowed to grow until cut for hay in June. The remainder of the land, half or more of most individual farms as well as thousands of acres of communal ground stretching up and over the mountain, was in rough pasture of grass, gorse, and heather. There were not many animals in that section of Teelin. Some sheep roamed out of sight at the edge of the mountain; the two or so cows that most families kept found enough grass on the rough pasture through the long spring and summer, and the small field of hay was sufficient for the winter.

Thus the average household provided itself with enough potatoes, milk, and butter for the year, and an unruly mob of wandering chickens gave eggs. It was hard to do more with the land, though at least one man tried. The few acres of rough pasture behind my own cottage were fenced off and let as grazing to a Kerryman who had married a local woman in New Zealand and then followed her back to this spot. He had seven cows on the patch of steep and stony ground: evidence by his lights of enterprise, but from the local perspective of folly. Francie would often comment on the poor ratio of grass to cows — and the animals themselves, it must be said, agreed. Among their number was a particularly assertive representative of a French breed, Charolais — "Charlies" they called them there — who would rake up the bottom of the wire fence with her horns and dig out the soft earth beneath like a dog — while her companions stood by and watched in dumb admiration. They followed her through the hole to freedom — which meant a roll through my garden, lunch in the meadow, an unannounced visit in my kitchen, and even, once — as Francie and I stood and watched in some amazement — a stroll to the pier, where they lined up as if waiting for a ferry that could take them to greener pastures. As a Clare woman said one night in the pub, taking the prize in a round of good-natured intercounty rivalry, "Donegal...is it? There's the place where they shear the horns off the cows so they can get the bit o' grass from between the rocks."

Then there was the bog — several miles to the west — where townland neighbors were neighbors again, in sections allotted to households as "turbary rights," a traditional claim to peat cutting recognized even under British landlords. By the mid-1970s, a new machine had only just begun to work in the region, sucking the wet turf from the ground and extruding long, rounded worms left in tangled piles to dry in the sun. However, by far most men — for the bog was generally a male preserve — "saved" the turf in the ancient manner, slicing blocks of wet peat and tossing them over their shoulders in a neat repetitive motion that produced a pile of shiny black bricks and another row of diagonal lines like brushstrokes in the earth. The newly cut blocks would then be "footed" — leaned up against one another in small groups to dry, with the help of God and good weather — then stacked and eventually hauled back home, where they were again piled in a great and always neatly arranged stack convenient to door and hearth. When the weather was fine, work in the bog was deemed enjoyable — an occasion for joking and communality over campfires and pots of tea. In this manner most families provided for their heating fuel, and for those who still cooked on the cast iron range and had not yet purchased a modern gas version, their cooking fuel as well.

A calf would be sold in the mart each year, but beyond that there was not much in the way of agricultural surplus. Nor did the garden and field provide all a family needed in the way of food, far from it. Women trudged up and down the road to one of several tiny local shops daily, and into the larger shops three miles away in Carrick on Sunday after Mass for their "messages" of bread, meat, tea, tobacco, sugar, tins, and — through the 1970s and 1980s — an increasing variety of exotic foodstuffs. For these and the other expenses of life — electricity, housing repairs, gadgets, necessities, bingo, and drink — other money was needed and was gotten, as it had been for more than an hundred years, through "little bits," a range of supplemental (but sometimes main) incomes from fish factories in nearby Meananeary and Killybegs and knitting mills in Kilcar. Fishing, though far from the major source of income it had been in years gone by, was still important to several families in the townland. Women knitted, usually on consignment from one of several shopowners who catered to the tourist trade. James "the Weaver" or Mickey Gara would drop off the wool — in whichever colors were selling — and pick up the finished product. At that time a finished sweater earned the knitter four or five pounds, for anything from one to two week's "spare time" work. Now the rate is several times that, but the price of everything else has gone up accordingly. Some of these women were acknowledged, even by outsiders, to be among the best in Ireland — indeed one of their number had, years before, won a contest open to knitters throughout the British Isles: the prize, to contribute to the trousseau of the present Queen Mother. Finally, there was government assistance: the old age pension and the ubiquitous "dole" for the un- or underemployed, a fit description of very many in the region.

This mix of incomes varied even through Teelin and the region, not only from family to family but more significantly by "zone." The distinctions were well put by the observant manager who had come from Dublin to run the fish processing factory in Meananeary.

> When I first came here I had terrible trouble in the plant. Workers were always missing or taking their holidays, but not returning for another several weeks beyond the two. You see, I didn't understand what was going on here, but I caught on eventually, and now I see that the people come in three kinds: those of "the water," those of the "mountain," and those of "the good land." The first want to stay away when the salmon are in season, and the second when they must take care of the sheep, and the third group — those who have a bit of good land — for the crops.

An unusually understanding plant manager, he adapted his production to local habits — scheduling for the respective agricultural routines rather than demanding the industrialization of his workers. Such differences could be noted even within Teelin, for in the more mountainy townlands there were bigger, but rougher farms, and families tended to keep far more sheep (increasingly for the Irish and European Community subsidy rather than for the market value of the animals or their wool). But the more marked differences were sub-regional. Teelin as a whole was known by the sobriquet "Teelin of the Fish," and there were men from every townland engaged in the fishery. Better farmland was found across the estuary in parts of Kilcar and in a few other spots within the parish. To the north of Carrick and beyond was the mountainy land where sheep were kept in great numbers. A favorite Teelin song celebrated the differences. "*Bríd Bhan*," "White Brigid," tells of the marriage of a Teelin woman with a mountainy man some generations ago. Alternate verses describe the unique pleasures and beauties of bay and mountain — the glorious leap of the silver salmon contrasted with the dew-soaked meadows. The song gives some idea of the perceived differences of life and experience — and also of place, as well as casting some doubt on assumptions about the practical, non-aesthetic perceptions of people who wrest a difficult living from the land.[3]

The other townlands of Teelin I would come to know over the ensuing months, and some of them years later on return sojourns, but the spring and summer of that year were spent mostly in the company of my neighbors in the townland of Rinnakilla. As Francie's visit announced, I was now a

householder, no matter how much of a "blow-in." Accordingly, I was generally welcomed, and by some encouraged, to enter into the reciprocal life of
the "town," a kind of rural neighborhood of which Teelin had seven. Em-
boldened by Francie's visits I soon realized that while I was not going to be
invited into my neighbors' homes — I was nevertheless welcome, even expected, there. As the weeks went by I eventually gave up the annoying habit
of knocking — which only inconvenienced householders by requiring them
to come to the door — and fell into the local pattern of announcing my
presence with a greeting as I entered. Inside, in terms of both family and
decor, each was caught at a different moment in the cycle of either domestic
life or national change — sometimes both.

Across the road from me was the home of Kathleen and Conal Phaddy.
Conal was about seventy and his wife somewhat younger. He had been a
younger, non-inheriting son in his own house and, to translate the local
phrase, "found himself a landed woman" — married into a family with only
daughters — in the event just across the road. Having married relatively late,
he and his wife had had time for only a son and a daughter, both around
twenty years of age when I met them. Father, mother, and children lived
along with two of the wife's older unmarried sisters. The lineal descent
of the household on Kathleen's side was preserved in the local habit of
naming: the young son Sean was known as Sean Kate, or Sean Kate Francie, rather than Sean Conal Phaddy. The whitewashed stone cottage was
crowned by the most brilliant gold thatch in the district; one often heard
tourists slowing their cars outside for "snaps."

It was a home in which I spent a great deal of time, though only in the
kitchen. A vintage Stanley no. 9 range stood splayfoot in the alcove that
once housed the open fire. Most evenings the trap door in the front of the
range hung open, revealing a row of vertical bars like dragon's teeth, and
behind glowed the inevitable fire — constant stoking kept an even glow and
rather intense heat, through weather hot, cold, or mild. On top of the stove
some five or six battered tea kettles were constantly shuffled: the supply of
hot water for the household.

But already the seat of honor was no longer next to the fire, but on the
edge of the leatherette sofa closest to the television. If not otherwise engaged, all the women of the house would be ranged about in their various
chairs — leaning toward the screen while their needles pushed wool into the
complex patterns of hand-knit sweaters. The television would be turned
on for the six o'clock news, but the Irish station preceded that with the
Angelus — televised church bells chimed as a rendition of Our Lady of

Perpetual Succour appeared on the screen. Knitting needles froze in mid-stroke and tongues in mid-sentence as everyone mumbled their "Hail Marys" through the ringing of the bells. My own eyes might rise at this point to take in the array of religious objects and pictures that adorned the wall of this — and nearly every other — kitchen. There was the Sacred Heart of Jesus, a print of Jesus with an open chest exposing a large heart encircled by a crown of thorns under which a small red electric bulb always glowed. For several generations it had been the custom, whenever a new home was built, to have it blessed by the priest and to light a candle — latterly the electric version — beneath this holy picture. Other pictures and small figures included what I would discover to be the usual run of Marian images — taken from the popular apparition sites at Lourdes or Fatima — and the widely popular Infant of Prague, Jesus as a young child adorned in royal costume. At certain moments, such as during the Angelus, during family rosaries (said nightly in some households), at "stations" (in this use of the word, masses held by the priest in the home, a traditional practice recently revived by some priests), and most profoundly at death, when the deceased would be "waked" in the bedroom, the religious character of the house was apparent.

Most often, of course, here as everywhere, the conversation was thoroughly secular, concerned with the progress of farmwork, the fate of the fishery, and especially the ongoing performance of local society. No movement, no passage of persons known or unknown through the townland, was beneath notice and comment. "There's Sean down to his mother. . . ." "A Ger-a-man goin' fishin', there's a terrible lot of visitors the year. . . ." The occasional anomaly — a battered white van with a Northern Irish license pulling up by some household — would set off a series of speculations that would end with utter conviction, "That would be the husband of Mary Kate's daughter, what moved away to the North." Sometimes the TV held sway–"the TV killed the conversation" (to translate the local slogan) — but I couldn't help thinking that the engagement with such popular American detective show reruns as Kojak or Columbo wasn't far off the traditional attitude toward an exciting story. Conal, Kathleen, and the others would interact with the narration as with that of a storyteller (*seanchaidh*), leaning forward in tense anticipation and entering into the scene — "Now boy, he's waitin' for you in there...now!"

Francie, my "agricultural instructor," lived immediately next door to me with his wife Maggie, his grown son, the son's wife, and the young couple's two small daughters. This classic "extended stem family" was in fact unique in the townland, and rare in Teelin.[4] Most of Francie's children had left the area and indeed Ireland, but one son had married across the bay into the next parish, and Colm, the eldest, had brought his wife home, probably because he led the relatively unusual life of a deep-sea fisherman, out on the water for weeks at a time. So his wife, who was also unusual in coming from three parishes to the east, was left at home with her in-laws to raise her daughters. As one might expect of a home with a young family in it, Francie's and Maggie's house was a a bit more modern than Conal's. But the core arrangement was the same — seats around the blasting range, Sacred Heart on the wall.

Most old fashioned and simple were the homes of what might be called "remnant" households — normally a lone bachelor or spinster, sometimes a pair of siblings — widowed or never married, living alone in their homes. None was alone for very long, for the neighbors constantly dropped in on one another, rarely staying long but keeping up a constant round of to-ing and fro-ing. The bachelors tended to visit more than to receive guests; their own accommodations might be rather spare. Sometimes the arrangements were formalized, as with the ninety-one-year-old woman nicknamed "Mary Kelly" who lived on the other side of the Gallaghers, and whom they watched over and kept in fuel. Mary lived in what was the most archaic house in Teelin. Alone among dwellings I visited there, her cottage had no iron range, and all cooking and heating was done in a great open hearth, in which she burned peat or coal. In fact the only concession to the twentieth century was one electric cable, which snaked in through the front door, up the wall, and across the ceiling, where it terminated in an unadorned light bulb. Mary deeply distrusted and resented this intruder, there at the insistence of Maggie Gallagher, who feared the old woman would upset her oil lamp and burn the thatched house down around her. I well remember my first visit. Mary's tiny form was bent over the fire and she turned her deeply lined, peat-streaked face to me. "So you're the Yank that's goin' to write a book about Teelin. . . . Well, that won't be much of a book."

She was a vital if ornery woman, this Mary Kelly. Like many of her generation, she had left for America around the turn of the century and had met her husband in Chicago. She now occupied his natal cottage. I asked her where she herself had been born, and she pressed herself against the window pointing up the mountain — less than a mile away in Croaghlin, another of Teelin's townlands. Evidently their meeting in Chicago had not been happenstance, and in their next moves, the young couple followed the already well-worn local immigrant path — west to the mines of Butte, Montana.[5] After another decade in that wild town, they returned to Teelin with a young daughter to take up "Kelly's" (for that, as it turned out, was her husband's nickname, given to him by American friends) stony little farm in Rinnakilla. It was not an easy life in 1912 Teelin, but it was made tragic for poor Mary by the death of her twelve-year-old child, followed by the blindness of her husband. Her own near relations had died out of or left Croaghlin, and the Gallaghers next door had taken up the role of close kin.

Just a few hundred yards from Mary's cottage, one could enter into an entirely new physical — and one might imagine, cultural, world. For the first time in about a hundred years, the population of Teelin was beginning to rise a bit. Relative prosperity in the late sixties and early seventies at home and a falling off at the construction sites in England, where many recent immigrant men had found work, had kept a number of young people home and even lured a small number of Teelin's emigrants back. Those who had saved the money built modern "bungalows" complete with carpeting and a "suite" of furniture in a front room, that had replaced the kitchen in several of its functions. There were still the religious pictures, but these would often compete for space with family photos, the latter usually achieving the more prominent position. The young occupants of these households might seem to represent an utter break with their neighbors. Their houses were modern; they drove cars; most of them had jobs; the men were building contractors, bus drivers, factory workers, and the women, if they had no children, often worked in one of the knitting mills of Kilcar. Yet a number of things mitigated this apparent generation gap. Almost all of the new households were connected to the older ones; in Rinnakilla every man who built a bungalow was a native of the townland, and the wives — even if married in England — came from no further away than Killybegs, and most often from Teelin itself. Thus these "new" families were generally tied into the old ones — often acquiring sites on or near the father's property — and the new habits of the young seemed to augment rather than disrupt the old. For example, Ellen, the new wife of Mickey Johnnie Beag (Little Johnnie's Mickey), could be seen wheeling her baby in a pram from in-law to in-law, spending most of her time in tea fueled conversation with her elders.

Young Ellen also exemplified another essential continuity between generations: the centrality of religion. Although the Church worries about declining Mass attendance, Ireland's younger population continue to "practice" their religion to a degree unheard of elsewhere in Western Europe. In such rural areas as southwest Donegal in the 1970s weekly Mass attendance was nearly universal — nor has it fallen off significantly since. Young women in particular were often very active in religious pursuits, and Mary, for example, was a local proponent of the cult of Saint Martin of Porres, receiving his devotional pamphlets and passing them on to her neighbors. Even the most traditional of religious practices, the Holy Well of Teelin, drew young and old alike, especially on the "pattern" day, June 23.

And so I spent the following months, visiting and being visited, tending my small garden and benefiting from those of my neighbors, watching the fishery and even doing a bit of fishing myself. Over the months I was, naturally, increasingly aware of both the distinctive character of the men and women around me — whose idiosyncrasies were always underlined and celebrated in nicknames and anecdotes — and the ways in which they were tied together in a complex, nested series of communities.

For if "community" was becoming an unfashionable word at the time among social scientists, it seemed in many senses a conceptual and social reality — or realities — locally. The townlands of Teelin — Rinnakilla, Ummerawirrinan, Lergadaghtan, Cappagh, Croaghlin, Ballymore, and Aghragh — were, with respect to much of the daily rounds of reciprocity and sociability, communities. That this should be the case was not peculiar, for a townland is a rural neighborhood — the remnant of the hamlet that had until the 1840s been the typical settlement type of the region. The Ordnance Survey Map of 1836 (Figure 4) still shows these settlements, usually one on each townland. In the days before the British, the "infield" around each such settlement was held in strips, access to which was rotated from household to household every few years. The "mountain" — extensive rough pastures — was also held in common, with grazing rights determined by holding in the arable zone. All this was to change in the eighteenth and nineteenth centuries, as we shall see in the next chapter, but the final result in this district was a dispersal of the one-time cluster into a row of households along the road, none separated from the next by more than a hundred yards or so, and each sitting on its own "stripe" of land comprising rough pasture and arable.[6] The common "outfield" survived all these changes, and while the significance of that portion depended on the varying importance of livestock, the "commons" was at the very least of symbolic importance, defining the continuing existence of the townland as a community.

Beyond the townland, the communality of Teelin as a whole was increasingly apparent through the summer salmon season.[7] The rotating boats I had observed on my first day implied a shared resource — common property in some sense of the term. The fishery, as I discovered, created a series of connections within Teelin. Most crews were primarily agnatic in

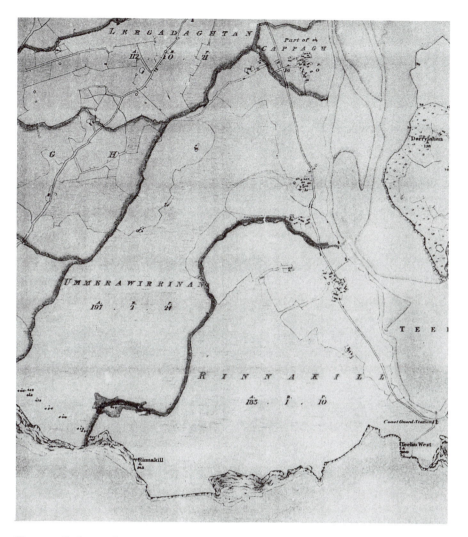

Figure 4. Ordnance Survey Map of 1836.

organization and thus offered a link in experience and a bolster for a father's authority in a place where agriculture was decreasingly important. There was also an intense competition within Teelin through the salmon season, more or less as if each boat were a team in a local spectator sport. Old Mary Kelly had not been down the thirty-yard path from her door to the road in twenty years, but if you visited her on any summer evening she would be able to tell you the score in Irish: "I heard the Cunninghams killed sixty today!" The sporting nature of the fishery also sharpened lines between Teelin and its neighbors. Although ties of affinity linked many Teelin households with households in the little market town of Carrick or across the river in the parish of Kilcar, during the salmon season the "Carrick ones" were seen as elementally different: non-fishermen. As for the competitors across the river, they were simply and disparagingly "far-siders."

Thus did the salmon fishery, through cooperation, competition, and conflict, contribute to the bounding and binding of the community. Up until the 1930s, however, most Teelin men fished not only for salmon in the protected estuary but through much of the year on the open sea for herring, cod, and ling. These fisheries had other effects on the local social world, such as the "cross-cutting ties" in the herring crews. In order to spread the risk — both of the catch and of the loss of life — these crews were less likely than were the salmon crews to be drawn from only one family. Instead, unrelated households would trade sons — as in the ancient Irish custom of "fostering."[8] The alliances created in this manner were social as well as economic, and I often found that a strong visiting or drinking relation between men of different townlands could be traced to the practice.

My discovery of the extent and character of communality in Teelin was also greatly affected by the fact that I was learning Irish, which I was busy through these months trying to adapt to the Donegal dialect — unfortunately for me the most distant from the so-called "standard Irish" taught in Dublin. The language changed my neighbors' understanding of me — of what I could or would be interested in, as I discovered one night, after an evening of drinks with Conal and Francie at the Slieve League Bar, Teelin's pub and a hub of community life for those who knew the way in. Strangers turned away from the padlocked and faded front door, but locals knew to go in through the kitchen on the side of the pub. There they would find old Michael Johnny seated, his long legs stretched out before him and his arthritic feet nearly through the open range door. When enough customers had entered, Michael would rise stiffly, heavy keys dangling from his bony hand, and lead the others through a side door into the bar. That was the most rustic of places — a few stools, and sacks against the wall for extra seating. There was no draft beer or stout — just bottles of whiskey and bottles of beer. Among the men[9] Irish was often the language of conversation. This was increasingly so through the salmon season — as if that pursuit could best be described and discussed in that language.

After the men finally left Michael Johnny's one night Conal Phaddy turned to me and said, "Come, there's some people you might want to meet." I followed him into a low thatched cottage near the pub. Inside, the kitchen had been made over entirely to its public purpose; besides the usual assortment of chairs, there were benches against the walls. About a dozen men were ranged about discussing the trials and tribulations of the fishery and sorting out the meaning of current and past events. Known only semi-jocularly as *An Pharliament*,[10] it was the Donegal version of what anthropologist Conrad Arensberg found in County Clare fifty years earlier. No one had thought to mention it during my first stay because the language was Irish.

Pubs like Michael Johnny's and institutions like *An Pharliament* were at the center of the lives of only a few dozen, mostly older men, however. The more general social life was certainly in the pubs a couple of miles up the road in Carrick, where no fewer than five public houses competed for the custom of the surrounding population of under one thousand. The presence there of church, school, shops and pubs made Carrick the center of a wider and more loosely bounded community, drawing people from three or four miles in every direction.[11] This larger unit, though less intimate, was, for those within it, a thoroughly familiar social world. Indeed the extent of social knowledge evinced by any older person — many could identify several generations of inhabitants in most households of two parishes — always served to remind me of one of the most crucial differences between their world and mine.

This larger community was manifest every Sunday, when for two successive sessions the church would fill to hear Father James McDyer celebrate the Mass and, often, regale the assembly with his latest plans for the community. Famous for his efforts to start and run cooperatives, Father McDyer was a very powerful actor in the secular and political world and had his avid fans and convinced enemies. One of the latter described the priest — with some justice — to a visiting official: "As a priest, he's a very fine businessman, and as a businessman, he's a very fine priest." Such a prominent figure in the local world had of course come to my attention in a variety of contexts: he had tried, for example, to get the fishermen of Teelin to buy the rights to the river and run it as a cooperative (see Taylor 1987). It was impossible to ignore his ubiquitous and imposing presence, and his political and economic, as well as spiritual, performance impressed on me the complex character of local religion.

Sunday after Mass was still the day for the ritual enactment of loyalties in the secular as well as religious sphere. As soon as Mass ended, the women and children streamed into the two grocery shops to get their "messages" and the men assembled in small clusters at various points along the main road, exchanging news. The men of Teelin gathered at the corner of the Teelin road, and after a half hour of chat filed into the pub known as "the Teelin house," because the owner's people had come originally from a town-land there. Through the week, however, Teelin men might be found at any of the Carrick pubs. The choices had been a function of personal affiliation, kinship, or politics, but were increasingly made on the basis of amenities. On weekend nights women were beginning to join men for a night out. Only a tourist woman would be found at the actual bar, but men and women of all ages mixed easily in the lounge, where the common apprecia-tion of traditional music spanned the generations (Figure 5).

My inquiries and perceptions were of course guided to some extent by my own developing interests. Since my first visit to Ireland, I had read what little there was of Irish ethnography, and that and the more extensive cul-tural geographical literature had convinced me that Donegal offered an interesting field site for several reasons. First, it was possessed of the na-tion's largest *Gaeltacht* or Gaelic (Irish) speaking area, which fact, along with the apparent late survival of Gaelic settlement forms and folklore (according to geographers and folklorists respectively) promised a "tradi-tional" local culture different enough to attract the attention of the anthro-pologist and perhaps able to shed light on earlier European cultural forms. The continuing importance of local communal forms — the management of the commons, the culture of fishing, the pilgrimage to the local holy well, and the continuing, if eroding, vivacity of the Irish language — all fit well enough with this picture.

On the other hand, a historical view suggested another reading of the local world, not as a vestige of a Celtic past, but as the product of a long and intensive colonial and postcolonial experience. After hundreds of years of partial control over a varying portion of Ireland, the British finally accom-plished a total military conquest of the nation in the course of the seven-teenth century. In the "Plantation of Ulster" most of the better agricultural land in the northern province of the country — including Donegal — was

Figure 5. Fiddler James Byrne and friends (photo by the author).

taken away from the native Catholic population and "planted" with Protestant tenants imported for the purpose from lowland Scotland. This ethnic /
religious divide, whose memory and reality continue to animate the current
conflict in what has become "Northern Ireland," characterized mainly the
eastern half of County Donegal. However, there had been Protestants within easy reach of every mountainy glen in the west of the county, and the
more radically changing world to the east continually and often dramatically affected even the most apparently isolated corner.

The potato, imported from South America by Sir Walter Raleigh,
became the human staple in the course of the eighteenth century, during
which time the rapidly expanding population further pressed the traditional rural economy, leading eventually to the disastrous potato famine of
the late 1840s. One response to increased pressure on the land was a constant and significant labor migration to the large farms in the east of the
county, and beyond to the potato fields and coal mines of Scotland. While
these economic adaptations were more characteristic of the northwest of
the county, even in the southwest, by the eighteenth century, cottage industries tied the very small tenant farms into a global economy. Linen and wool
flannel were woven on looms, and in those few coastal regions possessed of
safe ports, fishing supplied the money crop with which expenses were paid.
As is often the case in the early stages of industrialization, such activities
were part of a traditional adaptation to the local environment, but were
greatly expanded as once economically self-sufficient regions were drawn
into a larger market economy. In Donegal this process was greatly facilitated by some of the landlords.[12] Ordnance Survey maps, governmental
commission reports, travelers' accounts, the correspondance of landlords,
agents, priests, and bishops, and even a set of marvelously detailed photographs from late in the nineteenth century, taken together, depicted a local
world that had changed radically—especially over the previous one hundred and fifty years—and mostly as a result of external regimes. Not to say
that the region, any more than any other in Ireland, had been passive in the
face of forces beyond their ken and control. Through the late eighteenth
century and especially in the nineteenth century, local entrepreneurs traded
by whatever means were available, and a modest merchant class rose in the
small market towns, especially in the middle decades of that century. Places
like Carrick and more so Killybegs were also the home to a developing rural
intelligentsia in those same decades, typically the educated products of
those same merchant families. Priests, doctors, and, above all, teachers were
often remarkably literate and capable men (women enjoyed few oppor-

tunities for such positions) who played a part in promoting or interpreting for a local audience the larger cultural and political movements of their day. They read and occasionally contributed to the journals and magazines, like *The Nation*, which were critical for the development of the Romantic Nationalism that sustained literary movements as well as the urge for political independence. As several of the following chapters will show, local events echoed national ones — the fight for the repeal of the 1800 Union of Ireland with Great Britain, the struggle for land reform that succeeded in achieving peasant ownership at the end of the nineteenth century, the revival of Gaelic language and literature, and the fight with Britain for independence. When that independence was finally realized in 1922, the boundary with Northern Ireland, which remained part of the British state, was also the border of Donegal, now cut off from its natural metropole, Derry City. This proximity to Northern Ireland has ensured the continuing relevance of the larger political picture for even the most isolated of Donegal's mountain glens.

This colonial and postcolonial experience seemed to belie the traditionalist image portrayed by some folklorists; these people were far from isolated or insulated from the "world system" anthropologists were beginning to become (however belatedly) aware of at the time. The apparent paradox of a "traditional community" marked by early integration in a world market economy made this corner of Ireland an intriguing focus of study. Indeed both dimensions were manifest locally. While my fieldwork revealed more and more of the richly communal life of townland, village, and parish, my archival research — and, as I learned to see and "read" it, the landscape — testified to the presence and power of external forces in the life of the region.

My reference to the "colonial" past of the region — a usage at the center of current historical debate and, not coincidentally, the continuing search for national definition — implies the pre-eminence of the British state among these external forces. From another perspective, however, it is certainly the Roman Catholic Church that deserves the designation, as James Joyce noted years ago. For if religion in one sense is the most intimate expression of the local and the communal, the Church certainly qualifies as an international regime. In the guise of various elements, acting separately or even in concert with the Protestant state, the Catholic Church has also done much to reform the local culture and even transform the landscape. Nor, as noted in the case of Father McDyer, are priests inactive in the contemporary world.

I have already made reference to the fleeting but regular appearance of things religious — the sacred objects, the Angelus, and of course the universal pattern of Sunday Mass attendance and the forceful presence of the clergy. But there were two incidents, one in the course of fieldwork in Rinnakilla and the other historical and encountered in the Dublin archives, which began to reorient my interests toward religion. I will begin with the latter.

One of the most useful of the archival materials I discovered was the letter copybook of Arthur Brooke, estate agent to John and James Musgrave, Belfast entrepreneurs who had purchased most of Conolly's estate — which is to say most of the parish — in 1861. Brooke's letters include an account of a classic social drama — a story of conflict between himself and John Magroarty, the parish priest. In the end, and despite his reluctance to commit what he clearly recognized as a symbolically dangerous act, Brooke evicted the priest in 1877. Back in Teelin, I mentioned the Magroarty incident to an older man, who told me that this was a familiar story and that he would take me to someone who could tell it well. Some evenings later I found myself in the cottage of a ninety-one-year-old woman, a former schoolteacher, whose father had been present at the event in question. She proceeded to recite in Irish — to me and an assembled audience — the story of the priest and agent. That event and the story are the subject of Chapter Four, but it was this coming together of archive and field, of religion and politics, of competing "representations" of a past — which in Ireland, as someone once said, is not dead, and not even past — that began to pull my interests in new directions.

The other incident involved the search for a cure. One day I saw a family I knew piling into a borrowed car, on their way — as they told me — to a hospital sixty miles away to see Father McGinley, an old, former curate (assistant to the parish priest) in a nearby parish. They were going on this difficult journey to ask for Father McGinley's blessing for the father of the family, who had been recently diagnosed with cancer. Why, I asked his daughter — who was my own age — did they not seek the spiritual aid of Father McDyer, the manifestly powerful priest three miles up the road? She replied without criticism of Father McDyer, but said of Father McGinley, using an Irish phrase I would often hear, "he's a very *good* priest!" The cleric in question, as I subsequently found out, had been an apparent alcoholic and had been removed from his office as curate by the bishop years before. He had a reputation for cures, which is the sense of word "good" in that usage — as in "St. Martin is a very good saint." Like the story of the evicted priest, this incident momentarily lifted the veil on another world, of competing powers, of people appropriating priests as well as priests appropriating people.

But these matters were given scant attention in my earlier writings, wherein "history" simply meant what was recorded in the government archives. Questions of both religion and history as representation nagged at my consciousness until I finally took up again the story of the priest and the agent, supplementing my long-standing concern with the structural history of the region with an attention to the narrative world as alternative representation. My neighbors, I remembered, lived in the midst of their history —a physical "archive" surrounded them. The townland of Rinnakilla was named for what now was the merest vestige of a medieval church near the boathouse on the pier. The treeless landscape held imposing ruins of a much more recent past as well—a towering piece of wall of what had been a British coast guard station, burned down (as was the landlord's lodge), as I was told, in the "Troubles" (around 1920). There were also the ruins of abandoned cottages, whose thatched roofs overgrew and collapsed quickly, but whose walls remained for decades, even centuries, if their stones were not reused. And then there was the maze of mortarless stone walls—a spider's web thrown over the mountain—apparently the roughest of pasture had been worth enclosing and the number of families and crops on this townland had once been far greater than now. For my neighbors, that past was in fact living in the ruins and in the natural features of the landscape— for narratives and memories were "attached" to what seemed like every bump and hillock, every piece of wall or one-time field.

I returned finally for thirteen months in 1986–87, with my wife this time and once again on a bus. As in my earlier work, I combined archival research with ethnographic fieldwork, but focusing my attention on matters of religion and representation. Returning to a field site is always a mixed experience. Much had changed. The salmon fishery that had so interested me a decade earlier was moribund, and of course many of the older men and women I had known well had died. Old Mary Kelly and the publican Michael Johnny were among them, and the latter's heirs had sold that most rudimentary pub—The Slieve League Bar—to a German married to a local woman, who had turned it into a tastefully rustic restaurant bar where tourists and locals mixed. The Irish language had slipped further. The thatched roofs were almost gone and many new bungalows had been built. But now economic hard times were very much at hand, and the local factories had reduced their production and employment. Once again, young people were leaving the parish, as they were elsewhere in Ireland, going to London and, more often, New York and Chicago.

On the other hand, the place was still in many ways vibrant — traditional music was on the rise and there was dancing every Monday night at McGinley's Pub — and equipped now with an old Ford Cortina, I was able to participate in and observe far more not only in Teelin but beyond, as well as offer rides to my neighbors. In the course of the year, my wife and I lived and stayed in a number of places, in the Teelin townland of Aghragh, across the river among the "far-siders" in the parish of Kilcar, and just outside the town of Killybegs. Rather than limit myself to any one local community, I took the region as my "unit," getting to know people in all these locations who represented the range of life circumstances there. I followed them not only to the local holy well or Sunday Mass, but to charismatic prayer meetings in Killybegs, healing masses in Castlefinn, and as far as Lourdes in France and Medjugorje in what was still Yugoslavia. Clearly, even the most local Catholicism is part of a world system.

The time for such a study was propitious, for if older forms were — as they always are — slowly or rapidly disappearing, they were still to be found, coexisting not only with standard orthodox religion but with new forms of the miraculous. Nationally, as well as locally, the long heralded transition to a secular society was not going smoothly. Issue after issue, from divorce, to abortion, to Ireland's place in the European Community, was perceived as moral, and hence religious. The very notion of religion was being defined by its use in the discourse of contemporary conflicts. Thus an anthropological study of Catholicism open to this dynamic process — even if locally based — promised to shed some light on issues of more than local importance.

*   *   *

Although one would be hard pressed to suggest a feature of Irish culture more generally significant, Catholicism has received slight, and typically simplistic and reductive, treatment from anthropologists.[13] Irish historians and sociologists, on the other hand, have contributed much, if only in recent years, to the understanding of Catholicism, particularly in the nineteenth century.[14] For a much longer time, Irish folklorists have been collecting oral texts of great relevance to any understanding of local religion, including prayers and songs, legends, and auto-ethnographic descriptions of religious practices. All these reside in the extraordinary National

Folklore Archive in Dublin, but are, to say the least, underused by social scientists, who, understandably, worry about verification and context. Irish historians, however, have also been reluctant to make use of anthropological perspectives and methods that have so marked cultural history in France and Italy, for example. An anthropological approach that integrates and contextualizes the disparate bodies of evidence and perspectives referred to above, and interprets them in the light of developing cultural theories, might offer a useful bridge for both Irish studies and the anthropology of religion.

In order to accomplish that goal, this book does not follow the ethnographic strategy most typical in the anthropology of religion: that is, a cyclical tour through the life crises from birth to death and the days and seasons of the liturgical year. Such a presentation reveals a profound but limited aspect of the experience of religion and of its relation to or integration with other aspects of daily life. The notion of religion and religious time inherent in that view necessarily conveys a sense of "a religion" already and always there, monolithically assumed and unchanging.

In many ways this picture is neither unproductive nor entirely false. The assumption, since Émile Durkheim, of a basically synchronic — that is, one time frame — view of religion has allowed for the elaboration of two distinct but by no means mutually exclusive approaches within anthropology. One has emphasized the ways in which religious belief and, more, activity act to reinforce and reproduce social relations. In terms of the social world glimpsed in the preceding pages, we would expect that the household, townland, and larger community all to find their sacred support. And so they do. The household has its saints — its Lares — in particular the eternally lit Sacred Heart, and its communal rituals of Angelus and family rosaries. Larger communities — bounded and not — certainly loom into view at particular, recurrent occasions such as wakes for the dead (which are still held in the house of the deceased) and, of course, Masses and other church-centered rituals.

The other essentially synchronic approach to the anthropology of religion — also fundamentally Durkheimian in its roots — has been less concerned with the social function of religion than with how it acts to create meaning by providing a framework for experience. These "interpretive" approaches — the most influential have been those of Victor Turner and Clifford Geertz — have drawn attention to the dynamic of symbolism, of how words, acts, and objects manipulate conscious and unconscious thought and feeling and constitute, in their assemblage a "web of meaning," in Geertz's (1973) oft quoted phrase, the coherent whole of a particular culture.[15]

For those whose concern was the individual's and group's need for cognitive and emotional coherence, Geertz's definition was very appealing. However, shifting theoretical perspectives, even if dependent on Geertz's insights, have been increasingly critical of his formulations on several grounds, but particularly in terms of the consistency and uniformity perhaps suggested by the metaphor of the web.[16] The dominant postmodern tendancy has been to "deconstruct" culture—that is to see all culture as a reified illusion—the fleeting, frozen moments of a continuous process of human action characterized by conflict and contest between genders, classes, and so. At the very local level this process involves negotiation and invention, within and between individuals and groups. The postmodern words are all verbs: everything is in motion, all is contingent. From this perspective, the symbolic world that had been the territory of interpretive anthropology should not be viewed as the expression of a pre-existing system of meaning, but rather as a field for the ongoing, often contested, process of the creation of meaning. In that interpetive enterprise the world of contemporary literary criticism has exercised an enormous influence, as symbolic acts could be viewed as "texts"—written and read differently by local "authors" and "audiences" and part of conscious or unconscious efforts to establish or continue one set of meanings (and hence institutions) as opposed to another. This perspective demands fine-grained and sensitive analyses of the micro-process of the construction of meaning.

Our opening vignette of the bus ride hints at such a style of analysis. We first encounter the apparent uniformity of experience suggested by the incanted rosary, but further penetration reveals flux and variation: individuals coming from and going to very different places; groups of passengers with significantly different "readings" of what has and will happen. Of course every individual is unique in this as in other senses, but the ethnography of such occasions as that bus ride also reveals an intermediate commonality, a shared way of talking about and hence—one presumes—understanding a certain realm of experience that characterizes groups, or at least the illusion of shared understanding, an illusion that may have some of the quality of a self-fulfilling prophecy and that is, after all, a necessary ingredient, a belief and expectation, of that thing we call religion. I have called this shared aspect a "field of religious experience," which denotes a very loosely constituted "reality," a field like a magnetic field, strong perhaps at the center but not clearly bounded and defined at the edge.[17] Those inhabiting such fields can be likened to historian Roger Chartier's "interpretive communities."[18] Chartier's term was coined in reference to the distinct readings possible for a given text, while mine was in reference to the range of "readings" possible for a given occasion (like the Healing Mass). The same might be said for the other places and occasions we will witness in the following pages. They are not only "read" differently according to the "interpretive community," but are "written" by all the participants — in varying degrees — and each writing and reading contributes to the creation and maintenance of the field of religious experience in question.

What, however, of a more "macro" view of the same journey? Beyond the whir of discourse and representation — the momentary flux within and among the passengers — there is the external reality of that bus, and others like it, their routes now parts of a "system," another expression of religion that unfolds in historical time. For this bus, we remember, is one of several, each of which takes people on the first Tuesday of the month from a ring of market towns to the Healing Mass at Donneyloop in Castlefinn. This movement of buses and the Mass that follows it are the visible expressions of another dimension of what we call religion, wherein institutions and even churches come into existence. This sort of social formation — a system of power relations — might be called, following anthropologist Mart Bax (1987a), a "religious regime." Bax introduced his term in the context of competing political/devotional formations within the Catholic Church — most notably regular versus secular clergy. In the case of the Healing Mass and of the bus-routes that service it, making it a center for a series of prayer groups in two dioceses, there is something like a charismatic Catholic regime in question, participants in which may share to varying degrees a field of experience and thus constitute an "interpretive community." But the regime, while dependent, especially in its initial stages, on this experiential side, comes to constitute a visible, reified system, an alternative diocese if you like, whose existence does not depend on everyone believing the same things or sharing the same experiences, but rather on their behaving in a particular way.

This perspective is ultimately rooted in a Weberian sociology that has sought to understand and explain the changing forms of religion not only, or mainly, as beliefs but rather as systems of authority, power, and domination. There is of course as much danger of naive reification here as with interpretive models of religion. Imposing predetermined models of uni-linear evolution along any of the paths with which classical sociological thought has characterized western history is not the best way to discover nuance, much less novelty. Neither is our understanding of the complex and often compelling nature of domination helped by beginning with the assumption that all cultural forms are simply imposed "from the top," by cynically manipulative politicos, on eternally passive "local" ciphers.

However, this macro-view of religion as power has also benefitted from a postmodern critique which takes less for granted about the direction of change or, in fact, the very existence of such "essential" units as states, or in this case, Churches or religions. For example, Talal Asad's (1983) penetrating critique of Geertz's definition of religion calls for attention to the ways in which religions are historically constructed. This brand of historical ethnography owes much to Foucault's view of power as embodied in discourse and existing when and where it is performed in everyday life: a perspective that can be as easily applied to the church as to the state. Certainly the Catholic Church (in Ireland and elsewhere) has been and is the scene of contending discourses: particular ways of talking about reality (or some section of it) that perforce exclude other, different, and hence rival discourses. If states exist in their performances, than so does the Church. And if states inscribe themselves on the body (another recently favored field for the exploration of cultural power), than so, *mutatis mutandis*, does the Catholic Church in Ireland.

That perspective also suggests the utility — even urgency — of an intimate view of religion that looks locally for the so-called external, and, though aimed at uncovering the macro, historical character of religion as power, resists the temptation to abandon ethnography in favor of political economy. Attention to the actual and particular also leaves open the possibility of discovering that any number of social formations might use what we call religion to produce and reproduce themselves, and, in the process, significantly alter religious experience.

This view of religion was very much reinforced in the field. It was not simply that there was a general category or domain called religion that was significant among the people I was living with, but rather that at certain moments — such as the eviction of the priest and the recitation of his story — it was possible to observe the connection between religion as a large scale national or international process that has to do with churches, authority, and domination, and religion as a world of meaning, a set of beliefs, a style of discourse, a bodily comportment, a sensibility. It was also possible, indeed unavoidable, to discern not only that religion was often indistinguishable from political and social relations — an anthropological truism — but that there were specific and dynamic relations among these domains, as when a social class or nationalist political movement used a certain notion of religion to define itself, and in so doing contributed to the very definition of religion, nationalism, class, or gender per se.

Indeed, this historical construction of religion was vitally important in two senses. First, there was the "objective" historical time in which Irish Catholicism took and was continuing to take shape, without reference to which, to give one centrally important example, the contemporary role and meaning of priesthood was simply not comprehensible. Second, there was the subjective appropriation of "history" within the Irish religious sensibility — narratives of evicted priests or fire and brimstone missions that were invoked to interpret the present. Which is to say that among Irish Catholics, as among, to take another example, Jews, religious time is historical as well as cyclical: the "Faith of Our Fathers."

Further, field and archival evidence illustrated the dynamic and dialectic character of the interaction of locally and externally based powers and meanings. Asad, Foucault, and others are right to direct our attention to relations of power, which have shaped — and continue to shape — the form and very definition of religion in Ireland. Yet ethnographic experience — the critical importance of which is asserted here — suggests that there are other things involved: meaning can emerge from other sorts of power. Among the people of southwest Donegal — and surely everywhere else — there is something we might call a religious imagination. Propelled perhaps most often by basic fears and needs — searches for cures or help with the difficulties and profound disappointments that they and we face, the people seek solutions, tell stories, even occasionally invent (or reinvent) new forms.

Against this formulation, it will be cogently argued that in cases like the one at hand such individual and group quests are conducted within the frameworks created by "regimes," the political dimension of religious systems. This may well be so, but if the religious form or occasion is personally powerful, there is always an interactive play, a creative response. In several of the cases we will explore in these pages, even the most institutionally contrived, designed-for-domination forms, like the Parish Missions conducted by the Redemptorist order at the turn of the century, succeeded in gripping their audience only in so far as they left "creative space" for the imaginative participation of the audience.

In order to uncover and preserve the visibility of these relations, I have used *occasions* as the organizing principle of both research and presentation. That approach allows not only for the integration of interdisciplinary materials and perspectives, but also for a sustained focus on precisely the connection between religion as power and as meaning — points where power imposes meaning, and meaning enables power, and on the ways in which religion as a category came to be formed in the Irish case.

The order of the chapters — of occasions — is loosely chronological, beginning with that with the deepest temporal roots — the visit to a holy well. That most "traditional" of local religious practices is viewed not as a curious and static relic of a primordial Celtic past but as a dynamic element in the history of political and religious domination, resistance, and appropriation. From that we proceed to an exploration of texts and events that reveal the religious transformations of the nineteenth and twentieth centuries. A travelogue penned by a local schoolteacher is taken as symptomatic of the development of a new social class and an attendant religious, literary, and nationalist sensibility. The evolution of the Irish Catholic priesthood is explored in the next chapters, which treat the story and event of Father Magroarty's eviction in 1877 and the continuing fascination with the curing powers of alcoholic clerics. The range of priestly power is further revealed in an examination of the civilizing offensive of the centralizing Church as illustrated by the parish mission of the Redemptorist order. We next turn to three contemporary pilgrimages, the last of which — to Medjugorje in Bosnia — plays a critical role in the current genesis of the new regime and field of religious experience glimpsed in our opening bus ride. That world of charismatic Catholics is then further pursued in an intensive exploration of a contemporary prayer meeting.

Throughout these events, places, and texts two themes constantly reassert themselves — language and landscape — which are important, no doubt, to varying degrees, in many religious formations. In Ireland, however, it might be said, the value of language, of discourse in the construction of meaning, is particularly sharp. The landscape too figures centrally in the religious, as indeed in many other, aspects of local life. Ever wary of the romanticization to which both outsiders and insiders are subject (and which itself has an important part to play in the processes we will explore), perhaps it is not too much to say that the landscape of Ireland has never been thoroughly disenchanted. For Una — the kerchiefed countrywoman whom we met on the bus — and her neighbors whose lives are still thoroughly inscribed in the landscape, life is a series of regular and extraordinary movements — most often on foot — over a terrain thoroughly imbued with meaning. Memories both personal and collective are attached, as the Victorians liked to say, to nearly every rock and hillock and some of these are points of power, mediating between this and other worlds.

2. Sacred Geography: The Holy Well

> Oh there's great curing in that well. There was a woman brought her daughter to that well once and nothing could cure the child. She was that sick, and couldn't walk at all. She had brought her to all the wells, even Doon Well down in the North there, and nothing did any good for her. Anyway, her mother brought her here to *Tobar na mBan Naomh* and she spent the night by the well, and her mother took her away in the morning and she was cured. And by God, she stayed that way because she lived to a great age and she used come here to visit over the years — we all knew her as an old woman — and it wasn't long ago that she died.
>
> (author's field notes, 1976)

So Conal Phaddy told me, to the nodding approval of his neighbor and agemate, Francie Gallagher, as the three of us leaned against a stone wall by Francie's field in Rinnakilla. It was a fine June day, in fact June 23 — St. John's Eve — the day of the annual *turas* or pilgrimage to the holy well. I had already visited *Tobar na mBan Naomh* — the Well of the Holy Women — nearly invisible in a thicket of rough gorse and heather near Teelin pier, only a hundred yards or so from where we stood. The well was an unimposing hole in the ground recently covered over with a concrete slab, protecting the well from debris while allowing easy access to its special waters. For that purpose a couple of chipped ceramic cups sat by the lip of the well. About twenty yards to the east was a rough-hewn shrine: an enclosing structure of piled stones mounted by an apparently medieval, weather-worn, rustic stone cross (see Figure 6). Sheltered by the structure was a shelf on which were strewn an apparently random assortment of coins, pins, and broken bits of plastic and plaster Infants of Prague or Ladies of Lourdes. On the earth before the shrine sat three peculiar stones, each marked by a "waist" of what looked like wear marks (see Figure 7).

Later that afternoon, as I watched from a nearby hillock, several dozen men, women, and children followed the parish priest in a series of circles about the shrine and well. "Hail Mary, full of grace," the stentorian, nasal tones of Father McDyer's Glenties Irish rose above the murmuring voices

Figure 6. The Well of the Holy Women (*Tobar na mBan Naomh*) (photo by the author).

of his parishioners. As with every local *turas* I was to witness or read of, there was a prescribed route from stone to stone, precious things to lift or touch, and all of it accompanied by a litany of Our Fathers, Hail Marys, Glorias, and Creeds. At the Well of the Holy Women, the "stations"[19] — as the itinerary of stops and prayers are called — take the pilgrims around both shrine and well. In addition to the usual prayers, the ritual involves hoisting each of the three stones and passing it around the body three times and

Figure 7. Curing stones from the Well of the Holy Women (photo by the author).

touching it to one's lips. One also leaves something behind — the pins, coins, and other objects I had seen — "for what you take away." At the well, pilgrims drink the water from the ceramic cups that are left there and plunge whatever containers they possess into the well. This well water will be used for cures throughout the year.

*   *   *

Where is the Well of the Holy Women? It is in Rinnakilla, the last townland in Teelin, at the foot of Slieve League. It is also in Conal's stories, in the books and on the maps of surveyors and antiquarians, in the treatises of folklorists, and now in this book. Tobar na mBan Naomh dwells in the landscape and in discourse, but the two are indissolubly linked: the landscape speaks different languages, and the languages — the discourses — evoke, narrate, describe, and inscribe different landscapes.

If you stand by the well you can look beyond the massive rocks that shelter the estuary out into the open sea. Most often there is enough of a swell to send towers of spume into the air where the waves crash into the *Tor an t-sasanaigh* — the rock of the Englishman. The older men and women still remember the simple one-masted open sailing rowboats in which the men pursued herring, cod, and ling in the open waters of Donegal Bay — lowering their sails in salute as they passed the holy well before leaving the harbor. Near the Well of the Holy Women was *Tobar na gCórach* — the Well of the Winds — which could be propitiated against the storms that took so many lives on the wild seas. For wells are sometimes used to control such natural forces as well as to seek cures for diseases. But the Well of the Winds is no longer used, perhaps because men no longer fish under sail — though they still perish on the seas, now on the trawlers of Killybegs.

Also defunct is the *turas* that took the pilgrim through the townland of Ballymore and up the winding trail through scree-strewn gorse to the top of the mountain, Slieve League. There, not far from the scattered remains of what is thought (by scholars and locals alike) to have been monks' cells, is another well — attributed to Aodh (Hugh) Mac Bricín (see Figure 8). Aodh, the medieval annals tell us, was sent in penitence to live on the top of this mountain, and remained for seven years.

According to the locals, who like to link one well with another, one chapter with another, as they narrate the landscape, this same Aodh dwelt first on Rathlin O'Beirne, a small island just off the coast around the other side of the mountain, where another fertile estuarine niche shelters the

Figure 8. The Well of Aodh Mac Bricín, late nineteenth century (Lawrence Collection, National Library of Ireland).

settlements of Malin More and Malin Beg between sea and steep moor (see Figure 2).

> Aodh Mac Bricín was out on Rathlin Island and was put under a judgment of penance, and he left it to go to Slieve League. As he was going up he turned to take a last look at Rathlin O'Beirn. Tears fell from his eyes with longing. In the place where he stood a well sprang forth from beneath and to this day there is water there whether it is wet or dry. No one goes that way now who doesn't take a drink of the holy water. The well is the length of two boots, and one boot's width. People come from Malin Beg to the well to drink in the summer. There is an old custom with them when they come into the hills after sheep, to always go over to drink from the well, and to leave something behind—a coin, a piece of string, a stick, or anything at all to leave there. There's much curing in it—it is very good. No one goes there without finding a cure for every sort of thing. Warts or anything at all troubling on his hand he'll be cured of it, a good strength (*misneach maith*) there's to be gotten from Saint Mac Bricín. ("Hugh Bricin's Well," NFA, vol. 142: 1677–1678; my translation)

On Rathlin itself there is another well—no *turas*, but still used by a number of people, especially in Malin Beg and Malin More, for eye trouble. That one is attributed to another saint—Kevin.

> Saint Kevin was leaving the island and took a last look—a well sprang up under his feet. People come there from Malin now and leave sticks and rags and pennies there. (NFA, vol. 143: 1771–1772; my translation)

Further around the coast, to the far side of the parish, there is another, wider opening in the cliffs where the more sweeping valley of Glencolumb-kille faces the sea. On the floor of the valley sits a simple and graceful church, representing the Protestant Church of Ireland, built about 1828. On the church grounds there is a pillar-stone rising from a hillock and inscribed with celtic crosses that suggest a date of the eighth or the ninth century.[20] Across the road there is another one, in fact, they can be found at many of the thirteen stations of the best known *turas* of the region, Saint Columcille's, which takes the barefoot pilgrim on a three mile walk through streams and nettles and up to other stone artifacts reckoned to be associated with the great saint's life. Finally one arrives at the well—complete with mugs, offerings, and healing stone—high up the loose rock slope that leads to the sea cliffs.

There are other minor wells in the parish; most have fallen into disuse. In the next parish, Kilcar, there are wells associated with Saints Carratha and Keiran, and further east, in Killybegs—home to Ireland's largest fishing fleet—there is a well of Saint Catherine (presumably of Alexandria). Ardara parish, to the north, is home to the popular well of Saint Conal Caol.[21] The wells of southwest Donegal are mainly on or overlooking the coast — along the western edge of the world. It is a realm to which the wandering eremetic monks of the saints' stories came — sentenced themselves — pilgrims to the edge rather than the center. Aodh Mac Bricín was among their number: someone lived in those cells atop Slieve League. But this edge — and these wells — were clearly powerful before their arrival.

These Irish saints sailed west, following the watery paths of pagan Celts. The "outing" (*echtra*) of the latter was the prototype for the Christian eremetic's *perigrinatio*.[22] These were voyage tales, which told of islands real and imagined and the fabulous encounters of heros with forces of another world. A central goal was the land of eternal youth — a western isle that appears and disappears. The Other World — the source of power — lay on the horizon, not up, and was subject to liminal appearances, moments in time, points in space, when the inaccessible was suddenly there, though never easy to reach. Only a resolute hero could make such a quest and escape the thousand pitfalls that thwarted success. These journeys, or stories of journey, seem the model for the famous *Navigatio* of Saint Brendan, who also sought the Other World across the western horizon in some "Promised Land of the Saints." And the extreme landscape of southwest Donegal comes into the story. Brendan, according to the tale, hears about the island — the Promised Land — from a monk named Barrind, whose son Mernóc found an island near Slieve League called the Delightful Island, from which father and son sailed west to the Promised Land of the Saints (see Harbison 1991: 39). Rathlin O'Beirne, Delightful Island. But not only delightful; in the Celtic vision, the west is powerful, but ambivalent. After all, it was for the monks a site of penitence. Rathlin O'Beirne had been sought out as a site for a solitary life by Mernóc. And of the mountain Slieve League, we hear from Saint Munnu of Taghmon that he was told that, "if he ever wanted an unbearable trial or temptation, he should go to Slieve League in Tír Bogaine in south Donegal and there embark upon his voyage" (Harbison 1991: 47).

*   *   *

> "Have you ever seen such a west and farback place?"
> *An bhfaca tu aon áit chomh iargúlta?*

The question came from Conal Phaddy. We were standing on the low cliffs behind the well, looking "west." That is, we were looking toward the sea, which at that point in the landscape is pretty much due south. But to move toward the sea, toward the Atlantic, which is after all the very limit and definition of westerliness, is to move west; the twists and turns of the local landscape are overridden by the oceanic imperative. If you are walking toward the pier — again the main Teelin road runs north-south — then you are going west. "Larry, which way are you going?" they would ask me. "Are you going west (*siar*)? The phrase *iar gculta* adds "back" to west — truly backward, utterly peripheral. These people do not live in the center of the larger world, they know they are not the "middle country."

One evening toward the end of summer I was walking "up" toward Carrick with Francie, who was complaining to me about the shortening day. The breeze freshened: a sea borne wind that rolled down Slieve League and into the glen. "That's a west wind," he said. "There's rain on that wind, it's a good clean wind, not like an east wind. The east wind's a dirty wind — it brought us flu from the eastern world." I remembered a scene from O'Crohan's *The Islandman*, an account of life on the Great Blasket Island, off the coast of Kerry in the early years of this century. A small boat had landed on the island bearing word from the mainland harbor of Dunquin, "There's news from the Eastern World, a Duke's son has been shot and they say there will be war."

*   *   *

Aodh, Columcille, and the other saints came to the western edge, and in that they mirrored the eremetic tradition of monks on the opposite end of Christendom who found their exiles in the deserts of Egypt and the Near East. But they also followed the restless model of the Celtic West. They did not stay put, but wandered. The written "Lives" of these saints, and even more so the oral folk narratives, depict them most of all roaming with their cohorts, like the heros of the pagan Irish tales of the Fianna, through a wild landscape full of natural and demonic enemies. This "errand into the wilderness" — removed from the centers of secular or ecclesiastic power — put them in closer contact with God and the angels, with whom they had rather continuous communication. The *communitas* of this pilgrimage — as Victor Turner would call it — the feeling of unstructured communality — was restricted to a narrow band of monks. But liminality there was, for the wandering was a very extended middle stage in a rite of passage. Penitence — the impetus of the journey — is such a liminality of course, an extended transitional stage with the hope of a final "reintegration" into a state of grace — if not in this life then in the next. But there is another transition involved, for sainthood is not only about Goodness, it is about Power. The wandering Irish saints prophesy, cure, win battles, even raise the dead. They also curse. They are indissolubly associated with the landscape, and share its ambivalence and bouts of temper. In that they are more like the ancient Hebrew heros and prophets than the saint-martyrs of Mediterranean Roman civilization. Like the Hebrews they were tribespeople, not townspeople, the shamans of a pastoral folk who themselves moved in the landscape.

In the course of his wanderings in Ireland and Scotland in the sixth century, Columcille, the most famous of these saints, and the one for whom the parish of Glencolumbkille (The glen of Colm Cille) is named, had visions, made prophecies, cured many, and vanquished demons and associated features of the landscape. Among them were wells:

> . . . in the province of the Picts, he heard that the fame of another well was wide-spread among the heathen populace, and that the insensate people venerated it as a god, the devil deluding their understanding. For those that drank from this well, or deliberately washed their hands or feet in it, were struck, by devilish art, God permitting it, and returned leprous, or half blind, or even crippled. . . . Led astray by all this, the heathen gave honour to the well as to a god. When he learned of that, the saint went boldly to the well. . . . The magicians whom he often repelled from himself in confusion and defeat, rejoiced greatly when they saw this, since they imagined that he would suffer the like ills, from touching that noxious water. But he, first raising his holy hand in invocation of the name of Christ, washed his hands and feet; and after that, with those that accompanied him, drank of the same water, which he had blessed. And from that day, the demons withdrew from that well and not only was it not permitted to harm any one, but after the saint's blessing, and washing in it, many infirmities among the people were in fact cured by the same well. (Adomnan 1961: 350–51)

That, at least, is the story[23] as it is told in the oldest surviving written account of Columcille, the Latin Life written by Adomnan at the turn of the eighth century. It was over a hundred years since the death of the saint, and the monastery he had founded on the Isle of Iona off the Scottish coast was now the center of a "family" of monastic establishments — a religious regime with land and influence. These regimes, according to archaeologist Peter Harbison (1991), competed with one another by promoting the cults of their respective founder saints. This they did by capturing local pilgrimages and telling stories — re-narrating the landscape with a new protagonist. But it was not only pagans who lost their wells in these struggles, it was also more local saints. Thus, Harbison (1991: 108–10) reasons, did

the cult of Columcille come to the glen that now bears his name; so successful was the conquest that Columcille displaced Saint Fanad, a local boy.
Harbison dates the incised stones marking the turas of Columcille to the
eighth or ninth century, in a period of newly active Irish pilgrimage. But the
cult of Columcille was probably related to the spread of a secular regime as
well—the Ui Neíll. Whoever brought the stones to the glen also brought
the Life, which not only told of the miraculous power of the saint but
celebrated his connection to that powerful clan. Adomnan's Life begins
with a geneology that establishes Columcille's princely status among the Ui
Neíll, and further demonstrates the shamanic connection of the hero/saint
to the tribe by reference to the well-established power of magical speech
and song:

> This also seems to be a thing that should not be passed unnoticed: that certain
> lay people of the same blessed man, though they were guilty men and blood-
> stained, were through certain songs of his praises in the Irish tongue, and
> the commemoration of his name, delivered, on the night in which they had
> chanted those songs, from the hands of their enemies who had surrounded the
> house of the singers; and they escaped unhurt, through flames, and swords,
> and spears. A few of them had refused to sing, as if valuing little the chantings
> of the holy man's commemoration, and miraculously those few alone had
> perished in the enemies assault. (Adomnan 1961: 203)

The spread of the cult of Columcille at the expense of local saints is
an instance of the process described by anthropologist William Christian
(1972), whereby "local" is replaced by "generalized" devotion. But here
too, as in the Spanish cases described by Christian, the "local" strikes back.
It is still the place that is powerful, the landscape is not disenchanted,
merely renamed. Perhaps it was important to regimes—both sacred and
secular—to retain the charisma of blood and earth. So, in the end, Columcille is not an outsider, not the representative of external domination,
but an intimate. He is cthonic—an aspect of the landscape, which retains its
wildness, its points of power and strangeness.

Changing life circumstances as well as the new religious devotions of
the ensuing centuries did little to disrupt this pattern—this sacred geography. On the continent the switch from the bodies to the portable relics of
saints bolstered the growing power of bishops, who could concentrate such
trophies in their cathedrals (see Brown 1981). Even the rise of the Cluniac
regime, with its famous pilgrimage to Compostello in Spain, took the
pilgrim not only from relic to relic, but from imposing structure to impos-

ing structure. Within the cavernous severity of romanesque Vézelay the pilgrim's experience was doubtless shaped by the colossal Christ presiding over the Last Judgment, and the dozens of demons yanking sinners' souls from their dying bodies on every column's capital. To this were added sermons — a discourse of Sin, Judgment, and Purgatory.

Harbison (1991) argues that this religious form found its way to Ireland, where a system of pilgrimage centers replete with Celtic romanesque churches, high crosses, and round towers attracted a growing number of pilgrims. If so, these centers seem not to have challenged the older religious geography, but only added another layer. The old order — secular and religious — survived well enough to dismay Giraldus Cambrensis — Gerald of Wales — the twelfth-century Anglo-Norman cleric whose "Topography of Ireland" stands as the first of a centuries long, and continuing, tradition of "othering" the Irish. Gerald was struck by the aberrancy of Irish life and religion.

> The faith having been planted in the island from the time of Saint Patrick, so many ages ago, and propagated ever since, it is wonderful that this nation should remain to this day so very ignorant of the rudiments of Christianity. . . . The prelates of this country, secluding themselves according to ancient custom within the inclosures of their churches, are generally content with indulging in a contemplative life. . . . Hence it happens that they neither preach to the people the word of the Lord, nor tell them of their sins; neither extirpate vices nor implant virtues in the flock committed to their charge. . . . For as nearly all the prelates of Ireland are elected from the monasteries over the clergy, they scrupulously perform all the duties of a monk, but pass by all those which belong to the clergy and bishops. (Giraldus Cambrensis 1905:134–143)

Gerald was dismayed by a tribal rather than feudal social world, and by a religious structure run by abbots and monks rather than bishops and priests. As for the ordinary Irish, he found them barbaric, even savage. He praised the monks' asceticism, but complained that they did little to "civilize" (as Norbert Elias would say) the surrounding populace. He also correctly noted the interdependence of tribal structure and devotional life. Rather than saints' cults based on visiting the graves and relics of martyrs — of which, as he caustically pointed out, the Irish did not yet possess even one — he notes the importance assigned to other sorts of relics like the bells and staff of Patrick and other saints, and their role in swearing oaths.

For those swearing allegiance or cursing enemies, symbols of heroic authority were more important and more relevant than cathedral tombs. However, the Normans — sharing in varying degrees Gerald's perceptions — did what they could to change that. For example, in rather perfect illustration of Peter Brown's (1981) argument concerning the connection between saints' cults and pilgrimage and the power of bishops, the newly installed Norman bishop of Armagh "discovered" the remains of Saints Patrick, Brigid, and Columcille and had them translated to the shrine at Downpatrick, just outside of Armagh. The pilgrimage that he promoted, however, never seriously competed with that to the mountaintop in wild Mayo where Patrick — in evident parallel to Moses — spent forty days and nights in direct contact with God and a host of supernatural mediators.

Better use of Patrick was made by the Anglo-Norman Augustinians who, in the cooptive tradition of the early Christians, took over what was probably a local saint's shrine in Lough Derg and promoted a cult of a Saint Patrick that was more apparently in the Celtic mold yet subtly deviant. This was a saint of the landscape — an island in remote Lough Derg in Donegal where, the story went, Patrick entered a cave and there encountered the horrors of Purgatory. But Purgatory was at the time being promoted on the continent, along with the Last Judgment and the necessity of personal penance — all of which was represented in Europe not only in the discourse of particular orders but in the tympana of very many churches (le Goff 1984, Ariès 1981). It has been suggested (see Inglis 1987) that the penchant for penitance had in fact been brought to the continent much earlier by another group of wandering Irish monks — those that brought instruction to the Europeans in the eighth century. If so, by linking the practice and attitude to an evolving concept of Last Judgment and Purgatory, for which not only pilgrimage but Masses for the dead were the solution, the continental Church was able to harness the power of penitence and the experience of pilgrimage to the growing domination of a centralizing regime. It was a religious form and structure that achieved its most imposing and magnificent manifestation in the soaring, high Gothic cathedral. How different the experience of St. Patrick's Purgatory; it is difficult to imagine a more perfect inversion of the cathedral. Even from the Irish perspective Lough Derg was peripheral.[24] There the pilgrim confronted neither the architectural riches nor the holy relics of the institutional Church, but instead a cave — a definitively natural and liminal place.[25] This cooptation of the sacred charismatic landscape, in keeping with the Gaelic pattern, was more successful than efforts to make an episcopal see, by virtue of the alleged remains of Irish national saints, a point of pilgrimage.

The impact of Anglo-Norman religiosity, like Anglo-Norman culture in general, varied across the Irish landscape, but few places were more remote from such influences than west Donegal. Saint Catherine's well in Killybegs is the only evidence of "foreign cults" — having no doubt displaced some local favorite son or daughter. Further west the landscape — sacred and secular — remained what it was. The remains of medieval churches, in Kilcar, Teelin, Malin Beg, and Glencolumbkille are all to be found in the the small, fertile, estuarine glens ranged round Slieve League, in close proximity to the wells (see Figure 1).

The later middle ages saw the development of the first real episcopal regime, though it was hardly distinguishable from the chieftaincy. The bishop and his priests held hereditary land rights and relied heavily on the Franciscans for pastoral assistance. That order, though continental in origin, was by the mid-fifteenth century run by native Irish (Mooney 1952: 12), and was particularly strong in the west and northwest of Ireland.[26] From this period until midway through the eighteenth century, the writings of the scholarly Franciscans, but more so their preaching and pastoral ministrations, were perhaps the most important influences on daily religious life in the remote southwest of Donegal and similar regions in west Connaught and Ulster.

The Franciscans clearly stepped into the bardic role — in Donegal supplying chroniclers and poets for the ruling chieftains, the O'Donnells. Authors of the famous *Annals of Ulster*, the "Four Masters" of sixteenth-century Donegal Town clearly felt called to compile the heroic annals of warriors as wells as monks.[27] Among the notables mentioned in that text is one Philip O hUiginn, an Observantine Franciscan, who is described under the year of death 1487 as "best and most prolific devotional poet in these latter times" (as cited in Mooney 1952: 13). Franciscan historian Canice Mooney points out that, "just as St. Francis substituted Our Lady and Lady Poverty for the lady-loves of the troubadours, so he [O hUiginn] often substituted heavenly for earthly patrons and patronesses in the final verses of his poems." While the themes of the poems are traditional Franciscan themes such as the Crucifixion, Our Lady, and the Judgment Day, the treatment of the themes is "tribal," as Mooney points out. A twentieth-century Irish Jesuit, in a commentary that tells us as much about his own time and culture as it does about O hUiginn's, is worth quoting at length.

> Except for a few references to his Franciscan vocation, his poems are indistinguishable from secular bards of the time . . . but it is the manner in which he handles his themes that is most surprising. In addressing God or the Blessed Virgin or one of the saints, or in dealing with some Scriptural event or with some part of the spiritual life, his thoughts and emotions are not those which

arise spontaneously in the devout Christian heart. . . . They are exclusively the
conceits, fancies and far-fetched notions distinctive of the Bardic treatment of
religious subjects. . . . From a theological point of view, the strangest part of all
Bardic poetry is treatment of the Passion. In all ordinary Christian literature on
the subject Christ is represented as sufficient to redeem us from sin, offering on
our behalf to His Father the perfect atonement which He alone could offer. We
are urged to love Him in return and to repent our sins. . . . These ideas and
emotions are found in Bardic poetry, but are seldom expressed in a simple
straightforward way. . . . Far fetched analogies, the unnatural and often un-
theological conceits, and the unfamiliar points of view adopted by the Bards
make their verses on the Passion very difficult to understand and destroy
almost completely the devotional effect of their poetry . . . the love of playing
with paradoxes especially those arising from a confusion deliberately introduced between the Persons of the Trinity. . . . Since Christ is also God, He is
both angry with us and suffering for us. His wounds accuse us, crying out for
our punishment and yet saving us; inflicted by our sins and cure for those
sins. . . . Use of this paradox is the most disfiguring element in the treatment of
Sacred Passion. . . . Strange comparisons and overbold expressions arising
from them are distasteful to ordinary devotional feeling. . . . One of the most
common of comparisons is of Christ to a hero. He is often described as riding
on His Cross as on a steed, . . . that by His Passion and Blood Christ pays the
[bloodfine] *éiric* or *eineaclann* due from us to God on account of Original Sin
and our subsequent sins. . . . Commoner still and more calculated to cause
obscurity of language is the view that Christ's wounds . . . both cause and allay
the wrath of God. Thus if God charges the wounds against us, we can urge
them as pleas in our defence. By His Passion Christ is forcing his Father's hand
and thus acting unjustly. (McKenna 1931: xix)

I do not pretend that we can reconstruct the popular faith of southwest
Donegal in the fifteenth century from the writings of such poets, but it
is worth noting that the taste for the heroic sagas and for poetry, secular
and sacred, long remained a characteristic of the peasantry when the more
standard training of the clergy had long since produced a sensibility closer
to Lambert McKenna's, the commentator above, than to his subject, O
hUiginn. The National Folklore Archives are home to very many exam-
ples.[28] Clearly, a heroic, bardic version of Christian discourse was still to be
heard in places like Donegal up to the seventeenth century; one that may
have been created by, but was almost certainly not limited to, the elite. The
discourse adapted the classic Christian themes and beliefs to a social world
based on kinship, blood payments, and reciprocity. In this cultural universe,
penance, *aithrigh*, was a way of paying corporate as well as individual blood
fines.[29] As for survival of the charismatic landscape, consider the following
passage from the fifteenth-century Life of Columcille by Manus O'Donnell:

Another time Columb was admonished by an angel to go to uninhabited Seangleann [Glencolumbkille] thereafter and to deliver that tract from the wiles of demons, and to consecrate it to God. This is the extreme (western) portion of the country of Tirconnell; it extends into the ocean, and is horrible with craggy mountains and promontories which hang over the sea, and ascend towards (Slieve League) the heavens. It was dismal until Columb's time on account of its uninhabited state and the wiles of demons, for the evil spirits whom St. Patrick had expelled from "Cruachan Oighli," and precipitated into the sea, betook themselves thither, and remaining in it until the time of St. Columb they overspread it with a black cloud and a fog dense and impervious to human sight, and infected with poison the river by which that tract is divided from the rest of the main land, and made it impassible. To this place, therefore, by the admonition of the angel, Columb betook himself with a numerous retinue of holy men, and when he stood with his companions on the bank of the aforesaid river, a pole thrown by a demon from the opposite bank suddenly took away the life of his servant, who was called Cearc." (O'Donovan 1835: 117–118)

In this world of holy wells and Franciscan chronicler bards serving chieftains and God, there was an episcopal regime — a bishop ruling a diocese through secular (non-ordered) priests — in the making. In fact, there was even participation from this most Gaelic corner of Ireland at the Council of Trent, the set of great meetings on the continent wherein the Catholic Church framed its response to the Protestant Reformation. Bishop McGonigal of Raphoe — the diocese that includes most of Donegal — was one of three Irish prelates to attend the famous council and by all reports he supported the centralizing and reforming tendencies of the leaders. Realities back home, however, certainly militated against anything like the Counter-Reformation ideal of a bishop, independent of secular control, presiding over a diocese through a troop of well trained clergy. McGonigal was resident in Killybegs rather than the traditional diocesan seat at Raphoe because constant warfare made the latter unsafe and because his kin group had hereditary rights to church lands there under the rule of the clan Mac Suibne. Indeed the bishop was chosen by the ruling family — the O'Donnells. Even while in exile on the continent after the "flight of the earls" — (the end of the Gaelic chieftaincy in 1607 at British hands) — this privilege could not be completely wrested from the chieftain, for an O'Donnell living in Austria was consulted in the naming of the bishop well into the eighteenth century. Beyond that, McGonigal had few priests with whom to run a pastoral diocese.

Whatever changes the Counter-Reformation might have wrought in

Ireland, however, its progress was rather rudely interrupted by the British conquest and the imposition of a new Established Protestant Church. By the mid-seventeenth century in Donegal, as elsewhere, this meant the coexistence of two episcopal structures. The Protestant Church of Ireland, with their own bishops, dioceses, and parishes, was now in possession of whatever lands the Catholic Church had claimed as well as whatever medieval parish or monastic churches survived. They collected tithes from everyone but served a minority of new landlords and imported Protestant "planters," who, by and large, occupied the most fertile tenancies. The Catholic Church, especially after the passage of the Penal Laws beginning in 1703, continued to exist in a semi-legal state, and only three bishops were left in the country, not including the diocese of Raphoe (Brady and Corish 1971:9). The Catholics of Raphoe were, in fact, without a bishop from 1661 until 1725, and the infrastructure was, even in comparison with other parts of Ireland, particularly frail, as indicated by a return of the Church of Ireland bishop, dated 1731:

> The Bishop of Raphoe Returns one old Mass house one House lately built one Cabbin wherein Mass is said publickly and two sheds. Twenty six popish Priests and some Vagrant Fryars that preach and assist the Priests and four popish Schools. . . . One James Gallagher, a Reputed fryar has lately endeavoured to pervert some of the Protestant Inhabitants of Killygarvan but on the application of the minister of yt. Parish to the Magistrates to have him taken he has disappeared. (Report on the State of Popery 1731:173)

This number of priests and permanent places of worship in a territory comprising several thousand square miles of mostly mountainous terrain traversed by few and very poor roads necessarily limited the contact of priest and people. There could not have been anything like regular Mass attendance, even imagining the people were so inclined. Whether or not the popular memory has exaggerated the danger of arrest by priest catchers, the image of the priest on horseback, encountering enemies natural and supernatural, rather than in church, is no doubt based on experience. If less frequently attended, the open air Mass, so strongly etched in popular memory, was probably a more extraordinary occasion for that. A Protestant traveler, R. Pococke, described one in Dunfanaghy, in northwestern Donegal, in the mid-eighteenth century:

> In the side [a mountain] a sort of Amphitheatre is formed in the rock; here I saw several hundred people spread all over that plain spot and the priest celebrating Mass under the rock, on an altar made of loose stones, and tho' it

was half a mile distant, I observed his Pontifical vestment with a black cross on it; for in all this country for sixty miles west and south as far as Connaught, they celebrate in the open air, in the fields or on the mountains; the Papists being so few and poor, that they will not be at the expence of a public building. (Pococke 1752: 60)

The very movement of these clerics — "vagrant strolling Priests and fryars" from the Protestant perspective of the 1731 report — who appeared and disappeared, whose office was unfixed in any institutional setting, but who were instead encountered fleetingly and often in natural surroundings, certainly caught the popular imagination, hence the folk narratives of "penal days priests" and wandering monks — the *bráithre bána* — "white brothers." The open-air Mass figures in such tales, but most central to the popular imagination and memory is the story of a priest on his way to deliver the last rites to a dying parishioner. The number of tales that tell of such clerics, on wild horseback rides, led by divinity and thwarted by Protestant enemies or the devil, arriving in the nick of time for this crucial sacrament, says much about both the perception of priestly power and the crucial role of this rite of passage in popular religion. The "faith" as a whole was, by virtue of its very disenfranchisement and relegation to a nature still strongly associated with powerful wells and haunted moors, enhanced by an aura of extraordinariness — of liminal power.

Pilgrimages too were subject to legal censure from the Protestant state; Penal Legislation, beginning in 1703, forbade all pilgrimages, including the famous one to Saint Patrick's Purgatory, whose buildings and cave had been destroyed by an English general in the mid-seventeenth century, to which a fine of ten shillings was attached. But as Brady and Corish point out:

> Like much of the penal code, this law was enforced only very sporadically. There is evidence of the suppression of pilgrimages for a time, particularly in the vicinity of Dublin. . . . In general pilgrimages continued. St. Patrick's was never interfered with. The turas Locha Deirg [St. Patrick's Purgatory] seems to have been commonly imposed as a penalty for grave sin, and the great pilgrimage-centre continued to flourish. (Brady and Corish 1971: 78–79)

We can turn again to Pococke for a description of a contemporary place for sacred cures in Malin, in the north of Donegal:

> They showed me a hollow under a rock at the south end of a high small rocky Island, which at low water is a peninsula: Here people bathe with great success, the water being very salt, as not mixed with the fresh. And the Roman Catholicks plunge in with superstitious notions that the water receives some

virtue from the Saint (Terence Marialla) who lived in a cave in the rock of the
cliff, where poor people lodge, who come for the cure. (Pococke 1752: 48)

Pococke's most interesting description comes from Armagh, near the
site of the Downpatrick tombs of Patrick, Brigid, and Columcille we remember from above. In some cases at least, the Catholic clergy were directly involved in the turas:

> St. Patrick's Well under Struel hill a famous place for pilgrimages; the water
> rises from a spring cover'd over, and runs into two baths, one public the other
> private; at the spring they wash their eyes, and in the baths the people as a part
> of their religion, go in naked and dip themselves, near the well they go round a
> sort of an Altar, probably the side of an old Chapel by way of Penance, some-
> times on their knees; and near it a Chapel was lately built, but 'twas not
> thought proper to permit them to cover it: on the side of this hill to the south
> is a rock something in the form of a seat which they call St. Patrick's Chair, with
> a way round it over the broken rock, and to go in this way, sometimes even on
> their knees, is also a part of the penance; and on Midsummer day when they
> are performing their pilgrimages there are a great number of priests near who
> give them Absolution. (Pococke 1752: 12)

There is no mention of any pilgrimage associated with the bodies of
Saint Patrick et al. The focus is instead a holy well and a "chair" as in Lough
Derg; perhaps another saint has lost his seat. Or perhaps the provenance is
older still, for like Teelin's Well of the Holy Women, the turas date is not
Saint Patrick's day, but mid-summer, although there is no mention of Saint
John, whose feast day is Midsummer's Eve (June 23). And the priests are
on the scene, taking part in the occasion.

The presence of the clergy and the emphasis on penance and relief from
purgatory were probably related. The sermons of the clergy had long been
focused on these concepts, and the "Last Things" figure centrally in what
was undoubtedly the most popular Irish language book of the period,
Gallagher's Sermons (see Gallagher 1819). The author, Catholic bishop of
Raphoe in 1725, will reappear in the next chapter, as perhaps the first
architect of a newly centralizing — if still faltering — diocesan "regime." The
publication of his sermons in "the plain Irish of the people" in this period,
however, reminds us, as does the presence of the priests at Struel Hill, of the
coexistence of competing religious discourses in this period. Certainly it
was possible to combine the individual popular search for a cure with the
accumulation of indulgences, as had generations of pilgrims on the continent as well as in Ireland, and the Church had promoted cures long before

the vogue for Purgatory. Combined though they might be, the two goals of pilgrimage involve to some extent different notions of exchange. The cure was effected through contact with the powerful place or object — following the proper ritual form and requiring the correct moral attitude. The Irish pilgrim left something and took away the cure — immediate reciprocity. Penance, on the other hand, was in payment of a debt owed to God. Though earlier versions of this view tended to stress the one-time great pilgrimage as payment for a huge debt — particularly the kin-based model of a fixed bloodfine that had to be paid — eventually the post Counter-Reformation church was to raise the possibility that ordinary people could, like monks and nuns, live a life of regular penance.

At any rate, as their own religious regimes, based on Church and Mass and control over their own clergy as well as people, gained ground in the latter half of the eighteenth century, the Catholic bishops of Ireland began to oppose the holy well pilgrimages, most particularly for their "excesses."[30] "Patterns," as the patron day celebrations were called, and wakes were the two most frequent targets of censure, as Catholic bishops began to sound more Protestant than the Protestants themselves — to coin a phrase.

> It seems beyond doubt that pilgrimages, wakes and patterns, the most serious occasions of superstition, were much worse as the century advanced. Bishop Gallagher of Raphoe, e.g., after his transfer to Kildare and Leighlin, condemned the custom of keening at funerals and "the unchristian diversion of lewd songs, of brutal tricks called fronsy-fronsy at wakes," and threatened persistent offenders with excommunication. (D. Comerford, *Collections Relating to the Dioceses of Kildare and Leighlin*, 3 vols. [Dublin, 1883–86], quoted in Brady and Corish 1971: 81–82)

> Constant vigil against the superstitious usages in connection with wakes, patterns, and pilgrimages, the Bishop of Ferns in 1771 and of Ossory in 1782 forbade their priests to celebrate Mass on the actual site where a pattern was held. Mass was to be celebrated in public on such an occasion only if the day was a Sunday or holyday and it should be celebrated in the nearest chapel. (Brady and Corish 1971: 80)

The bishops were waging a war against "superstition," following, if belatedly, the Counter-Reformation move against all such heterodoxies. The attack against un-Christian diversion was also in keeping with the Counter-Reformation which, following the lead of the Reformation, had begun the narrow definition of religion that holds sway in the western world today. A religion was a specific approved body of doctrine to be sharply separated from "superstition", and to be practiced in a religious manner at religious times and in religious places. The contest between the chapel and the well — for that is clearly how these bishops saw it — was one of religious geography. The bishops wanted to replace one set of central places with another, just as they hoped to change both the discourse and sociability of local religion, and thereby constitute new social, as well as religious, worlds.

*   *   *

> Christenings — Marriages, Wakes, and Funerals are very numerously attended more so than in any other part of Donegal I am acquainted with. They are seldom attended with any unpleasant riots. . . .
>
> No RC chapel nor meeting house; no Protestant dissenters in the parish.

> The traditions respecting Columb Kill are very numerous indeed, but in general too ridiculous to mention. In a valley extending from Glen Bay about two miles into the interior fr W. to E. are 7 stones from 5 to 7 feet high and about 18 ins. broad inscribed with crosses and circles. They are held in very high veneration by the R. Catholics who perform Stations at them on Sundays[31] and holy days. St Columb's house and Bed are shown here-as also his well, the water of which the people think is possessed of great virtue in healing diseases of every kind — There is a stone of very particular use in curing head aches which must be lodged every night in St Columb's bed but is generally taken off every morning through the parish. I was not fortunate enough to see it tho' I called twice — but each time it was out on duty. (Ewing 1823: 2)

> There was a *gallta* [foreign] woman in Glen who was inhospitable to the locals [*gaedhil*] who were going on Columcille's *turas*. The cairns [piles of stones that marked the pilgrimage route] were on a piece of her land, and she went and broke every bit of bottle and glass she could find and threw it on the cairns, to prevent the Gaels who would be doing the pilgrimage from crossing her piece of earth. She fell sick. When she was dying, she was barking the whole time until she died as if she were a dog." (NFA, vol. 143: 1696; my translation)

Where is the holy well of Columcille? It exists — and has existed — in several landscapes and in several discourses. In the texts above we hear the Protestant and Catholic — sophisticated civil servant and so-called "primitive", each speaking of the "Other." The first text, dated 1823, is taken from John Ewing's "Statistical Return of Glencolumbkille"; the second is a short narrative recorded by folklorist Sean O hEochaidh in 1945 from Maire O'Beirne, a sixty-year-old woman from Malin Beg, who had heard the story in her girlhood. Each stands in his own landscape, viewing the other "through" a holy well, which therefore mediates, in a very real sense, their relationship. Each defines the other in terms of a perceived relationship to the well. For Ewing, the locals are the sort of people who believe in wells, while for O'Beirne and the other storytellers, Ewing might be the kind of man who not only disbelieves but interferes with or even desecrates such places. In their stories — *an ghall*, the stranger/Protestant. That role is, however, usually reserved for the same local Protestants mentioned in Ewing's report, in the context of a general description of the place.

> The coast is very bold rugged & precipitous was very much frequented by smugglers, but this has been greatly cramped of late by the Coast Guards who have three stations in this Parish — There are no plantations not one — in the parish. . . . No modern buildings; no towne or gentleman's Seats — the scenery an alternate succession of rocks, mountains, and improvable vallies; No inn, roads horribly bad — not a perch of good road in the Parish. . . . From what I as yet know of them I would say that the Inhabitants are quiet, peaceable, and inoffensive — there is neither lawyer, attorney, magistrate or policeman in the Parish. All the inhabitants speak Irish — all the Protestants and some of the R. Catholics speak the English language which is fast increasing since the establishment of the coastguards — who in general don't speak Irish. Children are generally employed in taking care of cattle — education here is very far back indeed — there is a school on Robinson's foundation which is numberously attended; another where the Master is paid directly by the pupils — the London Hibernian and Kildare Street Societies had a school here but during last winter the pupils were withdrawn — I now hear they are about to return to the school again. No libraries or manuscripts. . . . The tithes are very low let. There is an old church [established Church of Ireland] near which a new one is shortly to be erected. There are very few ploughs here, the crops are in general put down with the spade. . . . Black cattle and sheep numerous but of a small breed. Pigs increasing fast, no fairs or markets in the parish. Wages from 10d. to 1 s per day. Tradesmen neither numerous nor good. Flannel is the only manufacture, from this and butter and young cattle the rents are mostly paid. (Ewing 1823: 1)

Those few Protestant families — a tiny minority west of Killybegs had settled the few semi-fertile strips of Kilcar and Glencolumbkille parishes (see Figure 2). The church mentioned by Ewing was in fact built soon after his report and is still the place of worship for what remains of the Protestants of Glencolumbkille and Malin More. These families, with lowland Scottish names like Maxwell and Blaine, are the same noted by Ewing. Most of them arrived in the Ulster Plantation of the seventeenth century, taking up tenancies on the better land. The difference between them and their Catholic neighbors was perhaps most visible in Malin More, where one can still see a row of two-story dressed stone houses, each in the middle of a good block of land, while beyond in Malin Beg the rough stone cottages of the Catholic tenantry huddle for shelter in the rockier land—a microcosm of Ireland at the time of plantation. There were no Protestants —and no good land—on the Teelin/Carrick side of the parish, but acoss the river in Kilcar, the richer earth in the townland of Derrylahan ("broad oak forest") was, like Malin More, home to a number of "planter" homesteads. Little of this remains now. The beautiful church in Glen has an active congregation of a dozen or so, and it is the Protestant minister who now rides a circuit—in a Ford Escort—holding services in three different parishes for ever shrinking congregations. The two-story farmhouses in Malin More now house mainly Catholic familes and I myself met the last Protestant in Kilcar—a man whose family had been there for a bit over three hundred years. He died in 1990.

Ewing's report describes a world without great distinction of class and culture. It is he, the outsider, who sees the locals as Other; there is no indication that he feels kinship with the local Protestants. The storyteller, on the other hand, speaks in the language of local binary opposition. Three centuries of living together have not made one people—at least not in that discourse, not in that genre of story. The stark opposition of Gael versus Gall is in fact the one used in every such story in the archives, wherever the plot involves such characters.

One cannot take such stories as evidence of the quality of daily life; they are a response to experience, not a description of it. The religious narratives of the region—stories about wells, priests, and the like—are about power, and in the folk discourse of power, Gael versus Gall corresponds to experience of power and of difference and may also reflect a hostility and distance that increased in the period after Ewing's report.

The central theme of Ewing's account is the remoteness of the place: a world as yet little affected by external forces. Yet even the indirect commercial penetration of the eighteenth century had already had a dramatic impact on the region. The old adaptation based on small infields sown with oats and barley and extensive outfield supporting mainly cattle, supplemented with seasonal fishing in the estuaries and along the coast, had given way under a series of coordinated pressures in the course of the previous century. Potatoes were now the main crop and the population had grown rapidly. While the old *clachan*, or hamlet, with its "rundale" system[32] was still the dominant settlement pattern, such communities had grown and produced daughter hamlets, occupying less fertile lands. What had been rough pasture—"mountain"—was now growing potatoes, and the yet rougher grounds were increasingly grazed by sheep—from which was produced the "flannel" that Ewing notes. By 1823 the international herring fishery based in Killybegs had already collapsed, but local fishing and fish merchants were certainly an aspect of the economic life of places like Teelin. On the other hand, the formal apparatus of the British state, as well as the institutional forms of British, and even Irish, civilization, was not yet much in evidence.

The coast guard is of course an interesting and noteworthy exception. If the state had been anxious to foster the connection of such peripheral zones to the world economy by offering bounties on exports, they were equally anxious to prevent the "unmediated" access to that economy represented by the illegal "drug traffic" of tobacco smuggling. Hence the coast guard—three installations in a back-of-beyond parish not worth the investment of a road—the gaze of the state, of the colonizer. The illegal tobacco trade was, by all reports, reduced, but the continuing dependency equally noted by travelers must have meant profits for those few merchants in the region. Of course, whiskey—one of the relatively few English words of Irish origin—was produced at home, and so the campaigns of the "authorities" to end illicit distillation were of much more limited success. On the other hand, perhaps the most expensive drug was introduced by legal merchants, probably in the middle of the nineteenth century—tea.

At the time of Ewing's report, however, there was no tea and, more important, no town in which to sell it. The commercial and political regime of the Protestant English state had a limited presence: the coast guard station in Rinnakilla was not yet, I think, Foucault's panopticon. But the Catholic Church was also rather weakly present. Other religious occasions, wakes and *turasanna*, seem—perhaps in inverse proportion—very popular. Though disdainful of Irish "superstition," Ewing was interested enough to check three times for the curing stone. He was to some degree clearly fascinated by the "Other," but not a romantic. As long as such occasions were not the scenes of wild and uncivil behavior, which they seem not to have been,[33] Ewing was probably less inclined than the local priest, who was still struggling to cover two parishes on horseback, to see the turas as a threat. More likely, such behavior was for Ewing simply another symptom of a native irrationality linked, perhaps, to the "unimproved" state of those valleys, for moral and economic improvement, (social Darwinism clearly preceded the biological version) had already long been, and would continue to be the favorite refrain of government and private reformers. Ewing was, at any rate, hopeful that the economic transformation of the region by means of good roads, quays, and so on would promote a healthy enough trade to transform the people as well as the place. It was a question of geography, of making roads and towns that would civilize the wild west.

While neither Ewing nor the other representatives of the colonial/state regime was interested in launching an attack on any holy well, the centralizing episcopal regime of the Catholic Church was increasingly on the offensive. The wells and their gatherings fell under repeated clerical censure. Once again it was a question of the geography of power. As we will see later on, the Church was beginning to build chapels in this period and to increase its staff of clerics, subjecting the local populace to more direct social control, and redefining local religious geography—and with it, to some degree, social geography—in the process. The new Catholic chapels, built in the new villages like Carrick, were to be the central places, and the parish around it the clearly bounded social world. Thus the two "regimes," Catholic and colonial, were engaged, to some extent, in the same geographical project. And both would achieve the basic transformation in the 1830s and 1840s.

By 1835, when John O'Donovan arrived in the parish to fix the landscape on maps for the first Ordnance Survey, the first decent road already traversed the parish, and a combination of active landlords, agents, and government commissioners—a kind of state/colonial regime—were poised to change the most basic circumstances of people's lives.

O'Donovan too witnessed the turas of Columcille:

> What their forefathers thought, believed, said, and did a thousand years ago, they think, believe, and say at present. They are primitive beings who have but few points of contact with the civilized world . . . who live in what may be called the extreme brink of the world, far from the civilization of cities, and the lectures of the philosopher. . . .
>
> They are yet anxious to perform the lustrations and purifications, which so much prevailed in the early ages of christianity, and though the turas left by Columbkille in the old Glen is now condemned by the clergy, some of the natives go through it yet with reverence and solemnity, visiting each hallowed spot where Columbkille knelt or stood or left any of his sacred footsteps. . . .
>
> On the summit of the gloomy mountain of Slieve Leag are yet shewn the ruins of the little cell of Aodh Mac Bric. . . .
>
> A most solemn turas was performed here in the memory of the last generation, but he liveth not now who could point out all the hallowed spots to be visited and prayed at, so that it has been abandoned as a station of pilgrimage to the rapid oblivion of the name and fame of the solitary Bishop Aidus. (OSL, John O'Donovan, 1838, "Donegal," pp. 120–21)

TEELIN HARBOUR, Co DONEGAL. 14-59. W.L.

Figure 9. Turas, Well of the Holy Women, Teelin Harbor, late nineteenth century (Lawrence Collection, National Library of Ireland).

John O'Donovan, Irish scholar and antiquarian, was one of several surveyors working for the first Ordnance Survey of Ireland. His vision and voice are clearly different from Ewing's; O'Donovan "respected" the well, in a way not unlike that of an academic. He represented, instead, another sort of desacralization, or perhaps disenchantment — and one as equally likely to be Catholic as Protestant. Indeed O'Donovan's antiquarianism can afford to be more tolerant than that of the Catholic clergy he mentions, for example, because there is no need for him to separate "religion" from "superstition" in such cases:

> I hope that all these places are carefully set down on the plans of the parish of Glencolumbkille, as they will appear very conspicuous on the map of so wild a parish. The Tree, the grave of Kerk, all the holy wells and all the ruins should be shewn and their names given. The theatre of the solemn pilgrimage of Columbkille which extended for three miles along the Glen should be carefully shewn, such as the hole made by the bell when it fell from the sky, the ruins of the monastery, and all the wells and other footsteps of the Saint and his followers, the pilgrims. (OSL, John O'Donovan, 1838, "Donegal," p. 127)

But why, one might ask? And does this apparently respectful and interested cataloguing of the sacred landscape have some part in the domination of the locals? O'Donovan answers:

> Man looks with veneration upon every spot that has been hallowed by sincere religion be it ever so deluded and feels anxious (when possessed of true learning) to preserve every trace by which the turas of the pilgrim and the progress of the human mind in art, religion, or enthusiasm can be followed (traced). (OSL, John O'Donovan, 1838, "Donegal," p. 127; emphasis added)

The act of mapping and commenting on these sites was clearly part of the "progress" of which O'Donovan speaks here. In fixing these sacred spots on his maps he was also fixing them in time: an ancient practice, which if unchanged for a thousand years, was in relation to the history of the Western World — his history — a *survival*. So the evolutionary anthropologists of the latter part of his century would term it: a survival of a former stage and valuable in its *sincerity* (thus showing an underlying religious truth) as well as in the way it was illustrated by means of contrast with modernity, progress. Indeed, the contrast is plainly, and intriguingly, exaggerated:

> They are primitive beings who have but few points of contact with the civilized world . . . who live in what may be called the extreme brink of the world, far from the civilization of cities.

This exoticism no doubt added to the excitement of O'Donovan's "fieldwork," as it did those who would follow him. The making of maps, the self-consciousness of history in this sense — this understanding of where *we* truly stood in time and space — was for O'Donovan an important part of that progress.

Clearly, he was right. In southwest Donegal, the world he mapped was about to change, or rather to be changed, by the concerted effort of land-lords, agents, and government officials. Beyond the holy wells, O'Dono-van's maps (see Figure 4) showed how people lived — the arrangement of their houses, still in clusters, surrounded by scattered bits of land — an ar-rangement known as "rundale." These tightly clustered hamlets must have been communities — and were certainly largely composed of related fam-ilies, as an analysis of names by townland shows in the 1850s.

First the coast guards — just after the turn of the nineteenth century. Then roads. Then O'Donovan and his maps and letters. More was to fol-low — commissions, reports, and institutions issuing from government, lo-cal landlords, and their agents, or the two acting in concert. It was an expanding regime, intent on transforming the human relation to the land-scape. The issue was power. The Protestant power was that of the new law backed by military force, but also of rational economic and scientific dis-course, for O'Donovan was a surveyor, one of those given the herculean task of translating the Irish landscape into a series of documents, the Ord-nance Survey Maps of 1836. His map sought to fix and thus control all the vaguaries of that Irish landscape, even to the holy wells, each of which he noted in its place.

For both surveyor and storyteller, landscape and language are interde-pendent. Reading the map objectifies the landscape and the objectified perception of the landscape makes the map possible. Just so with the folk narratives. The stories preserve the enchanted landscape; the well and other places like it literally hold the stories. Those raised with the stories need only hear the name of a given place or else see it to rehear the story that is tied to the place — or at least know that there is a story that someone else "has." Perhaps it is less a question of whether or not one "believes" the story than of a landscape that has stories in it — stories it can tell you — versus a landscape that talks about other things or is mute.

Just as the Ordnance Survey, in depicting a world, contributed to its change, so too did a series of government commissions interrogate a world they thought needed "reformation." The reports of these commissions re-veal much about both the conditions of the locals and, more subtly, the intentions of the inquirers. The First Poor Law Report dates from the same period as the Ordnance Survey. The commissioners sought information on the state of mendicancy, evidently expecting to find that the general poverty of the region had produced an underclass of wandering landless souls, marrying and/or procreating with abandon, committing crimes, and dunning honest locals for money or food. A proposed poor law was to change all that, institutionalizing the poor in workhouses supported by a tax. In Donegal, the commissioners encountered general resistance to this idea, except from merchants in towns.

By far most tenant farmers favored continuing with the old system—testifying that they and all the others felt it both good and right to give food at the door to the destitute. The idiom they used does not separate religious, ethical, or so-called "magical" formulas. They give "for God's sake," in order to avoid like suffering themselves, and because it is right. The shopkeepers, a feature in the more developed regions to the northeast, did not share this reciprocity-centered view—the great wheel of life (*an rotha mór an tsaoil*), as Mickey MacGabhainn called it (MacGabhainn 1959).[34] Interestingly, the Catholic bishop agreed with the shopkeepers, favoring an institutionalization of the poor supported by a tax, if it could be fairly distributed so that the burden fell on the large landowners and not the struggling tenantry.

Perhaps the bishop understood that state institutions were not necessarily against the interests of the Church; clerics could and would be assigned to poorhouses, fever hospitals, and other state institutions. Perhaps the Church and the state—as Tom Inglis (1987) argues—shared a common goal in civilizing the wild Irish. Perhaps—more subtly—both commissioners and bishop understood that the ethic of reciprocity acted out in mendicancy was inimical to progress and improvement (from the state's point of view) and to the formation of a new set of dependencies (from both Church's and state's point of view). The old attitude toward beggars, supported by religious hopes and fears, does seem an instance of what Jane Schneider (1990) calls "equity consciousness."[35] The outer ring of relationships—with the unknown beggar—thus fell under the auspices of indirect reciprocity, wherein you gave with the expectation of a return, not from the receiver, but from some other when and if you found yourself destitute as well. But the very basis of daily "equity consciousness" was no doubt the hamlet community—the *clachan*—with its rotating right of access to fields and its carefully managed commons, and that social world was even more the subject of attack by rationalizing landlord and agent.

While the famine of the late 1840s is justly remembered as the national watershed in transforming Irish life, in areas like western Donegal perhaps the most profound social transformation was in fact the break-up of those small hamlets of related households that had for centuries been the basic element of the local social fabric. According to his evidence before the Devon Commission in 1844 (pp.175–80) Alexander Hamilton, agent to Thomas Conolly, the owner of most of Glencolumbkille parish, was by that time engaged in the process of breaking up the hamlets and their system of divided and scattered inheritance. He regarded the arrangement of both households and fields as the height of irrationality, the obstacle to progress and improvement, and the seething breeding grounds of every Irish vice. He "squared" the land — creating what he hoped, with constant vigilance, would be a rational unit that would pass, undivided, from one sober tenant to the next. It can be well imagined that the tenantry took a different view of the matter and indeed, as both Hamilton and subsequent agents complained, often ignored the new rules and divided as they wished what they stubbornly regarded as their land.

Thus the complete transformation of the landscape, natural and cultural, was accomplished by the concerted action of landlords, agents, and government officials — the colonial/state regime as I have called it. But the holy wells were not on the agenda. Ewing thought they were ridiculous, O'Donovan "respected" them, others ignored them. They were perceived as primitive — either romantically or not — but never, I think, understood to be connected to the "equity consciousness" for which they may well have been a sacred manifestation.

Perhaps, however, the locals understood the well as both symbol and embodiment of their relationship to one another and to the land that was under attack. The folk stories describe a landscape that not only resists disenchantment but strikes back at those who seek to alter it, divide it, objectify it, deny its inherent power. In every story, the enemy of the well is *an Ghall*, the foreigner/Protestant. This enemy interferes with the turas, as in our story, or — in another favorite sub-genre — puts a foot in the well both to desecrate the holy water and to demonstrate its powerlessness. But the evil-doer is punished — by being unable to remove the foot until a priest is summoned to "unbind" him or her. Sometimes conversion is part of the exchange. There are also stories of moving wells. A Protestant landlord plugs up a well only to have it burst forth in another place — sometimes in his own house!

*   *   *

Although the stories tell of Protestant desecrators, it would seem that the far more direct and consistent enemy of the wells was the Catholic Church. The diocesàn regime, built on and in churches, trained clergy, and the centrality of Roman devotional cults that historian Emmet Larkin christened the "devotional revolution" was already beginning in the east of Ireland, and moved in fits and starts across the country, eventually achieving a dramatic re-orientation of local religion.[36] The religious changes of the nineteenth century were critical elements in a general socio-cultural shift that involved both a "civilizing process" in Elias's (1982) sense of the term — wherein models of civility were adopted by a growing Catholic bourgeoisie, and what Kitty Verrips (1987) has dubbed the "civilizing offensive" — a frontal assault on the behavior of the poorer classes.[37] Assemblies at holy wells were anathema from either perspective. The aspiring bourgeois might eschew it as peasant superstition, while the peasants themselves, and the growing class of landless laborers, found themselves increasingly subject to clerical censure. Not that they listened. For much of Ireland, it was the massive death emigration caused by the famine that broke the backs of the lower classes, and this, combined with the increasing presence and power of the clergy (see the next chapter), eventually succeeded in taming, if not altogether halting, such assemblies.

In southwest Donegal, however, the famine did not strike as deeply as elsewhere, and the population continued to rise until the 1870s. The parish priest by the 1830s had already suppressed the great local turas of Columcille, but, as O'Donovan noted, many continued to seek the healing powers of the well. Other holy wells fell into disuse by the early years of the nineteenth century, or at least lost their organized turas. By the 1870s, however, a more securely Victorian clergy was beginning to view the holy well devotions — stripped of the embarrassing secular "excesses" — through the lens of a Romantic nationalism that celebrated the distinctively Celtic in whatever form in appeared. Writing in 1872, Monsignor James Stephens — a man who will reappear in subsequent chapters — included a chapter on holy wells in his tourbook of the region. Stephens himself was from a well-to-do family in Ballyshannon and had been recently installed as parish priest of Killybegs. From his sophisticated point of view, wells — especially if associated with ancient ruins (he was a member of the Kilkenny Archaeological Society) — were of historic interest as well as an appropriate topic for sentimental verse, both being typical ingredients for the form of Romantic Nationalism he endorsed — evincing the continuing connection of an ancient Celtic soul and landscape, both animated by an innate religiosity.

Under the influence of the ensuing Gaelic revival, and even more in the independent Ireland of the twentieth century, priests were in a position not only to tolerate or approve the well cults but to lead the turas themselves. In the early years of this century, priests in many parts of Ireland began to coopt the pilgrimage, presiding over the procession and sometimes holding an outdoor Mass near the well, after which the pilgrims went peacefully home. Indeed, many clergy so successfully captured and tamed such devotions that some began to look further, reviving defunct pilgrimages in order to reinvigorate what could now be perceived as quaint local custom. Once securely positioned as patrons of the pilgrimages, local clergy would sometimes promote other devotions at the site, with lay support, making major iconographic modifications. Especially during the papally declared First Marian Year in 1954, local communities not only built the grottos — usually replicas of that of Our Lady of Lourdes (with or without Bernadette), but sometimes added a statue of Mary to their well, obscuring or displacing, at least visually, the local saint. At least one well-known well — Saint Brigid's near Liscannor in Clare — has become a veritable cornucopia of "generalized devotions." It is difficult to find poor Brigid among the Marian images and Sacred Hearts (see Figure 10). Then again, that is probably no more than what Brigid herself did to whatever goddesses preceded her.

*   *   *

No such newcomers have yet overtaken the wells of southwest Donegal. To judge by the names of the saints, the most recent instance of a generalized devotion capturing a local well is that of Saint Catherine in Killybegs, whose cult was probably brought there by Augustinians in the twelfth century. The other saints are autocthones — still inextricably linked to the landscape through which they wandered. There are even wells that have resisted the saints. At *Tobar na mBan Naomh* — the "Well of the Holy Women" — it is still *Ciall*, *Tuigse*, and *Náire* (Sense, Understanding, and Modesty) that preside; there is no sign of Mary or even Brigid.

Nevertheless, the all night vigils exist no longer[38] and, watching the magisterial Father McDyer lead his people from station to station, one is

Figure 10. St. Brigid's Well, Liscannor, County Clare (photo by the author).

tempted to conclude that the once wild pilgrimage so often condemned by the clergy is now but an extension of the church. The earth, it seems, has been disenchanted and sacred geography has once and for all shifted away from the western edge and into the town—where the institutional and social center—post office, school, police, five pubs, and the large shops—are joined by the religious center of church and cemetery. But the notion of a different sort of power, and perhaps a different sort of social world, is kept alive at the wells and in the discourse of the wells—the stories people tell about them.

The turas, or "stations," as they are called in English, of Saint Columcille in the parish of his glen—"Glencolmcille—begin and end in what is now the Protestant churchyard (see Figure 11) and wend their three mile way across a stream and through fields and thickets. The stations themselves are early Christian monuments, rough standing stones whose smooth faces bear the same Celtic designs as eighth- and ninth-century metalwork,[39] and a variety of fragmentary early Christian ruins, including Columcille's bed. The most important leg of the turas takes the weary pilgrim up a steep hill to Columcille's well, a natural spring of sacred water. Surrounding the well is great heap of stones, according to locals a legacy from the great numbers of souls who have "done the stations" over the years. Condy Seamus, whose little farm is in the townland just below the well, explained, "They used to carry three stones up to the well with them—as a penance, do you see—and some of them would want a big penance and they would carry big stones, like this." He stooped forward with the weight of the imaginary stones, one great one in his right hand, balanced behind his back, and two more crammed between his right hand and pointed chin. His eyes flashed with admiration as he mimed the poor penitent's encumbered stride up the hill.

The well itself is housed in a rough stone altar, a series of slabs that include two shelves. On one sits a mug and a cup for taking up the water, and on the other are arrayed the "little bits" left by the pilgrim as tokens. "You must leave something for what you take away." There are coins of every denomination, pins, and myriad small and often broken religious objects: scapulars, miraculous medals, plastic and ceramic Infants of Prague, Our Ladies of various loci. These rest rusting or crumbling in apparent careless disarray. In all this there is nothing to distinguish this well from the many hundreds of others that can be found throughout the Irish landscape.

There is, however, one nearly unique addition to Columcille's well. Propped next to the altar is a life sized "primitive" statue of the saint himself. This corporeal presence is not ancient but the recent work of a local folk

Figure 11. Turas, Colmcille, Glencolumcille, 1987 (photo by Maeve Hickey).

artist, "John the Miner," whose passing in 1985 at the age of eighty-one left his region bereft of a most singular individual. Workers in stone, concrete. and wood in this part of the world usually bend their skills to practical jobs. They build houses and walls, and for those who cannot afford the milled granite of respectability, such local craftsmen make gravestones. But even in that task there is rarely much in the way of whimsy or adornment. Not so with John, whose gravestones in several local parish churchyards are graced with niches in which he placed tiny images — saints or something like them. In his old age John was an artist in concrete. Having succeeded with the gravestones, John made full-sized saints for two of the local holy wells: Saint Kieran's in the neighboring parish of Kilcar, and this one of Columcille.

The presence of John the Miner's rendition of Columcille — the fact of its oddity — forces a reflection. Images of saints are common enough elsewhere in the Catholic world, indeed they are to be expected. One thinks, for example, of the Italian, Spaniard, or Latin American kneeling before the image — at home, in church, or at the shrine — of the saint him- or herself, addressing entreaties to this personal mediator. Anthropologist Michael Kenny (1960) argues that in such a religious system the saint was a mediatory patron that mirrored the local large landowner. A sacred version, in Durkheimian fashion, of a vertical power system with ancient roots in Mediterranean urban class-structured society. In either case the poor dependent bargained with the patron for intervention with forces great and remote. There is, however, at least one salient difference. One bargains directly with the living patron and indirectly with the saint, access to whom is itself mediated by the image — the statue or picture that adorns the niche or shelf. The saint is in heaven but he is also there in the image or icon, and lives as well in stories, not just the "traditional" legends of interest to folklorists, but the narratives concerning his or her record as saint-mediator. While one's mother might not tell the story of the saint's miraculous life, she is likely to tell of her personal experience of the saint's favors. These narratives also figure in the books and pamphlets published by various arms of the church to promote their saints.

The importance of images and places in the cult of the saints is pursued in far greater depth in the work of William Christian (1972, 1981). In his discussion of religious life in rural northern Spain, Christian distinguishes between shrine images whose uniqueness is owed to their connection to the landscape and those images understood to be mere renditions of some other image, itself a miraculous residue. These latter images are foci for "generalized devotions," and in such cases the particularity of the object would seem to be less significant for the devotee. To put these observations into a more theoretical format, we might say that in the case of generalized devotions we are dealing with symbols of symbols, or even symbols of symbols of symbols. Take, for example, the mass-produced lithograph of Our Lady of Lourdes to be found on many a Catholic's wall. For the devotee, that lithograph may reproduce a master image to be found at Lourdes, which in turn represents Our Lady as she "appeared," which, finally, represents Our Lady as she *is*, in heaven next to Christ unchanging through time.

In Ireland, however, images are not nearly so common, at least in public spaces. The holy wells which were, up until 1954, the only form of local shrine not inside churches, are sometimes dedicated to Our Lady, but more often to the early Irish saints of Columcille's ilk—Kieran, Conall Caol, and of course, most often, Patrick and Brigid. The wells themselves, like the one described above, are typically simple affairs: rude, dry stone constructions with a slab of rock, by way of altar, on or near the well. At best an ancient, nearly stub-armed cross stands over the shrine. The religious objects, as described above, are not objects of devotion but rather items left in exchange. The early Irish saints are not often pictured, although lithographs of Patrick appear in the nineteenth century; perhaps it is the well itself—the sacred landscape—that retains the mediatory power.

Such a view is suggested by the way people talk about the wells and the turas, for in stories of cures associated with them the saint is often not mentioned. Other saints, those more recent additions to the pantheon, whose cults arrived with images, relics, and pamphlets—*are* viewed as miraculous intercessors/curers, and are consequently named. The contrast is clear in the "quest for therapy" story told to me by a middle-aged woman of Kilcar parish.

> That girl [she nodded toward her twelve-year-old daughter] was that sick. . . .
> I took her to Kieran's Well and to the other wells, even to Doon Well, and
> nothing helped her. They told me in the hospital that they could do nothin' for
> her. Well, a neighbor of mine had given me a relic of St. Martin [St. Martin of
> Porres, a popular saint whose cult was being promoted by missioners and
> pamphlets] and I prayed to Martin and prayed to him, and I promised to name
> my next child after him if he cured the girl. Well he did. And that's how Martin
> [her next oldest and favorite] got his name.

This distinction is typical. The new saints are pictured, talked to, dealt with. The old Irish saints are addressed only in traditional Irish language prayers—formulaic injunctions. "You don't really have to think about them," a forty-year-old man from Teelin told me, "they're just there, like." Part of the landscape, through which they moved, and through which the modern pilgrim moves—for a variety of reasons.

Mrs. Kennedy sat with her nephew—a boy of eight—on the stone flags outside the Protestant church in Glencolumbkille, rubbing her damp and sore feet before replacing her shoes. Her close-cropped silver hair and slacks seemed incongruously modern and middle class for someone who had just completed the ancient round of "stations" of Columcille. The turas used to begin for all pilgrims at dawn on June 9. It was three miles long, proceeding from one ancient cross to another through boggy fields and up a rocky hill to the well and "bed" of the Saint. The true devotee, like Mrs. Kennedy, went barefooted and so usually incurred, especially in the dark, a variety of minor injuries. Now pilgrims did the stations throughout the day—whenever they felt like it. As a result, rather than what must have been the more impressive show of a large assembly walking and praying together, there was a more or less constant trickle of pilgrims from dawn to dusk, usually in small groups of family or neighbors. Certainly a larger group would have gone together if Father Eddy, the curate, had gotten back from his trip in time to lead them, but he had not. It was nearly six in the evening when Mrs. Kennedy and the four others who had gone with her completed their rounds. Her accent, like her dress, were decidedly middleclass (in local terms); her eyes and voice were pure contentment:

> I live on the main road to Kilcar and I've been coming here to do the stations since I was a girl. I would say it's just good for you to do it—I have a great time with it.

Later that evening on my way to Killybegs and my weekly charismatic prayer meeting, I saw Una walking a bit uncertainly in the boggy grass alongside the road. "I'm just after doing the stations at Glen," she told me. "I always try to do them, like when we were girls." Una was from a fairly remote farm in the hills north of Carrick and now in her late thirties had only been back a few years from a decade of work in Glasgow. She was married now and lived with her Scottish husband and several small children in a housing estate outside Killybegs. This more modern setting was only about sixteen miles from her natal home, but was in some senses in another world—"in through" as they say in Killybegs. Her childhood language had been Irish, while her Killybegs neighbors were all English speakers. As small a place as it is, fewer than two thousand souls, Killybegs is very much a town, and dominated by an extremely active waterfront. The fishing fleet is the largest in Ireland, and the social profile is far more akin to that of parts of Dublin than the rest of Donegal. For Una the stations at Glen are a return to her childhood and to a very different world — indeed, to a different religion. I wondered what she made of the charismatic prayer meetings at which she was a regular attender.

Kathleen, on the other hand, had never lived in Killybegs or Glasgow. She had not shifted in fact from the cottage overlooking Teelin Bay since her birth some sixty years before.

> When I was a girl, I met up with my friends up in Glencolumbkille — I had relations there do ye see — to do the turas. We began at midnight and it took three hours. Well, I was all covered with cuts and bruises. In those days the people came from the two parishes mostly, as far as Crove. Those that came from Carrick walked all the way there, and of course they'd walk through the night to arrive in time to do the turas. We did it for our intentions. We'd also go to Teelin there on bonefire night [June 23] and you'd do the stations there and put the three stones there around you. The stones were very good for back and leg trouble. I've done that turas many times, sometimes for a pain of some kind — do ye see — and sometimes, if there was nothing in particular wrong with your health, for an "intention."

In Kathleen's account we see the usual mixture of motivations: although she feels herself no longer physically able for the turas, it is for her, as for Una, a definitive memory of girlhood, an annual walk across the parish, an enactment of kinship; in short, an intrinsic aspect of the place and being of the place. Note also that the place so defined is loosely bounded. Columcille is not a patron saint whose cult defines a clearly defined local community set off against rivals, with their own saints. Columcille wandered. So do his devotees. Kathleen went to all the wells in her region, each on its day. But there was also the special search for a cure, which might not wait until the day of the turas, but which had the best chance on that day. When she went to the well of Columcille or of the Holy Women, like the others Kathleen left something — a rag, pin, religious object — for the "cure" that was taken away.

For the cure is there — at and in the well — a direct mediation to a world of power and a world of stories. In telling me the story with which this chapter began, Conal Phaddy's tone was nearly off-hand, but assured. Nor was he a particularly religious or credulous man when it came to other claims of the miraculous. When talk of "moving statues" swept Ireland some years later, he wryly suggested that Rinnakilla might well learn from the "cute" people of Ballinspittle and spread similar reports in order to boost tourism.[40] While claims of moving statues seemed ridiculous to Conal and Francie, the record of cures attributed to the Well of the Holy Women was firmly rooted — embedded in the earth itself, in local knowledge, and in the narratives that linked the one with the other.

For Conal, Francie and others like them, it is perhaps not even entirely a question of the "supernatural" or the "sacred" at work in such cures. Rather, for them, the local geography "signifies" in a way that links rather than separates "sacred" and "profane" knowledge — joining the mundanely practical to the morally or magically instructive. A fisherman or a shepherd — sometimes the same person — must know more than his own fields. If a fisherman like Francie, for example, needs to refind a fishing ground, he will triangulate his position with two shore points — perhaps *Tor an t-Seolaim* and *Tor an t-sasanaigh*. The first is named for its shape — the sail rock; the second, "the rock of the Englishman (Saxon)" refers to a story of a shipwrecked Englishman of some previous century and the aid he received at local hands. Every bump and hole, every twist of the nearly treeless wild bog and mountain landscape, carries its own name. Not everyone knows as many names and narratives as Francie does (Referring to an Irish PhD student who had collected much place-name lore from him, Francie said, "It's me that put the title doctor on him.") But many know dozens, and nearly all the people know some, and know that such stories exist, even if they do not know them themselves. They know, in other words, that the landscape contains narratives — that they are there, if you will — and that there are individuals, local sages, who "have" that knowledge. But if much of the earth signifies, carries narratives, holy spots like the well of Francie's story are more than that; they are powerful places, and their stories are powerful as well.

The stories about the saints are set in "dream time" and tell of their wanderings, their feats, their bouts of temper, and their discovery or creation of the wells. The stories about the wells and their cures, however, are often linked to particular people, with assurances of veracity. The saint does not come directly into the story, but one might hear of the sacred trout or salmon that appears to signal the successful mediation, the bridge to the other world.

*   *   *

There are other stories about other spots on the landscape, also powerful, but dangerous. Such places — called *uaigneach* — lonely — are also portals to another world, the world of fairies ("the people of the hill") and/or ghosts. The remains of earthen forts and certain trees or places carry this notion, and were generally thought to be dangerous for any who interfered with them. Writing in 1938, the folklorist O hEochaidh, himself a native of the mountainy Teelin townland of Croaghlin, told of the belief in Teelin that any local dún (presumed by archaeologists to be iron-age forts) was a prime habitation of the "people of the hill"—fairies. There was such a place in the townland of Lergadaghtan, from which it was thought very unlucky to remove a blade of grass; a cow left there to eat the grass of the fort would soon die. This negative reciprocity—if you will—reminds one of the wells, for here is another window into the other world, although in this case death or diaster can be taken away.

There are, however, other stories about meetings with the people of the hill in which a more positive exchange is sought—a special skill or riches—but that is always tricky, and most tales end with disaster. In the case of this *dún*, however, if the exchange is initiated from the other side, as in the following story, no evil befalls the mortals.

> There was a woman of the Cunningham clan living long ago at *bún a' dúin* [foot of the fort] in Lergadaghtan townland—a very lonely (*an uaigneach*) place it is—and there were not many other houses around. The woman was home sitting late one night, and as was the rule, all the men of the houses there were out fishing. She'd taken in a young boy from one of the neighbors to keep with her till morning.
>
> They were sitting by the fire with a pot of porridge when they sensed people coming toward the house. They had a nasty dog there, but he didn't feel them there. The door was opened and in came three lads, well dressed fishermen they were, and they stood by the fire.
>
> The old woman asked them to sit and offered a spoon for the porridge. One of the men asked her if she had put salt in the porridge and she told them that she had. They told her then that they couldn't take a drop of anything with salt on it, but if she had any without it they'd drink that. They told her then that they had to hurry home to their people. She asked them how far they had to go, and they told her not far; they were her neighbors every day of the year. The three then walked out the door and she never saw them again. She recognized those three lads—she said—and they had been drowned in the year she had seen them. (NFA, vol. 539, pp. 10, 271–72; my translation)

This is the ancient and common theme of the returning dead—apparently hungry: "trick or treat." They could not take food with salt; perhaps it would hold them in this world, for salt (central to both official and popular Catholic rituals here as elsewhere) contains and holds, as we shall see in other chapters. At any rate, they are offered hospitality, and later on, as the

Figure 12. Turas, Well of the Holy Women, 1992 (photo by the author).

story tells, others return to that house — perhaps fairies this time — to play pipes at a wedding. Finally, many years later, a mysterious and well dressed stranger comes to the same house for a wake and leaves a two shilling piece on the church altar. He is followed out of the house, but disappears. As in well stories, tales of lonely places speak of powerful, but more often malevolent, spots on the landscape and of the crucial role of exchange in gaining favor and averting disaster.

The enemies of such balanced exchange, as we saw earlier, were those who held onto their resources, who saw life not as a "great wheel" but as a straight line — progress. They were not all strangers — *na gaill* — and while it was such outsider Protestants who usually felt the wrath of the well, at least one local Catholic "gombeen" — the derogatory term for an aquisitive merchant — also got his comeuppance. So Francie told me.

> Do you see that gate there? [He spoke of a turnstile next to the road — a break in the fence surrounding the rough field in which the Well of the Holy Women was located.] Well, it was old Boyle that put it there. Do you see, that field with the well, all the way down to the cliffs, was land attached to the coast guard station that was there. And the coast guarders us't let the fishermen dry their nets on it — it was common land for them, do you see. Anyway, when the British pulled out, everyone thought that land would be common again, do you know, but old Boyle — seems he went to the coast guarders and he bought it from them, and next thing you know he had a fence around it, and his cows in it. So you couldn't put your nets in it, and you couldn't get to the well — now do you see? Anyway, it seems that one of this cows of his — it was his best cow, and she was in calf — wandered over the cliff one night. She was found dead on the beach below. Well old Boyle put that gate in then, do you see?

Indeed I saw — and whatever or whoever exacted the retribution, the link between commons, reciprocity, and wells was clear enough.

*   *   *

On June 23, 1992 I made my way back to Teelin from Galway where I was living and teaching for the year. I went to the well in time to meet Brigid, my neighbor and friend from the townland of Aghragh, who, followed soon after by three young girls from Croaghlin, had come to do the stations at the Well of the Holy Women. I watched and photographed them (see Figure 12). Brigid did everything one should, lifting each stone, and passing it around her body, saying every prayer, and filling her plastic liter soda bottles with water. The girls had been sent by their mother, and they too followed the prescribed route and filled their bottles before turning their faces for Croaghlin. Brigid walked out through the gate with me and paused for a moment, her eyes dropping to the vinyl bag in which her water bottles lay. Apparently satisfied, she turned to me and said, "And if you should leave anything at the well — by accident like — you can't go back and get it. Oh no, it would be very unlucky to go back and take it away."

3. The View from Slieve League: Intimate Alienation

> Sliabh Liag, that awe-inspiring mountain—"horrid, vast, sublime,"
> whose sharp edge you see in bold outline against the ruddy glow of the
> evening sky. The feelings suggested by the appearance of Sliabh Liag
> on a clear evening, a little before sunset, are utterly indescribable. Be-
> hind, the sinking sun . . . the sombre side, shadowed in gloom behind,
> shows his dark mass through the gauzy transparency, like the face of an
> Ethiopian Bride peering through a veil of softest lace.
>
> (McGinley 1867: 32)

Even with the mixed metaphor obscuring the gender of the mountain, this passage from *The Cliff Scenery of South-Western Donegal*, an ostensible guide book published in 1867, falls within the expected range of Victorian travel prose. Writers had been exoticizing the west of Ireland for more than fifty years by then, and this orientalizing of the western edge—an "Ethiopian bride"—would have fit well enough into the popular discourse of British salons of the period. Some might have found the sensibility a bit old fashioned for the time, but the quotation marks around "horrid, vast, sublime" indicate a self-conscious reference to an earlier romantic idiom that fixed on the power of mountains in a new *natural religion*. And the mountain Slieve League, so powerful—as we saw in the last chapter—in the imagination of both pagan Celt and early Christian—loomed large again in the nineteenth century, when tourists, as opposed to travelers, began to "discover" west Donegal's "highlands" (a term, one imagines, used to make the connection—quite legitimate in geological and to a degree cultural terms—with the Scottish highlands, an ur-ground for romanticism).

The tourist might come, of course, mainly for "sport" or in a spirit of adventure that often combined with a sardonic and exaggerated view of the "primitiveness" of local life and circumstance:

> . . . the wild district we are about to enter on. This, one would say, is almost
> the end of the world—the termination of terrestrial travel: even Fishbourne is

now at fault, and car-borne Banconi can proceed no more; "the force of nature can no further go," and locomotion dies out of itself. We left the rail at Strabane — the van disappears at Killybegs — and all posting is extinguished at the next stage, which is very appropriately termed Kilcar. (*Dublin University Magazine* 1860: 262)

But the tourist might also be there on a pilgrimage of sorts — to experience one or another of the "landscapes" available for "reading": the all-purpose romantic moor and mountain, or the specifically nationalist version. The patriot Thomas Davis is reputed to have stood on Slieve League and, admiring the panoramic view, said, "This is a country worth dying for." If the landscape was a "text," it was rarely encountered unmediated. The tourists, like the pilgrims, arrived with a variety of predispositions and often explicit directions on where, what, and how to feel about the ground over which they traveled.

I had discovered a photocopy of *The Cliff Scenery of South-Western Donegal* in the basement of University College Galway's library and at first sight took it to be such a guide. Considering the title and the shape of the text — an east to west tour enhanced by frequent bouts of poetry — it seemed the standard Victorianization of the wild west of Ireland, and the pseudononymous author no doubt yet another British traveler come to undergo, and contribute to, the prescribed and predetermined literary experience of the scenery; nothing he encountered failed to provoke him to verse. A closer look, however, immediately revealed something more interesting and perhaps important. The author was clearly very familiar with the landscape and, more unusual yet, the people.

The reader of *Cliff Scenery* is not only told what to see and when to feel transported by the sublimity of Nature but also treated to a series of very local narratives, each "attached" to a spot on the landscape. These stories are both "traditional" legends of the sort one finds in the folklore archives or still hears — mainly in Irish — and nationalist disquisitions. The latter, though the larger point may be explicitly nationalist, are always anchored in the very local — typically a ruin rather than a natural feature of the landscape. Like the described vistas, the narratives are followed by verse, much of which is nationalist as well — the world renowned Irish poet Thomas Moore is the best represented — but which also includes Shakespeare, Byron, Scott, and many minor poets of the period. This narrated landscape reminded me of my neighbors in Teelin, but the structure of the text — even to the combination of historical nostalgia with a religious experience of nature, and the soupçon of nationalism — was certainly all within the standard repertoire of literate Victorian prose. And the language of "Kinnfaela" —

the pseudonymous author—is certainly Victorian English. He cites the occasional Irish word or phrase, but so does John O'Donovan of the Ordnance Survey, whom we encountered in the last chapter. Yet it is the body of local stories, replete with the standard traditional guarantee of authenticity—"the grandchild of the woman to whom this happened is yet alive."— that made me think that the author was not only Irish Catholic, but local.

As usual, the "people of the parish" knew more than I. A Carrick-born antiquarian informed me that "Kinnfaela" was one Thomas C. McGinley, born in 1830 in Meenacross—one of the more "farback" corners of the parish of Glencolumbkille—but educated in Killybegs and then Dublin.[41] A remarkable man, McGinley had returned to southwest Donegal to teach and while so employed had authored two books: a biology text[42] and *The Cliff Scenery of South-Western Donegal*. The author's local roots made the versification and orientalizing of the local landscape both strange and intriguing. A transcultural author had produced a transcultural text: a "reading" of the local landscape that from a historical and anthropological view could be taken as an artifact of the cultural field of which McGinley was to some extent representative—the small but influential local group of newly middle class Catholics.

But there is evidence of a more active cultural role for the text; there are strong indications that McGinley's tour was not after all mainly intended for, or read by, tourists. The book had been published by the *Derry Journal*, as the preface informed, only after serialization in that newspaper—among Catholics, at that time, certainly the most read periodical in the northwest of Ireland (a very different perspective on local life could be found in the virulently Protestant *Ballyshannon Herald*). The *Derry Journal* certainly found its way into all corners of the parish, where, by all accounts, interesting bits were read aloud in pubs and elsewhere. According to the editors, however, the extraordinary local popularity of McGinley's work went beyond that mode of dissemination:

> There was scarcely a reader of the Journal resident West of Donegal who did not duly forward his paper to some friend in America, Australia, or other foreign land, to give him, even in fancy, one other glimpse of his native hills. . . . The desirability of having the "Tour" re-produced in a more compact and enduring form . . . has been pressed upon the publishers of the *Journal* by numerous correspondents. (McGinley 1867: iii)

Such an audience for a tour book suggests a very interesting and even important role for McGinley's work. For both McGinley and his readers, the book recast the familiar — deconstructed and reconstructed the landscape. The editors go on:

> The Irish exile is proverbially attached to his native land. . . . Family affection will, doubtless, despatch many a copy of this little work, as a herald to loved ones living under other skies to them "all about the old country." . . . A thrill of pleasure stirs the exile's bosom, . . . as he reads of the scenes of his early days, and the well-conned old stories which he had often heard repeated round many a happy fireside. (McGinley 1867: iii–iv)

McGinley himself adds:

> . . . my little opusculum . . . may bind their hearts still more strongly to their native hills. . . . Should the perusal of this little volume awaken in any one a higher love for the land of his fathers, or soothe the sorrows of a lone exile of Erin, I shall feel amply rewarded . . . [for having] set forth beauties of my native highlands. (McGinley 1867: iv)

The emigrants' nostalgia is central to the enterprise. The landscape about to be toured — though it is described as though encountered for the first time — is, for the readership claimed in the preface, absolutely familiar, though now gone. The book, like the landscape itself, will trigger memory not only of the emigrants' own experiences but of the collective past, as Halbwachs (1992) called it — mediated now by the printed word. But to the familiar will be added geological instruction, a wider historical view that connects local grievance to a developing nationalist tradition, and a general Victorian sensibility that combined romantic ecstasy, sentimental domesticity, and a respectable, moral Catholicism. That manipulation of sentiment in which the landscape is made to evoke not only local but generalized devotions perhaps requires a certain prior removal, a detachment preceding that "proverbial attachment" the editors speak of. The text might be seen as the meeting place, at a certain distance from the landscape, of the emigrant and McGinley and, to varying degrees, the members of his developing class. Among them, this special distance was most particularly characteristic of the rural intelligentsia of teachers, priests, and doctors — living alongside their "peasant" relations, but increasingly separated from them by a distinct domestic world and a mentalité that might be called "intimate alienation."

*   *   *

In 1830 Thomas McGinley was born into a parish on the verge of transition. As we saw in the last chapter, the first decent road and bridge had

just been completed, opening this virtual island to concerted outside influence. During McGinley's childhood those "influences" came thick and fast.
Before the famine of the late 1840s, state, landlord, and Catholic Church,
separately and in various combinations, rearranged the social organization
of the local landscape. Catholic churches began to replace the crude thatch
roofed "Mass houses" (*scathlain*), and were better manned with priests.
The state manifested itself in an institutional structure based on Poor Law
Unions — the workhouse, prison, and fever hospitals for the district were
built in Glenties. Locally, the police barracks represented and constituted
state discipline, and schools — as we shall see ahead — were brought under
the direction of a new National School Board and subject to "inspection."
The domination of these external regimes was certainly aided by the transformation of the social geography; the *clachan* hamlets were broken up and
the small but crucial street-town of Carrick was built.

The landlord, Thomas Conolly, was responsible for both those projects, as the commission reports of the period note, but as is also recorded in
the local memory. Of the dispersal of *clachans* Francie Gallagher told me,

> It was in Conolly's time. A man named Kelly came here and striped the land.
> He said, "These lines will stand forever." and by God so far he's right.

A more detailed account of the rise of Carrick and the local Catholic
merchant class was given to me by Anthony O'Donnell, at the time a man of
sixty-three. He was, like McGinley, a local schoolmaster and himself a scion
of those people. He had heard the story in his youth from a much older
cousin and neighbor, who like Anthony's own father, was one of the pub
owners in Carrick.

> I learned the history of Carrick from Johnny Condy Rua. He's a McShane,
> and his father was the brother of my father's wife, so we're *seisear aghaol* or
> *clann a dha dheil* — sixth of kin.
> Johnny Condy Rua's pub was there on the main road, where the chip shop is
> now. He came into Carrick from Glen. . . . That was the way the village grew.
> The landlord, Colonel Conolly, came to his lodge, where the Golden Gate
> [another pub] is now. . . . Later it was made into Musgrave's Hotel. That was
> Conolly's summer home, do you see, and he wanted to build a village there. So
> he offered anyone willing to build a house in Carrick a plot of land for free.
> Only the better class of tenantry would build. Two of them came in from Glen:
> Eoghain O Canain — where Gallagher's electrical and furniture shop is now —
> and the other was McShane — Johnny Condy Rua's grandfather, and my own
> great grandfather came from Carrick upper [townland]. There was another
> McShane pub belonging to Tommy Mór. He was born in 1830 and his father
> had a pub in that house, probably before 1800. Tommy Mór went and bought

property in Carrick — the site of the Garda barracks and Mona's house. He was called *mór* (big) because he was wealthy — very wealthy.

Others too — like Paddy Bhartley — were invited by Colonel Conolly in the 1840s to come to Carrick and build shops. In those times they had fine horse and cartmen, do you see. They'd go to Derry with seven carts; they'd all go off together at daybreak on a Monday morning and on the third day they'd come into Derry — they talked of the cobblestones in Derry — the sound of their wheels made from the best metal. The shopkeepers in Derry knew by that sound that it was the Carrick ones. They were made by two families of black-smiths, my great grandfather — he died in the 1850s — was one of the carters. They would stay at Biddy's of Barnes Gap — its still there [see Figure 13]. Biddy's was famous for carters coming and goin'. The carts would take a sixteen hundredweight load — an odd horse would take a ton. There were highway-men in Barnes Gap, and they would attack the carts as they went through. That's why they traveled together and had "loaded whips," with bars of lead at the ends, do you see.

Trading in Derry continued until the railroad was extended as far as Drim-amore in the 1880s. In 1891 it came to Killybegs, and then they carted to Killybegs. My brother was a cartman at twelve-years-old — around 1920, for my father's shop — until the lorries came in — in the mid-1920s.

Neither these merchant carters nor their wives were likely to have been Victorian gentlefolk. But just as a publican family had produced a school-master in Anthony, so did most of the merchant families of Carrick — like those elsewhere in rural Ireland — produce not only heirs to the business and respectable daughters to marry others of their class but the profession-als who still enjoy such great respect in the countryside: teachers, priests, and doctors. Such offspring did not take the rugged road to Derry, but went instead to Dublin for an education. In the second half of the century they lived in two story homes with parlors in the front. They played pianos and danced waltzes as well as jigs. They read, and some of them wrote, books; the sort of antiquarian history related by Anthony was also their preserve. And the local priest, always chosen from within the diocese, would have been raised in a similar family and with similar values; now ensconced in the new churches and parochial houses of such villages, they were the very model of civility (see Inglis 1987).

While Carrick was being formed, the already extant town of Killybegs was also attracting some Catholic entrepreneurs and it was there that the parents of Thomas McGinley went. Though far from being a cosmopolitan center, they encountered in Killybegs a social world significantly differ-ent from that of Meenacross, or even Carrick. The surrounding land — as in the case of Glencolumbkille — was owned in a large estate by an absentee

Figure 13. Barnes Gap, Donegal, late nineteenth century (Lawrence Collection, National Library of Ireland).

landlord: in this case Alexander Murray of Broughton, resident in Scotland. But Killybegs was a sort of border town between the western zone of poor land and the more fertile drumlin hills to the east, where much land was held in smaller estates by a resident Protestant gentry. The non-inheriting sons of that class had become lawyers and professionals and congregated in one of the three towns set up two hundred years earlier in the Plantation of Ulster: Killybegs, Donegal, and Ballyshannon. Each of these towns had a harbor and, at its center, a "diamond," which still marks its origin as an English settlement. There were also Protestant tenant farmers in the region, although the mass of the tenantry was still poor, Irish, and Catholic. The total population of the parish of Killybegs in 1831 was 4,287, of which 672 were Protestants of the Established Church and 3,615 were Roman Catholics. The town, however, had a much higher percentage of Protestants.

Like Colonel Conolly in Glencolumbkille, Murray was interested in "improving" both his holdings and its occupants, and among other projects he caused a school to be built in Killybegs in 1834 at a personal cost of £200. Like his other assets in the region, Murray's school was under the supervision of his agent, George Venable Wilson, who was resident in town. It was, in fact an era of activity on the scholastic front. In 1831 the National School Act had provided government finance for local schools all over Ireland, an arrangement in which the Catholic Church cooperated only when assured that management of the schools would be under clerical control according to the religious faith of the student population.

Mary Daly (1979) has shown the degree to which the apparently new national schools were pre-existing local schools that applied for government funds under the new legislation. This is true for southwest Donegal as well, where an intriguing and valuable glimpse of local education is available in the various reports of the Commissioners of Irish Education and in the applications made in behalf of pre-existing schools for funds. By 1825, according to the Commissioners of Irish Education Inquiry,[43] three schools were in operation, and the particulars are instructive. Two of the schools were in the western end of the parish, in the area of Protestant habitation, and the third was in Teelin.[44] In 1825 the Catholic Church had only one priest for both parishes of Glencolumbkille and Kilcar, and hence little control over the education as well as daily life of the parishioners. Ewing's "statistical return" of 1823 (see Chapter 2) remarked that English was being taught in a Protestant school in Glen, and the mixture of Protestant and Catholic children in that end of the parish may have made for a less divided society than that indicated by the tales of Gael versus Gall.

But the facilities of the best of these schools were paltry and the attendance limited to a small proportion of the children of the parish — and was spotty for them. While the commissioners list no school in McGinley's native Meenacross, an application for funds for what must have been a very crude "hedge school" does show up in the Dublin Education records. In those same records an application for national school status from landlord Murray's school in Killybegs reveals the gap, and the opportunity afforded McGinley and his fellow town dwellers there:

The Common School — established Feb. 1834
1 mile E. of Kbegs
   The school was never connected with any society and never received aid from one. It was erected on the property of Alex Murray of Broughton Esq., and not upon Church or Chapel ground. It is substantially built of stone and lime and slated, measuring 34′ × 22′, at the expense of Murray. No rent. There is also an apartment for the teacher. The schoolroom measures 30′ × 18′. The house is new and in the best state of repair. Four desks and 12 forms are capable of accommodating 70 or 80 children, supplied entirely at the expense of Murray.
   Saturday religious instruction of both persuasions using respective catechisms. . . . There never has been any complaint or interference by parents to this arrangement.
   Instruction 6 days, 7 hrs., 9–4pm
   270 students weekly, nearly equal number of boys and girls . . . much greater attendance in winter than in summer, no doubt in a few years will increase. Teacher, Mr. John Dargan — not educated at a model school, reference from Mr. Edgeworth esq. of Liverpool, salary £40 in Sterling paid by Murray, children pay nothing, one penny a week nominally demanded but it is rarely ever paid.
   The Roman Catholic clergy has attached his signature [to application for National School status and funds], the rector [Protestant] of the parish was applied to but did not attach his signature.
   The school is under the direction of none except Murray or his agent.
   There is one school within 3 miles, but in the Parish of Killaghtee and another in the town of Killybegs. Both are to best of my knowledge parish schools.
   The population of the parish is between 4000 and 5000.
   ref. — Edw. Murray, esq. attorney, Dublin.
   The clergy have access to the school as often as they feel inclined and indeed the clergymen of both persuasions in the parish were personally requested by Mr Murray to visit the school.

It is Mr. Murray's wish to have the school placed entirely under control of the board and to be endowed by them, but he will expect to be allowed a part of the expense of building the house, It having cost him 200 £. sterling. signed,

Prots. [Protestants]
Murray Babington
Oswald Wotheerspoon
Alex Babington, J.P.

RC [Roman Catholics]
Wm Drummond PP
Hugh Mulvany

The figures reported in this application—the cost of the school, the salary of the teacher—are by far the highest in the district. The circumstances of the application were, however, typical. A landlord had given support (the amount varied) and was the chief applicant, along with the local Catholic priest. In all cases, the Protestant clergy of the Established Church were not signatories to the application and, despite being invited to take part, withheld any kind of approval of or involvement in the new National School system. Having been guaranteed control over the education of schools with Catholic students, the Catholic clergy had for the most part[45] gone along with the new system, no doubt hoping that the state would finance an essentially Catholic education under their local control. This was the case with Father Drummond, parish priest in Killybegs from 1833 until his death in 1864 and a signatee to all requests for school funds from Killybegs parish. He was in fact an active cleric—the "architect" of the Devotional Revolution in Killybegs. Drummond managed to build the new and quite substantial Gothic Catholic chapel—St. Catherine's—perched triumphantly on a rock outcropping on the main road of the town, overlooking the bay and harbor. Something of what went on in that church is conveyed in the following entry for August 15, 1841 from the *Irish Catholic Directory*:

A solemn high mass was offered in the Catholic church of St. Catherine Killybegs, honourable Rev. Dr. Drummond, high priest; assisted by Rev. Mr. Stephens who sang both the gospel and the Epistle. The silver thurible was carried by Master Browne, third son of Alex Browne, Esq in commission of Her Majesty's cutter, Racer, and Masters Magrath and Conwell, acolytes. The altar was superbly decorated, over which immediately were six massive candlesticks, 17 in. high, supporting wax lights. Around the tabernacle was a large profusion of flowers, in handsome Chinese vases; and covering the sanctuary was an excellent carpet (red and black), the same as that used in the great chapel of Glasgow, which had been presented a few years ago by an "Anonymous," who, in a note, merely requested to be reimbursed in the prayers of the ever-faithful Catholic people of Killybegs. The church and yard were densely crowded, many having come from Inver, Ardara, Kilcar, and even the distant parish of Glencolumkill. The nature of the festival was explained by the Rev. Dr. Drummond, and the devotion of Catholics to the Blessed Virgin, Mother of God, ably vindicated. (*Irish Catholic Directory* 1842: 417)

Aside from the opulence of the church and the presence of some moneyed Catholic patrons, it is interesting to note once again the border status of Killybegs, which in terms of the Church as well as landlord and state regime, stood on the edge of one world and cast its shadow westward. The Feast of the Assumption was clearly not something familiar — at least to the contingent from "the distant parish of Glencolumkill" — and needed to be explained. While thus consolidating the presence of the Church in Killybegs, Drummond, like his colleagues throughout southwest Donegal, was willing to cooperate with the landlords in order to provide a clerically controlled education for their parishioners.

And Thomas C. McGinley, according to the local memory, was fortunate enough to receive the best education available in the region — Murray's well endowed and equipped school. He excelled at his studies, and took the typical route to the teaching profession, becoming monitor at Fintragh National School (just to the west) and then, at age twenty, the untrained principal of Meentinadea School. After qualifying as a teacher in Dublin's Marlborough Street Preparatory College, McGinley took a post in Belfast, but was only twenty-five when he returned to Donegal to become the principal of the national school in Croagh, a mountainy corner northeast of Killybegs. While there, the schoolmaster wrote not only *The Cliff Scenery of South-Western Donegal* but an introductory biology text published by Collins in London and Glasgow, and purportedly a text of instruction in Kensington, London. Certainly the "most distinguished educationalist of the region" — to use the language of an award committee — he was made principal of the first secondary school in the area, the Niall Mór School of Killybegs, in 1879 (Patrick McGill 1974: 53–54). McGinley died in 1887, at the age of fifty seven.

Thomas McGinley was a man of substantial influence in the region, and it may have been the author as well as the subject that made *Cliff Scenery* so popular. His reputation as an instructor lived on in the district, and his fellow teachers thought enough of him to select him as delegate to a national meeting in Dublin. To judge by columns in the same *Derry Journal* in which he first published his tour, McGinley was particularly active in the local schoolteachers' association, which comprised all the parishes of southwest Donegal. Another of his cultural heirs, P.J. McGill, schoolmaster, antiquarian and author, tells us that McGinley taught many who went on to join the clergy, including Canon McGuire (1920), who wrote a two volume history of the diocese (McGill 1974). In fact, McGinley and his wife, Mary Synott, produced two clergymen of their own, one of whom went on to become a bishop in the Philippines and, retiring to Killybegs in what is still known as "the bishop's house," by dint of ecclesiastical grandeur eclipsed to some extent the memory of his father.

This network of teachers and priests — each training the other — was critical in the evolution of a cultural field of "civil Catholicism." Beginning in the 1830s, but quite fully developed by the date of publication of *Cliff Scenery* in 1867, this field was produced and reproduced in three critical settings: church, school, and bourgeois parlor. The first two were of course open to the general public, and the cultural forms encountered there entered their consciousness to varying degrees and were appropriated — again, to varying degrees — to fit other perspectives and experiences, as we will see in subsequent chapters. The parlor, of course, remained the more specifically bourgeois arena, a setting for piano and upholstered furniture,[46] and a place of books. Here, as well as in the hands of the emigrants — whose numbers by the late 1860s were considerable — McGinley's "little opusculum" could find a home.

* * *

The Cliff Scenery of Southwest Donegal begins with a selection from Byron that sets the stage for McGinley's theme: the human relation to the landscape:

> to sit on rocks to muse o'er flood and fell . . . where things that own not man's dominion dwell and mortal foot hath ne'er, or rarely been . . . wild flock . . . alone . . . this is not solitude . . . but to hold converse with nature's charms. (McGinley 1867)

The reader is escorted from east to west, and from view to view. The panorama from each elevation is treated to a painterly description, often followed by geological observations. In the local manner, history, in the

form of narrative, is recounted in relation to those features of the landscape
that provoke it. Such history includes everything from a story of executed
Vikings to the unfortunate drowning of a boy in a lake the year before. To
such accounts McGinley occasionally adds a more pointed conclusion:

> If you feel your soul elevated by the contemplation of the beauties of nature
> all around you, it must experience a saddening reaction when it fixes on the
> woe-begone appearance presented by the wretched looking village before you
> [Inver Port] . . . the ruin of what was once a rich magazine of fish. . . . Yonder
> may be observed what seems to have once been a long row of neat cottages,
> prettily situated, and looking out upon the rippling wave. Now nothing is left
> but the bare broken walls as if the entire range had, at a former period, disas-
> trous conflagration. Yet, gentle reader, it was no raging flame that tumbled
> down the roof-trees of the cottages at "The port." While the Irish Parliament
> embodied the feelings and aspirations of Irishmen; while it, like a tender
> parent nurtured with fostering care every department of Irish industry; when
> "Ireland for the Irish" was the motto of all classes and of all creeds in Ireland —
> then it was that such places as "The Port," Inver, Rutland, &c. were the busy
> hives of prosperous industry. But all this is at an end. Ireland has lost its native
> legislature and with it its institutions of industry. These the unemployed Irish
> must seek in other climes, and not under their own genial sky. Industry has
> taken its flight from Ireland and the unemployed, starving Irish, must follow
> to where it has found a home.
>
> Such must be your reflections, gentle reader, when you gaze upon the de-
> serted village before you. . . . The only [house] left standing, with any ap-
> pearance of comfort about it, is that of Mr. John Meehan, where, if the reader
> may happen to call, he is sure to meet with hearty Irish welcome. (McGinley
> 1867: 20–21)

McGinley indulges in few sorties of this kind; the book is far from
being a political tract. But when nationalism is the theme, it is always
expressed in the idiom of landscape. Irishness is, in fact, defined in terms of
a proper relation to the landscape and hence open to "all classes and creeds."
McGinley shifts between an ethnic classification of Anglo-Saxon versus
Celt and a nationalist one of Irish versus English. It is not logically consistent. Irishness is at once derived from Celticness but open to those transformed by a proper relation to the landscape:

> Of the inhabitants of Malinmore, a considerable number are Protestants and of
> Scottish descent, but who are now noted for being "more Irish than the Irish
> themselves." They are particularly endowed with large, generous sentiments
> towards their Catholic fellow-countrymen, and distinguished for their truly
> Irish hospitality. (McGinley 1867: 133)

Reading these lines one cannot help but think of how different the idiom of the folk stories for which these same Protestants were always *na Gall* (in the plural form) — the foreigners — who, at least in stories with religious themes, were stereotypically opposite to the laudable picture drawn by McGinley. It may be that the author wanted to echo the national political position, which sought to define Irish nationalism in non-sectarian terms; he probably also wanted to maintain good relations with his entire local audience.

At any rate, for McGinley, all local evil is caused by and results in the disruption of the local relation to the land. This is true at the national level — no Irish parliament — and locally, where oppression and misfortune are due less to landlordism per se than to absenteeism. It is the distant English landlord who — thoughtless and uncaring — wreaks a havoc that, in the end, leads to the severing of other relations to the land: the destruction or abandonment of settlements, and finally emigration.

The schoolmaster could not help but follow his commentary on "Port" with verse — Goldsmith's "The Deserted Village." The choice of an Anglo-Irish poet follows McGinley's definition of Irishness, but the culturally very English portrait of a village in the plain near Athlone is somewhat disconcerting as a literary image of southwest Donegal. Thus the author sounds the note of universal nostalgia for a way of life lost in the face of progress:

> Near yonder thorn, that lifts its head on high,
> Where once the sign-post caught the passing eye,
> Low lies the house where nut-brown draughts inspired,
> Where village statesmen talked with looks profound,
> And news much older than their ale, went round. . . .
> No more the farmer's news, the pedlar's tale,
> No more the boatsman's ballad shall prevail;
> No more the smith his dusky brow shall clear,
> Relax his ponderous strength, and lean to hear;
> The host himself, no longer shall be found,
> Careful to see the mantling bliss go round.
> (Goldsmith in McGinley 1867: 21)

The notion of a powerful relationship with Nature — as we saw in the last chapter — is also a central concern of the folk idiom. But in that cultural universe such "communion" can be dangerous if uncontrolled. Something of the disjunction between these two views of natural power — and perhaps of McGinley's own transcultural ambivalence — is conveyed at a few points in the text. As he approaches the open, dreary moor between Kilcar and Carrick, McGinley remarks:

> Continuing onward on our journey . . . we breast a steep hill for some distance, till we arrive at a part more level, and surrounded with moor. It is looked upon as a very lonely spot, as numbers of ghosts are said to have been seen there. But in reference to such ghost-stories, it may be said of the native inhabitants of these wilds, as of a personage celebrated in Scottish verse, that
>
> "The desert gave him visions wild,
> Such as might suit the spectre's child . . .
> The mountain mist took form and limb
> Of noontide hag, or goblin grim;
> The midnight wind came wild and dread,
> Swelled with the voices of the dead;
> Far on the future battle-heath
> His eye beheld the ranks of death . . ."
> (Scott in McGinley 1867: 70)

Who is better suited than Sir Walter Scott to put the local notion of *uaigneas*, loneliness, into romantic perspective? Scott's verse itself appropriates folk concepts in a cultural landscape very similar to that of Donegal: blood soaks into the earth, and places of death — of fallen warriors — are haunted. But both Scott and McGinley distance themselves from "native inhabitants" subject to such visions; the authors are, rather, prone to verse.

The other place that evokes the contrasting impulses of the local and the educated Victorian is on Slieve League. The mountain, in McGinley's tour as in the local version of natural power, dominates both the landscape and the imagination. As we follow the author from east to west Slieve League appears from a number of vantages, ever closer and more imposing. When finally standing atop the ridge overlooking the sea, McGinley informs us of the local perspective on such heights:

> The native inhabitants of these romantic localities state, that persons going near the brinks of these lofty cliffs, particularly if they sit upon them and look down, are subject to morbid sensations in the brain, which the people term *glas ailt* [weakness of cliffs]. . . . While under its influence, the patient, instead of moving inward to save himself, invariably takes the opposite course — he projects himself outward, forgetful, apparently, of the direction of gravitation. When the first symptoms of the feeling are found to be coming on, the parties

affected cautiously place themselves out of danger. Sometimes they are delivered from impending destruction by their companions, who notice . . . the wild glare of the eyes, and the show of helplessness evinced by the despairing sufferers. (McGinley 1867: 89–90)

McGinley's medical idiom — "morbidity of the brain" — is itself an interesting recasting of the local notion of landscape-induced temporary insanity. The cliffs of Slieve League are still a frequent local choice for suicide.

Apparently unafraid of *glas ailt* himself, McGinley recovers his composure in the very next passage, where he asks us to follow him in.

Looking down from this lofty elevation upon the rolling ocean that noiselessly curls and chafes 2000 feet below, one almost imagines himself as if raised high above every terrestrial consideration, and a succession of spiritual feelings, thrillingly delicious, and approaching rapture, take full possession of the sated soul. (McGinley 1867: 90)

While the book is replete with stories and verse, thus constantly confronting local narratives — themselves already Victorianized — with nineteenth century poetry, it is on the mountain itself that we encounter the most striking and revealing "rereading" of the landscape. McGinley retells what is still one of the most often recounted and locally interesting narratives, very much attached to the mountain Slieve League. Here is a version collected by folklorist Sean O hEochaidh in 1936 from a ninety-year-old fisherman from Malin Beg, Sean 'ac Fionnlaoich (Sean McGinley), who heard the story himself fifty years before (c. 1886) from "the old people" of that place.

There was a Spaniard long ago, and it was in Spain he was brought up, and one day he told his mother that he wanted to leave Spain and make his living as a mariner.

"Well, if you do, my darling," said his mother, "say your rosary and whenever it is, you'll have a priest at the hour of death." He said he would do so. But he shipped out and the whole time he was at sea he was saving money, and the money was in a belt he had around his body — in a broad belt.

But in the end he knew death was coming to him, and he asked the crew of the merchant ship to put him out, up there in back of the height by For Rónach. Well they did that then; they put out a small boat — from the merchant ship — and they put him in the small boat, and they landed him out on *For Rónach*.

Well, he crept up the steep glen there until he found a place to sit and then he was weak after that and sick as well.

There was a priest in Glen in those days, and the priest came to that townland to give the last rites to someone at the point of death. Then the priest was going out to Teelin to do the stations [to celebrate Mass in someone's home there], and he and the boy were going up Slieve League and when they came over the top of the mountain they heard a moan.

"There's someone weak there," the boy said to the priest. "Go see him," said the priest to the boy. The boy looked and found the man sitting there, and the priest went then to him. The priest asked him then what was his condition and where was he from. He told the priest then that he was from Spain.

"Well, my mother asked me," the Spaniard said to him, "to pray my rosary every morning so that I should have a priest at the time of my death."

"Well, you have that now" said the priest. . . . They took him then. When he had done his confession and the priest had readied him, he put the oil on him and he took him with him, himself and the boy, and they took him to a certain house that belonged to people from Malin Beg up on the mountain. They left him in that house. He gave his belt full of money to the priest and he asked the priest to build a chapel with that money.

Well, we saw two houses the priest made, no doubt: the chapel at the foot of the three streams, and another little chapel that was done over in "Farmac-bride." (O hEochaidh, NFA: 1762–1765; my translation)

There are other local versions of the story, with some variation in detail—including the number and locations of the chapels built with the Spaniard's money.[47] In all versions of the story in the folklore archives the main plot is the same: a young man goes to sea having promised to say a particular prayer or the rosary every morning or night. After a life at sea, and with all his money in his belt, he falls ill (or the ship wrecks) and is rowed (or washed) ashore on a beach below Slieve League. A priest is on his way across the mountain, having been (or on his way) to give last rites to a parishioner, when he and/or his servant hear the moans of the dying Spaniard. Last rites are administered, and the Spaniard gives the belt full of money to the priest in order that he may build a chapel with it. In one version the priest is named—"a priest of the Carr clan" (there was a priest named Owen Carr who served both parishes of Glencolumbkille and Kilcar from 1768 to 1782).

Beyond explaining several ruins in the two parishes, the story fits the important genre of pre-nineteenth century priest stories (as we saw in the last chapter), when the clerics were always on horseback, moving through their wild domains and either pursued by enemy soldiers or attempting to arrive in time to administer the last rites to some dying parishioner, sometimes both. There is no doubt that this sacrament was the most important to the people and always figures at the center of such narratives. The storyteller, Sean 'ac Fionnlaoich—Sean McGinley—was born in 1848, only eighteen years after Thomas C. McGinley. The McGinleys of Malin Beg are distinct from those of Meenacross, but distantly related, and it is not at all unlikely that the author McGinley would have heard a similar version of this important local story.

This makes Thomas McGinley's rendition the more remarkable. I will only offer a few small samples of "The Dying Spaniard—A Legend of Sliabh Liag," for McGinley makes the story last for nineteen pages, including some eight long verse passages taken mostly from Thomas Moore. McGinley begins with a historical framework utterly uncharacteristic of folk narratives, telling us that the story takes place about the beginning of the eighteenth century on board a vessel bound for the Spanish coast when Spain and Austria were at war over the succession to the Spanish crown and the English admirals were "particularly anxious to capture any Spanish argosies that might be found." Thus the story is given an appropriate political framework. The Spaniard is then somewhat de-exoticized—given a name, Don Antonio, and a more recognizable life.

> This man was a Spaniard by birth, born of respectable and pious parents, but having become possessed of a spirit of adventure, he emigrated to the West Indies, where he soon amassed considerable wealth. Like most men who have attained to sudden opulence, he became less mindful of his religious duties, and so got entangled in the mazes of pleasure, dissipation and vice.... Notwithstanding his vicious habits of life, he never omitted, even in the very climax of his excesses, to repeat every day a prayer which his good mother had taught him; namely that he might have the ministration of a priest at his last hour. The obligation of saying this prayer he regarded as a sacred duty, because it had been imposed upon him by his saintly mother on his parting with her; and she dying soon after, of grief for the losing of her son, he repeated it every day by way of reverence to her memory. On hearing of his native country overrun by the hostile confederates and Charles, Archduke of Austria proclaimed king— his patriotism took fire. He grew impatient to return to his mountain home, repair his shatered frame, and strike for the freedom of his native land. (Mc-Ginley 1867: 98)

The Spaniard is now an emigrant rather than a seaman, who, no doubt like McGinley's emigrant audience in the New World, left pious parents and sank into profligacy. This favorite Victorian theme—with biblical roots of course in the Prodigal Son—is used to "fill out" the Spanish character. He is no longer the simple and mysteriously foreign Spaniard of the folk legends, but a recognizable romantic hero, a political ally, and an emigrant returning home for patriotic reasons. Then there is the mother—now elevated in this Marian age to a more critical role, dying herself of a broken heart. Perhaps unable to choose between shipwreck and illness, McGinley gives us a gravely ill Don Antonio suffering below as the ship tosses in a violent storm, during which he has a dream or vision: his mother appears (in an era of Marian apparitions), asks him to repeat the prayer, and points out a lofty precipice on which, she tells him, he will die the next day. "After some other consoling remarks, she disappeared, telling me that she longed to see me in heaven" (McGinley 1867: 101).

If the sanctity of mother and the reassurance of heaven is not enough to achieve the full Victorianization of the Spaniard, the work is completed some pages later when Don Antonio is landed on the wild Irish shore.

> On reaching the base of the cliff, the good crew tenderly raised the enfeebled Antonio in their arms, and carried him to the pebbly beach. Here they would have laid him down, but a supernatural strength seems to have come to his aid, and he stood up firm in their midst. He then embraced each of the crew most affectionately, all of whom wept like so many children, feeling that the being on whom their gaze was now riveted would, before the rising of to-morrow's sun, be a blessed citizen of heaven . . . taking a small ivory crucifix from his neck he placed it in the hands of his friend Diego, saying "Remember me in your prayers Diego; keep this for my sake, and for the sake of Him whom it represents." (McGinley 1867: 105)

This apotheosis of the Spaniard is reminiscent of *Uncle Tom's Cabin*—which, given its immense popularity, may well have been among McGinley's readings.

The author then turns to the priest, who is named as Cannon (in fact a priest in the early eighteenth century, appropriate to the setting during the War of the Spanish Succession). Father Cannon struggles through the same storm, and having discovered the Spaniard, converses with him in his native tongue, the cleric having been educated in Salamanca (historically possible). As in the folk versions, the Spaniard gives the priest the belt full of money—"a large number of Spanish dollars"—and dies. The priest builds a chapel at Fochair in Glencolumbkille.

In this Victorian version of the "Dying Spaniard," nationalist politics is given a place, and the role of religion much expanded and matrialized—the narrative has undergone what historian Larkin called the "devotional revolution." And the American emigrant audience is pulled right into the story. If that were not enough, however, there is the matter of the verse—eight passages, five of them from Thomas Moore. While Moore wrote many poems on Irish themes, all the verses used by McGinley come from "Lalah Rook,"[48] a verse narrative set in the Orient. McGinley takes some liberty

with Moore's lines, rearranging their order of appearance in the original
and changing the gender of the central character, in order that the verse
narrative match to some extent with his story.

Perhaps this orientalizing, like the descriptive passages cited earlier, is
not meant to recast the local landscape for the locals or the emigrants, but
rather to assert its literary merit by showing the appropriateness of Moore's
popular verse. While unlikely to much affect those who perceived the landscape from within the oral tradition, McGinley's version may have encouraged the new middle class to reframe the immediate world of place and
narrative in the Victorian idiom taught in school — and of course to na-
tionalize the landscape as well. As for McGinley's religious idiom, the sacred geography against which growing priestly power was sometimes directed could be accepted through sentimentalization. This amounts to a
devotional revolution of narrative, and a case of "generalized" devotional
idioms being attached to "local" discourse.

McGinley was not alone in this enterprise. And it is interesting to note
the clerical connections. His contemporary, the Rev. Dr. James MacDevitt,
at the time professor of mental philosophy at the Foreign Missionary College of All Hallows in Dublin, had published the year before his own regional guide, *The Donegal Highlands*. MacDevitt, who was born in Glenties
in 1832, spent much of his childhood in The Rosses — a west Donegal district to the north of the southwestern penninsula — where his uncle, the Rev.
J. MacDevitt, was parish priest of Templecrone. After some years as a professor in Dublin, the younger MacDevitt was appointed to the see of Raphoe
in 1871. According to his brother and biographer, the Rev. John MacDevitt:

> His heart was where he spent his early days, and every year, as the long vaca-
> tion came round, he hurried home to his native highlands. Here, with light-
> ness and perfect freedom of spirit he spent his time in wandering over the
> mountain scenes, and catching the traditions, and legends of the country
> "which," he said, "interpret the echoes of the olden time." He was passing fond
> of the beauties of nature, especially when history, like the very ivy on the the
> ruin, gives to them a venerable and religious association. Hence his enthusi-
> asm for descriptive poetry, and in a particular manner for Wordsworth's "Ex-
> cursion." (MacDevitt 1880: 35)

A familiar enough sensibility; MacDevitt even pauses in his travelogue to
tell the story of the Spanish Chapel — not a long version, however.

Most interesting, however, and most locally significant, was the work
of another cleric, Monsignor James Stephens, the curate in Killybegs when
McGinley was growing up there, who returned to take up the position of

parish priest at the death of Rev. Drummond in 1864. Stephens was from a very prosperous family in Ballyshannon — landed Catholics — and privileged far beyond McGinley. He was a world traveler, taking leaves from his parish duties to visit Rome and the United States. Irish priests were no strangers to either place, of course, but when they came in those years to America it was often because they were sent to collect money. Stephens came to spend it. He wrote long letters describing his travels to the *Derry Journal*, and these would certainly have been read aloud to at least his own parishioners. But Stephens also wanted to rewrite the landscape of his new home, and his *Scenery and Antiquities of Southwest Donegal*, published in 1872, covers much the same ground as McGinley's, but from a significantly different angle. There is, proportionately, far more verse in Stephens' account, and — unlike McGinley's selections — it is almost exclusively Irish Catholic. Much of it would have been read in *The Nation*, the nationalist periodical, which began publication in 1842 and enjoyed a very healthy circulation. Even more given to explicit political statements than his friend McGinley, Stephens promised great things for the region if tourism were developed and the government of Ireland returned to its people. As for McGinley, for Stephens those people included Protestants, and indeed he evinces great comfort with the local Protestant gentry as both governors and friends. It seems that he gathered more of his information from them — no doubt over cups of tea or glasses of sherry — than from the "peasantry." He was an active antiquarian and less concerned with the grandeur of the scenery than the heroic past implied by the occasional ruin. Ironically, this drawing room priest was most taken with Niall Mór Mac Suibne, a fifteenth-century chieftain of the area whose ruined castle stood just east of Killybegs at St. John's Point. Aided by strong verse, Stephens devoted considerable space in his slim volume to resurrecting this local figure.

Resurrect indeed, for unsatisfied with simply writing about local antiquities, Father Stephens used his considerable authority as parish priest to "edit" the historical landscape. Having enhanced his predecessor's work on the parish church and especially the parochial house, Stephens took his hero Niall Mór's elaborately carved tomb cover from the ruins (much of what remained of the castle was apparently used in constructing his parochial house) and placed it upright — set in concrete — just outside the door of St. Catherine's Church. It can be seen there today. He also set up a memorial plaque to his popular predecessor, Dr. Drummond, and to his most notable ancestor in office — the Bishop McGonigal — who attended the Council of Trent in 1530 and had made Killybegs his seat while avoiding war-torn Raphoe. And since the area lacked that most famous type of early medieval church ruin, the round tower, Father Stephens supplied one, causing an example of that impressive symbol of resistance to invading barbarians[49] to be raised outside a new Catholic church in Bruckless, several miles to the east of Killybegs. Now local schoolchildren, as Canon McGuire noted in his parish history (McGuire 1920), had no need to go to Tory or Devenish to see such an important Irish structure.

Of course, Father Stephens knew Thomas C. McGinley very well, and in fact appointed him principal of the Niall Mór School—the first Catholic secondary school in the region. Working alongside McGinley was a younger local man, John Ward—or Seaghain Mac a 'Bhaird—the author of *Leabhar Filidheachta fá Choinne na Scoil,*[50] a collection of Irish language poetry for school use, published by Ward himself. Both McGinley and Ward were instrumental in bringing Irish language instruction to the area. In fact, Ward was one of only four certified Irish language instructors in the county, where the Protestant plantation described in the last chapter had produced an especially bifurcated world: oral Irish in the west and literate English in the east. Killybegs stood precisely on the border of these two cultural regions and was thus particularly suited to the development of a reflexivity necessary to the reinvention and rediscovery of an Irishness that combined nationalism, civil Victorian Catholicism, and the Irish language. This cultural field then spread through the developing rural intelligensia to the west—to places like Carrick.

*   *   *

Dr. Conal Cunningham, born in Carrick in the 1930s, is now a doctor in Connemara, County Galway. His home sits high in the rocky moors that are as common here as they are in southwest Donegal. Conal Cunningham trained in the University of Galway—just fifteen miles to the east—and, having married a Galway woman, decided to forsake his ancestral turf for this similar terrain. But his homeland is with him, for Dr. Cunningham has searched out every archival nook and cranny on the Island in order to assemble the neatly bound historical record of the parish of Glencolumbkille. It was he who told me about Thomas C. McGinley, and about of his own family as well:

My own grandfather was born in 1850 and lived to 1929 in Carrick Upper. His father had died when he was fifteen, and he was, from the age of sixteen, a monitor, or assistant to the headmaster, then assistant teacher, and then teacher in Glen and Meananeary, where he finished teaching in 1914. He and his wife, also a teacher, had thirteen children: two priests, one doctor, four teachers. My father told me that he, my grandfather, had heard Mass in the scalan in upper Carrick. The priest, Father McDermott, stayed in Charlie Cunningham's three room thatched house, built in 1838. The scalan [thatch-roofed Mass house used before church was built] was within one hundred yards of that house. The scalan in Glen was at the crossroads.

It is interesting that both the grandfather and the grandson chose to relate the family connection with the priest and scalan. No doubt the story marked the early intimacy between the local clergy and "the Cunninghams of Carrick," as this particular "clan" was known — to distinguish them from the many others of that name in the region. But also, as with Anthony's relating of history according to Johnny Condy Rua, this story evinces a linear sense of the past marked by significant dates and a sense of the importance of the transition from the days of informal scalan and priests staying with families to that of town church and parochial house. I asked Dr. Cunningham if, by any chance, he knew what books his grandfather had owned or used. "I've got them here," he said, and returning from the "archive" with five volumes: an 1877 edition of *Gallagher's Sermons* in both Irish and English (the former owner being "Dan'l McGettigan of Inver"), an 1848 *Dunlevy's Catechism*, also bilingual, and an 1898 *Cuimhne Columcille* (Columcille Memorial), the very popular book printed for the Gartan Festival held that year on the Thirteenth Centennial of Saint Columba — that is, Columcille, whose stories we heard in the last chapter, there was a copy of John Ward's collection of school poetry (noted above) in a 1909 edition, and a 1904 version of *The Epistles and Gospels for the Sundays and Holidays*, translated into Irish by the same John C. Ward (Seaghain Mac a'Bhaird) "under the revision of the Bishop of Raphoe." I thumbed through Ward's Irish poetry volume. Dr. Cunningham explained, "Many of them were written by a local man, an O'Beirne from Malin Beg — John Ward married his sister. We learned four of them off by heart: '*An Sean Troid*,' The Old Fight [against England], '*Mó Mhaire*,' My Mary [a simple love poem], '*Mó Phiopa Deirid Dhonn*,' My short brown pipe, and '*Pilleadh Aoidh Ruaidh Úi Dhomhnaill*,' The Return of Red Hugh O'Donnell [the local and national hero of the Nine Years' War 1594–1603]."

*   *   *

Thomas Moore — Thomas C. McGinley's most quoted poet — replied to a charge of rabble rousing as follows:

There is no one who deprecates more sincerely than I do any appeal to the passions of an ignorant and angry multitude; but ... it is not through that gross and inflammable region of society a work of this nature could ever have been intended to circulate. It looks much higher for its audience and readers — it is found upon the pianofortes of the rich and the educated — of those who can afford to have their national zeal a little stimulated without exciting much dread of the excesses into which it may hurry them; and of many whose nerves may be now and then alarmed with advantage, as much more is to be gained by their fears than could ever be expected from their justice. (Moore: 194)

If McGinley's work was intended to appeal to such an audience — at least in its local, modest incarnation — then it did so through demonstrating the erudition and sensibility of its author along with the articulation of specific nationalist positions. Clearly, the reader was meant to associate the character of the writer with his politics — a respectable, civilized, nationalism. But *Cliff Scenery* is not just a pastiche of cultured posings and political discourses; it is a tour, a movement across the landscape that follows the sacred geography and rediscovers the stories that are attached to it. Such a tour was possible because, for both the folk mentalité and the civil Victorian, the powerful, narrated landscape played a central role. There was, however, — as we saw above — a difference. It was a difference that could be ignored by the urbane author satisfied simply to appropriate both landscape and inhabitants into his own romantic fantasy, but one that produced in McGinley a certain ambivalence — an ambivalence, one can imagine, shared to an even greater extent by the other newly middle-class readers of southwest Donegal, most of whom were less "educated" than the author.

These class differences — with their respective cultural fields — persist, and as can be gathered from the above account, many of the current members of the native, local middle class are descendants of those who reached that status in the mid-nineteenth century. Their degree of distance from an older sense of the social and natural order of things varies, of course, from person to person. The most important factor in this variation is, naturally enough, the extent of childhood involvement in the local world. Anthony O'Donnell, the schoolmaster who related the history of Carrick he had gotten from his own older cousin, was educated in Dublin, but only after a totally local childhood. After a few years of teacher training he returned to his native turf. Though his grammar is far more "standard," his accent and idiom are not much removed from the countryside in which grew up and to which he returned. He had committed many a Victorian poem and song to memory, but that idiom did not invade his speech in either Irish or English.

No doubt the fact that he encountered the history of his village in oral form — in Irish — in his childhood did much to help him retain the "old fashioned" character of his language. The history by kinship — an idiom of the local farmer or fisherman — is combined with a great interest in dates, each one pronounced with great stress and implied significance: a significance of age but also of exactness, of pinpointing in a linear and lineal narrative. But it is still a local history, a history from the local perspective, tied into the landscape — or at least the built humanscape. Each building on the one street town of Carrick provokes a narrative. Those, however, who go away to the Loretto Sisters or the Jesuits in another county — much more frequently the case today for the children of teachers and doctors — find themselves in a very different milieu, and it shows both in their view of the local scene and in the local sense of who they are. But their very removal allows — if they so desire — another approach to the "locality," another appropriation of the landscape that links the personal to the collective experience and memory. Thus did Dr. Lochlann McGill of Ardara, son of the local schoolmaster and celebrated local antiquarian P. J. McGill, choose to follow — as his wonderfully detailed 1992 volume is titled — "in Conall's footsteps."

4. The Priest and the Agent

> Father Magroarty is it? That's the priest that Brooke put out of his house. Did you hear a report on that name? Well, here's the story the old people heard about it. . . . My father was there, and my mother, and here's the lore about it that they had.

Máire Ni' Cunnigean warmed to her task, which was to tell the story of Father Magroarty and Arthur Brooke—the priest and the agent—two figures I had met in the Dublin archives. Arthur Brooke was agent to John and James Musgrave, who had purchased most of Glencolumbkille parish from the estate of Thomas Conolly in 1868, through the Encumbered Estates Court. Brooke was a lawyer and well enough organized to keep a copybook of his correspondence—tissue thin paper that absorbed the ink beneath his letters. Two brittle volumes of the correspondence, spanning the years from 1876 to 1880, had been found in Killybegs and deposited in the National Library. The letters cover the mundane business of running a large and poor estate in the west of Ireland. There is also a story, a narrative, in the letters concerning the parish priest of Glencolumbkille, Father John Magroarty. The story weaves in and out of the letters for nearly two years, beginning with a disagreement concerning the payment of rent, turning into a prolonged struggle over fences the priest had erected to enclose a portion of commonage, and leading to the priest's eviction. The eviction is not the end of the story, for Brooke's troubles really only began with that event.

I had read the story with interest; it seemed a classic social drama of the sort that might reveal much, not only about the history and social organization of the estate but also about the character of the priesthood and the very definition of religion. There were enough details in Brooke's letters—to the landlord, to the priest, and even to the bishop—to piece together a notion of what had happened and why. There was more, however, for beyond Brooke's copybook, the conflict had left other written traces. The Musgraves and their agent, Brooke, were so anxious to avoid the eviction—but to settle things in a way acceptable to themselves—that they wrote several times to Bishop MacDevitt (whom we met in the last chapter as the scholarly author of *The Donegal Highlands*), enclosing the correspondence between Brooke and Magroarty. Evidently they hoped that the bishop would bring round his errant priest. The *Derry Journal*, the *Ulster Examiner*, and the *Freeman's Journal* (the most important national Catholic paper) all carried accounts of the eviction, as well as subsequent correspondence from the aggrieved priest, Magroarty, and the Musgraves: a series of letters in which each party took to this public forum to defend himself and decry the perfidy of the opponent(s).

That exchange made it clear that the actors in this local drama were as interested in its "representation" as in the legal outcome. The struggle was not only over land, tenants' rights, and the privileges and powers of priests and landlords, but over the story. Perhaps the most important question to be decided, in fact, was the genre of the narrative. Was the eviction to be remembered and told as a tale of firm justice, of equality before the law in a modernizing, rational estate — as Brooke and the Musgraves urged — or would Magroarty's version prevail — a religious tale, a saga of the resistance of heroic good against the dark forces of evil? The contest was hardly equal. Those who might have preserved the landlord's version of the story are mostly gone. But that is not to say that Father Magroarty's performance was unnecessary, that the collective memory of the events and of the priest himself were foregone conclusions. As the archives — and occasional spurts of alternative popular memory — reveal, Magroarty was a difficult, aggressive man who made enemies among his coreligionists as well as among landlords and agents. The eviction, however, provided him with a stock role in a classic confrontation; the story that would follow fell naturally within the genre.

That much was clear to me as I sat in Máire's kitchen. When I had mentioned to a Teelin friend my discovery of Brooke's copybooks and the drama they contained, he told me that he knew of the eviction and would take me to a woman who could tell me the story. Her account, to which we will return below, told of the dramatic events of April 4, 1877 and the particularities of the actors; but Máire also evoked a more apparently timeless frame, a world of heroic, magically endowed priests and their faithful followers, of poor, moral, Irish Catholics versus wealthy, "black" Protestants, of Gael versus Gall.

*   *   *

The historical context of the events can be pieced together from historical sources. Most of the parish of Glencolumbkille had been held by the Conolly family since the seventeenth century, and according to both commission reports and local testimony, the Conollys were the very type of the old style landlord.

> The management was formerly of the old-fashioned, free-and-easy, feudal type; rents were low, they had not been advanced for fifty years, were irregularly paid, and never pressed for. On many townlands, especially round the coast, subdivision and subletting, and the introduction of squatters unchecked ran to a ruinous extent. Forty years ago [c. 1840] Colonel Conolly vainly endeavoured to reduce this over-crowding and double up his smallholdings. He is stated to have built 1,000 slated or well-thatched houses, or contributed 10 l. [pounds sterling] to tenants who would put their cottages in decent order. . . . Under the able agency of Mr. Alexander Hamilton, on many townlands the farms were squared or striped. (Dun 1881: 171)

This view overlooks the possible trauma—certainly reported elsewhere in Donegal—involved in the "squaring and striping," which, as we read earlier, meant the destruction of the basic social world of the peasantry. The tenants did seem to like Conolly, however, who is also consistently cited by them in commission reports of the period as one of the better landlords, among the most "improving" of the region. General economic difficulties in the years after the famine, however, were landing many landlords in the Encumbered Estates Court, a clearing house set up to sell estates burdened by debt, and Conolly was among their number. Apparently, "horse-racing and gambling brought serious difficulties on the generous-hearted but improvident county family" (Dun 1881: 172).

The Musgrave brothers, John and James, fit the stereotype[51] of the buyers. Whereas the Conolly family were substantial gentry whose estate was a political base—the Colonel's grandfather had been speaker of the Irish parliament in the eighteenth century, and he himself had been a Member of Parliament and a county officer—the Musgraves were Belfast merchants whose principal interest lay in that world. Over a period of twelve years they purchased several portions of both the Conolly and Murray Stewart southwest Donegal estates—eventually amounting to about 52,000 acres, for which they paid £27,000. Whether for personal profit or out of a genuine concern for the region, the Musgraves were certainly active and vocal landlords. Letters from them appeared in various Irish newspapers over the years, urging improvements in fisheries, roads, and so on. They themselves invested substantial sums in capital improvements and in wages. The Musgraves were also clearly interested in taking up a certain role in local and regional society, and with the completion of their purchases in 1879, they entered the ranks of the county's largest landowners: in the top ten by

valuation and third in terms of acreage, behind the Marquess of Coyning-
ham, who held a colossal 122,300 acres, and Lord Leitrim, with just over
54,000. These three estates, together with what was left of the Murray
Stewart holdings, comprised the greater part of west Donegal, and though
much of the land was wild moor and mountain, it was a very heavily populated region.

The "mountainy" farms, market villages, and fishing hamlets of the
Musgrave estate supported more than 8,000 persons in 1880, a population
not much reduced by the famine. A set of maps and rent rolls put together
at the time of purchase in 1868 has survived (see Figure 14), showing the
state of the holdings at that time.[52] The hamlets and rundale holdings are
gone—compare Musgrave's map with that of the 1836 Ordnance Survey
(Figure 4)—but the townland remains the critical local unit, with common
lands attached to each. Tenants in a given townland are entitled in the lease
to "mountain grazing" and the right to cut turf (turbary rights) in bogs,
usually several miles distant. In the years since the "squaring" of rundale,
the loosely controlled tenantry had probably continued to subdivide some
holdings, and in several townlands, as the rent rolls show, individually held
farms could not be distinguished. Elsewhere, small holdings apparently
supported a number of sub-tenants. Though the vast majority of the inhabitants were "tenants at will," paying a pound or two for a few acres of land,
and subject to renewal—or discontinuation—annually, they had been in
the habit of concluding their own land deals without interference. They
inherited tenancies like private property and sold access to rented lands by
virtue of what was called "tenant right," a custom found through most of
Ulster (the northern nine counties of Ireland). This payment was considerable, amounting to at least twenty times the yearly rent ("twenty year's
purchase"), but sometimes far more. The practice ensured that tenants
could realize something for their labor over the years; it was a frequent
source of emigration money, for example. But, as unsympathetic landlords,
agents, and officials pointed out, it also meant that the incoming tenant,
having been impoverished by the purchase of the "good will," was not in a
position to indulge in any improvements in the holding.

It is clear from his letters to his estate agent that James Musgrave, the
brother who took the most direct role in the estate, was determined to
"improve" and rationalize his newly acquired domain. In this he relied on
Arthur Brooke, hired in 1875 to manage the estate, who had been agent to
Murray Stewart and was probably of the planter family with substantial
holdings near Donegal Town.[53] Judging from his letters and the oral his-

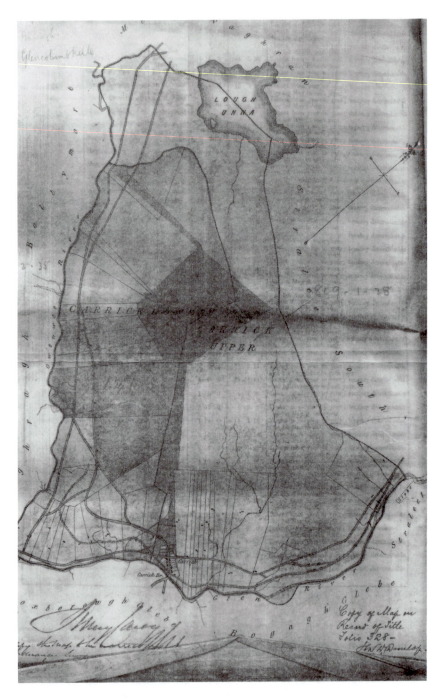

Figure 14. Estate map, 1861.

tory of the local populace, Brooke was diligent in pursuit of his employer's goals, but just as concerned with establishing his own authority. In any event, he was certain that the one thing depended on the other. Resident in nearby Killybegs, and weekly present in Carrick conducting estate business, Brooke was a new type of broker. Locals in Killybegs today "remember" him as a difficult and proud man who required tenants to leave their boots outside his office when paying the rent. Armed with the authority of both the landlord and the local government (to which he was also well connected), he could effectively mediate a range of local disputes, and in that way challenge the secular power of the priest. Indeed, Brooke's letters show that many of the locals were quick enough to realize that a case well presented in the appropriate idiom to agent Brooke might find quicker and more favorable resolution than with priest Magroarty.

Something of the appearance of the region under the Musgrave regime is conveyed by the Lawrence photos (Figures 15–20), taken late in the 1880s. Figures 15–18 show, respectively, Teelin as a whole, a section of Rinnakilla, a group of fishermen standing before a Rinnakilla cottage, and the new pier, financed by government grant and some landlord investment, just below the coast guard station. The photos show the narrow stripes of land that persist to this day, though they now bear only a fraction of the crops. The cottages are small and rough, whitewashed with lime, and all thatched. Figure 16 shows one two-story slated dwelling, the house of one of the Hegartys, an early merchant family. The photo of the fishermen probably shows them at a point when they were somewhat better off than in the late 1870s. This was the Musgraves' empire, and the contrast between the fishing family's cottages and the vacation home James Musgrave built for himself just west of Carrick (Figure 19) must have been even more striking to the locals at that time than it is to us now. Figure 20 conveys something of the geographical as well as social position of the landlord in his estate — a new "center" with a view of his wild and expansive domain, including, of course, Slieve League. The Musgraves also improved and expanded the small Glencolumbkille Hotel built by Conolly in Carrick, hoping to attract tourists to their piece of the "Donegal Highlands."

By the late 1870s, as we saw in the last chapter, there was also something of a middle class in the region. There were a small number of farm families — some Catholic, most Protestant — with holdings valued at substantially more than those of their neighbors and, to judge by valuations and census data, boasting two-story slate-roofed homes. Most such dwellings, however, were to be found in the developing market villages of Carrick

TEELIN·Co DONEGAL. 1455·W· L·

Figure 15. Teelin, late nineteenth century (Lawrence Collection, National Library of Ireland).

Figure 16. Rinnakilla, Teelin, late nineteenth century (Lawrence Collection, National Library of Ireland).

Figure 17. Fishermen, Teelin, late nineteenth century (Lawrence Collection, National Library of Ireland).

Figure 18. Teelin pier, late nineteenth century (Lawrence Collection, National Library of Ireland).

Figure 19. Musgrave's lodge, late nineteenth century (Lawrence Collection, National Library of Ireland).

Figure 20. View from behind Musgrave's lodge, late nineteenth century (Lawrence Collection, National Library of Ireland).

CARRICK LODGE. Co.DONEGAL. 1448. W.L.

Figure 21. Carrick, late nineteenth century (Lawrence Collection, National Library of Ireland).

(Figure 21) and Cashel (Glencolumbkille), where they huddled together on the main road defining a townscape that, however modest, was a different world from that of Rinnakilla, for example. It was the world of teacher and merchant, but it was also the natural habitat of the parish priest, John Magroarty. At the far edge of the photo one can discern his "seat," the newly built Catholic church, just west of the village and on the way to the Musgrave "cottage."

That church was only built in 1862, the most visible mark of the penetration into this world of that other regime, the diocese of Raphoe. The evolution in southwest Donegal of a diocesan regime with strong parochial organization was, naturally, a local expression of broader patterns. As we read in Chapter Two, the British conquest and subsequent Penal legislation had left a crippled and impoverished Church. In 1703 only three dioceses in the country were left with Catholic bishops, and Raphoe was not among them. When James Gallagher was consecrated bishop in 1725 — as we remember from Chapter Two — the "infrastructure" of the Church there was in pitiful state, with few churches and priests to minister to his poor and scattered populace. Gallagher began the consolidation of his diocese and attempted to enforce some doctrinal uniformity as well as Tridentine orthodoxy through the publication of his famous Irish language sermons in 1736 in "easy and familiar stile": the only devotional book in Irish, apart from Catechisms, to be published in Ireland in the century (Brady and Corish 1971: 70). These sermons, intended for use by his clergy, emphasized the "last things" — particulary Purgatory — and the need for the sacraments. Promotion of this Church-centered devotional practice was complemented — as we saw in Chapter Two — by attacks on patterns and wakes. While the book was certainly a publishing success, and the sermons themselves found an eventual place in the folk religious culture,[54] his efforts to seriously alter the structure of religious behavior could have had only limited success among the general populace in the period. This was particularly so in regions like west Donegal, where the lack of priests and "Mass houses" was matched by the popularity of non-clerically dominated religious occasions — such as patterns and wakes.

The first bishop successfully to impose a strong diocesan regime — though not without great difficulty — was Anthony Coyle, consecrated in 1782. In 1786 Coyle reported to Rome on the state of his diocese, which was still far from ideal. He estimated that there were about 40,000 Catholics, almost all of whom lived in "the hills," while about the same number of Protestants inhabited the lowlands and towns. He reported a great shortage of priests, and the inadequate preparation of those he did have: many had very little education and no opportunity to attend any of the Irish colleges abroad, in Paris and Rome. As a result, they were unfit to minister satisfactorily to the people. Coyle also decried the continuing scarcity of houses of worship — barely a real parish church in the entire diocese. Apparently, the fault was not all with the "gall" — for Coyle complained that, during his predecessor Bishop O'Reilly's term, the clergy had not met regularly, no visitation of parishes had been made by the bishop, and even the sacrament of Confirmation had not been conferred. According to Coyle, O'Reilly — who had for years been very ill — had spent most of his time with relations outside the diocese, and had left the running of the diocese to his vicar general, a Franciscan named Dominic MacDavett. Coyle accused Mac-Davett of taking advantage of the shortage of priests in order to secure parishes and curacies for some of his fellow friars (Giblin 1980: 13).[55]

Whether Coyle's portrayal of O'Reilly and MacDavett is strictly accurate, it is clear that these men were engaged in the classic struggle between regular and secular clergy, a conflict for control of parishes and dioceses going on elsewhere in Ireland, and in fact symptomatic of structurally similar situations elsewhere in time and space.[56] Coyle also attempted to train a more disciplined and dependable clergy by sending prospects, at his own expense, to the Irish College in Paris. With this better educated and more controllable priesthood, he hoped to replace the older clerics, whom he described as addicted to alcoholic drink. According to Giblin (1980: 14), Coyle made headway against this "abuse which was very prevalent and did serious spiritual and physical harm to both priests and people." The bishop, who was assisted in this campaign by those clergy he recruited himself, was specially thanked for his efforts by the civil authorities.[57] Apparently Coyle found it necessary to deprive two unregenerate priests of their parishes. Such reformation, if motivated by a distaste for drunken comportment, also assured Coyle's political control of the diocese. In an effort to bureaucratize that control, Coyle reinstituted annual visitations of his parishes and the administration of the sacrament of Confirmation, and presided over monthly conferences of all his clergy. The *smacht* (controlling power) of the bishop — a favorite popular phrase depicting bishop/priest relations — is here felt strongly for the first time. His clergy more firmly in hand, Coyle also turned to doctrinal matters, publishing widely used tracts on purgatory and the real presence of Christ in the Eucharist and other points of Catholic doctrine (Giblin 1980: 27).[58]

At the time, the Rev. Edward MacNulty, a Paris-educated Coyle supporter ordained in 1775, was parish priest of both Kilcar and Glencolumb-kille. The two very extensive parishes had been joined in 1665, and maintained as a single unit—first by Protestant decree and later through an inability to provide staff—until 1831. The long-lived MacNulty presided from 1781 until his death in 1829, during much of which time he was assisted by Friar Anthony, a Dominican. It was MacNulty who had suppressed the turas of Columcille, but with what degree of success it is difficult to know. His successor, MacDermott, also a graduate of the Irish College in Paris, was the first parish priest charged with Glencolumbkille alone, and so his influence was likely to have been more concentrated. In fact, the situation in the diocese as a whole had materially changed by 1842.[59]

> Although 20 years ago, at the commencement of the present Bishop's appointment, there were only 23 priests in the entire diocese, there are now 50 on active duty, and work for 10 more. The cause of Temperance has here produced a most extraordinary effect in the promotion of peace, order, and religion. The new College at Letterkenny is in a flourishing condition. (*Irish Catholic Directory* 1842: 267)

In the southwest, this meant the addition of one curate only, for now Cornelius MacDermot of Glencolumbkille was assisted by Charles Ferry. In extensive Kilcar, John Gallagher still labored alone, while the Rev. Drummond of Killybegs was assisted by James Stephens.

On the other hand, the diocesan archives reveal problems in this period, not only with those parishioners recalcitrant before efforts at "medalling them" for pledging abstinence, and—not surprisingly—with resistance to the cause from publicans, but with the clergy as well. Through the entire period covered by the archive (1840–1880) there are occasional reports, from clergy or parishioners, of the serious drinking habits of some local clergy. Though never a majority, in any given decade there were at least two or three priests in the diocese whose drinking was bad enough to incur such censure. Apparently Coyle's reforms were not permanent.

Despite such lapses, the overall impression conveyed in the bishop's archive—corroborated by other evidence—is of a "diocesan regime" comprising priests of very similar backgrounds and education increasingly under the control of the bishop and in control of their own parishioners.[60] Many priests were from the same families, and by far most went to the Irish Seminary in Maynooth (County Meath), where they were subjected to a similar curriculum and general culture. They were civilized Victorians and inclined, even before the primacy of the pro-Vatican Paul Cardinal Cullen,[61] to bring new devotions along with their "civilizing" efforts.[62] We remember, for example, that Father Drummond, the first Maynooth graduate to serve in the region, had already brought the dramatic display of Assumption devotions to the church he built in Killybegs in 1842.[63]

Further west, however, the full force of the new regime and the "devotional revolution" did not arrive until the Rev. Charles MacNeely took up the curacy in Carrick in 1858 (parish priest from 1860). It was Maynooth educated MacNeely—from a wealthy Mountcharles family—who contributed most to the rearrangement of the local religious geography. First the new pastor launched an attack on the remaining pattern at the Well of the Holy Women in Teelin (*Tobar na mBan Naomh*):

> The celebrated pilgrimage, that used to attract thousands of people to this inspiring hillside, continued to increase in throng and attractive excitement, till Father Mac Neely's time, but excrescences of abuse, and especially drink and unseemly dancing, brought the celebration into degraded repute, and ultimately entailed ecclesiastical prohibition, about 1860. (Cannon McGuire 1920: 454)

Soon after, in complementary fashion, MacNeely erected the "very respectable" Gothic church that still graces the main road in Carrick. While Cannon McGuire (himself a student of Thomas C. McGinley of Chaper Three and a professor at Maynooth) describes MacNeely as "goodhumored," he is remembered locally as powerful and hot tempered. I was told a story of MacNeely demolishing a local drinking establishment by pulling down the beams with his bare hands. By way of contemporary corroboration, one letter survives from the period in which an obviously well educated Teelin man named Edward Kennedy complained to the bishop of "the violence of his [Father MacNeely's] temper . . . bullying every person who comes in his way" (Armagh Archdiocesan Archive; MiCH 51/g/31/73).

As Kennedy's complaint shows, the increasingly intrusive priests might run afoul of their middle class parishioners, with whom no doubt they sometimes vied for local influence. In one letter, a northern Donegal merchant complained bitterly, and at length, that the parish priest vigorously favored a rival merchant (and a relation of the priest) over the complainant. Priests did not as a rule define their province narrowly, and the practice of recruiting all priests from within the diocese, coupled with the pervasive power of kinship, not to mention the general practice of priests' farming tenancies of their own (opposed by many bishops), combined to make the local priest something other than the ideal "stranger/mediator."

Suffice it to say that when John Magroarty arrived on the scene in 1870, the local populace were used to aggressive clerics who defined the role of pastor literally and broadly. Magroarty was born in Keelogs, Inver, where he studied classics in Patrick Mac Goldrick's academy. The future bishop, James MacDevitt — who figures in this story — was among his classmates, as was MacDevitt's brother and biographer, the priest professor John Mac-Devitt. Magroarty matriculated in Maynooth in 1849, again a fellow student of both MacDevitts and, according to McGuire (1920: 463) John was his sole rival in brilliance. Magroarty's political interpretation of the priest-hood — as the literal pastor of a flock — was evident long before his arrival in Carrick. As a curate in Doe (1858–62) he found himself involved in the cele-brated sheep stealing accusations there and, according to Cannon McGuire,

> a more competent champion of the down-trodden and calumniated peasants it would be difficult to find in any age. . . . So immensely popular had he become that the congregation barred the doors and windows of Doe church against Father Diver in 1862, when the latter was appointed parish priest in succession to the Rev. Joe Magee. (McGuire 1920: 463–64)

Magroarty went on to a curacy at Glenswilly, where he came to the defense of a local man accused of murdering a Scottish bailiff. In an even more telling sign of his judicial ambitions and his notion of the priesthood, Magroarty

> established a tribunal in Glenswilly for the trial of all local cases, and sur-rounded it with all the paraphernalia of a public court of justice — a judge, jurors, advocates, and a secretary. During his residence in Glenswilly, no in-habitant dare venture to bring any alleged offender before a petty Sessions or Assize Court. (McGuire 1920: 464)

For all his brilliance, Magroarty was not made a parish priest until his appointment to the pastorate in Glencolumbkille in 1870, and Glen was hardly a choice location, being one of the poorer and more isolated parishes of the diocese. In fact his forcefulness — or arrogance, depending on one's point of view — made him enemies not only among the "gall" but among his own colleagues. The following is extracted from a letter addressed to Bishop McGettigan from a Rev. Peter MacDevitt[64], curate in the parish neighboring Magroarty's. Apparently, MacDevitt's own family lived in Magroarty's curacy.

> May the 30th — '65
> My Lord I humbly beg to submit to your consideration the manner in which it has pleased the Rev. Mr. McGrorty [sic] to treat my father and every member

of the family for the last three Sundays. He has done everything in his power to destroy their character. He has gone back for generations and everything . . . whether true or false he has publicly accused them of from the altar. (Armagh Archdiocesan Archive MiCH 51/g/27/6)

The letter identifies what MacDevitt believed was the cause of the problem. Magroarty's predecessor had planned to dismiss a schoolmistress, and Mac-Devitt's father, who owned the schoolhouse, was insisting she vacate the premises. Magroarty evidently disagreed enough to "read them from the altar," that is, publically criticize them in church. This practice is, in fact, directly indicated elsewhere in the archives for a number of priests — and is very vivid in the local memory. Other priests elsewhere went so far as to deny the sacraments to those who carried on in defiance of priestly authority.[65]

The people of Glencolumbkille, whose pastor Magroarty, already well beyond fifty years of age, finally became in 1870, were by that time accustomed to an increasingly imposing Church and authoritarian priests. Given MacDevitt's letter, the general practice of priests at the time, and the surviving memory of Magroarty as an aggressive man in street, house, and pulpit, it is likely that those among his own parishioners who crossed him felt his wrath.

On the public stage, however, Father Magroarty was to be found defending the oppressed tenantry, and there is no doubt that the people of southwest Donegal were hard pressed in the late 1870s. He was not long in his new office before taking up their cause again, and heading once more into a courtroom. This time the priest was fighting for the Teelin fishermen, for whom he sought to establish the right to catch salmon in the open sea. Once more he was facing off against landlords, this time the Musgraves — who were also new arrivals on the scene, as well as several other smaller landlords who held fishery rights that extended out from the river to the three mile limit. There was in fact mention of these matters in a letter from Magroarty to Bishop MacDevitt:

3 August, 1875
My Lord,
. . . The Musgraves are here now and are very active in their opposition to the poor fishermen. I appeared in the Landed Estates Court by council and opposed on behalf of the fishermen to resist the Musgraves' claims to certain fishing stations which have always been in the possession of the people, and which Mrs. Hamilton and the Musgraves claim as an exclusive right. The case was postponed until November, this has set the Musgraves into a complete rage.

I am your Lord a faithful servant, John McGroarty. (Diocesan Archives, Raphoe)

A year later, with Magroarty further enmeshed in his struggles with the Musgraves, Bishop MacDevitt apparently offered him the pastorate in Dungloe. It is difficult to know whether the scholarly MacDevitt was rewarding Magroarty for his efforts or was nervous about his way of tangling with landlords and courts and just trying to get him out of harm's way. Magroarty replied:

27 September 1876
My Lord:
I am in receipt of your very kind letter and feel more grateful than I can express. I note Dungloe is a much more important and extensive Parish than Glencolumkille, but there are local circumstances that incline me to remain here. There are improvements to be made which if circumstances had been favorable, should have been affected.
Thanking your Lordship most gratefully, John McGroarty. (Diocesan Archives, Raphoe)

*   *   *

It is hardly surprising that the Musgraves were ill disposed toward this very assertive priest. When they hired Brooke to manage their estate, they warned the punctilious lawyer that Magroarty was up to tricks with his own land, and Brooke was probably wary when Father Magroarty walked into his office on January 24, 1876 to offer the rent on his farm in the townland of Upper Carrick.

Having received the correct amount, Brooke proceeded to write out a receipt in the name of "representatives of P. Gallagher," for Gallagher was the name Brooke found listed in his lease records. Magroarty protested that he could not accept a receipt except in his own name, adding by way of proof of his own rightful tenantry that he had paid a substantial sum to Gallagher, before the latter had emigrated, and in the presence of the Reverend Logue, parish priest of Kilcar. That argument was not one that could possibly find favor with Brooke, for whom the presumed lofty status of priests was — as is increasingly clear through the letters — the real problem. Magroarty refused to pay the rent without a proper receipt, and Brooke could not "recognize" a claim unsanctioned by the authority (of landlord and contract) upon which all his own power depended.

This, however, was not the only or the main transgression of which

Magroarty was guilty. Brooke noted that the fences about which Musgrave had warned him were still up. Apparently, the priest had enclosed a portion of the townland's commonage. Brooke's account to landlord Musgrave of his confrontation with Magroarty on this issue is interesting:

> He says he acted "bona fide" in putting [the fences] up, thinking he had a right to do so in order to protect his grazing, and not until some of the other tenants had first done so and asked him to do so also. . . . He is willing to acknowledge in "black and white" [that he is in the wrong] but he cannot recede from his position by taking down the fences as he would lower himself in the eyes of his parishioners. . . . He maintained that you had promised four years ago to take steps to protect his grazing from trespass by making some regulation about the quantity of stock to be kept. (Musgrave Estate Papers; 4278 n. 784)

Increasing population in the parish must have put growing pressure on accessible pasturage. The "irrational" commons were usually targeted for enclosure by landlords who wanted to create more valuable individual tenancies wherever possible. In this case, however, the press for enclosure seems to have come from the better-off tenantry. Magroarty had complained of trespass—which on a commonage could only mean that his poorer neighbors had more animals on the commons than their holding warranted. Traditionally, the size of the holding dictated the number of animals one could keep on the commons, and the fact that Magroarty had asked Musgrave to "make a regulation" to that effect certainly indicates that the poorer tenants in the townland were keeping more than their share. But if Brooke and Musgrave favored the general principle of enclosure (as did all "improving" landlords), they were clearly not happy about tenants taking the initiative by carving up commonage without first securing the contractual right to do so.

"He was arguing," continues Brooke's letter to Musgrave, "as if priests were to be treated differently from other tenants, and that if you gave in to him it could not form a precedent to your harm." Indeed, both the priest's hope for special treatment and Brooke's fear of giving it testify to the priest's position in that social world. Beyond their specifically sacred role, such rural priests were almost alone among local Catholics in such regions in their ability to communicate and even mobilize for political ends. As Samuel Clark notes (1979: 197), the Catholic clergy, particularly after 1873, took an active part in parliamentary politics, and were, in fact, "time and again accused of having improperly interfered in politics."

Brooke was concerned, however, with more local matters, such as the election of the Board of Guardians, whose jurisdiction over county affairs most affected the running of the estate.

> Nathaniel Walker has been returned as Guardian for Glen and Malinmore though John Blaine pushed him very hard, to within 8 votes. . . . I have not heard the particulars of the election yet but I think the Priest must have interfered for Blaine as Walker told me more than two thirds of the voters had pledged themselves to him. I purposely avoided anything like interference for fear of raising his back. (Musgrave Estate Papers; 4278–4279 n. 774)

The "fear of raising his back" shows Brooke's sensitivity to the power of the priest and the possibly adverse effects of a direct confrontation — particularly over a public issue and in a public arena. Brooke hoped for a legal contest where the issues were contractual and settled in court, but his letters show quite clearly that he was aware that such a battle would, in the final analysis, be difficult to keep within judicial limits. Accordingly, Brooke offered Magroarty £200 in compensation for the property in question — covering his "tenant right" plus the £40 the priest had spent in "repairing the house."[66] However, the priest refused the offer, insisting instead that the proper "tenant right" was £700. Brooke was shocked by the amount — certainly rather high for a farm whose annual rent was £3, 13s, and 2p per year. In December 1876 Brooke (or Musgrave) hit upon what seemed an inspired strategy and made the following proposition to Magroarty:

> The Messrs. Musgrave have often thought of providing a free residence for the parish priest and I am now authorized to inform you that although in the indications of rights as landlords they have been compelled to resume possession of your holdings, yet having regard to the position which you occupy in the country and not wishing to cause you the unpleasantness and indignity of being evicted from your residence, they are willing, provided you quietly cede possession of your older holdings, to execute to you as parish priest the lease of the house together with the garden in front of it as a parochial residence for the parish of Glencolumkille for one shilling per annum. . . . You will observe that by this arrangement the Musgraves will virtually be making a present of the house and garden to the parish. (Raphoe Diocesan Archives; Brooke to Magroarty, Dec. 20, 1876)

This offer was rejected by Magroarty, who claimed its acceptance would prejudice his case in the courts, and so Brooke went straight to the bishop with the same offer, enclosing the entire correspondence between the priest and the agent. Evidently Brooke assumed that Magroarty would look unreasonable in the exchange and that the Bishop would be tempted by the offer of a perpetual parochial house at a nominal rent. But Bishop MacDevitt wrote to Magroarty about it, who insisted once again that the offer was only designed to undermine the credibility of his case and added,

> I have considered the matter over and think that too much condescension has been shown to Brooke and the Musgraves. And I could not think of wishing your Lordship to write again. (Raphoe Diocesan Archives; Magroarty to Mac-Devitt, 5 March 1877)

The Bishop apparently followed Magroarty's advice, as there is no reference to any future correspondence. Brooke felt that he and the Musgraves had no choice but to proceed to act on the ejectment order they had obtained many months earlier. Brooke may have entertained faint hopes that the people would not support Magroarty, as he had it from his network of spies that the local opinion of the priest was not altogether favorable; he was often described as avaricious. However, reports from reliable sources ultimately made him nervous.

> Magroarty is determined to be put out, I am told, as it is his avowed object to make the place impossible for you. That it is which makes him refuse your offers. . . . He will not give up until put out, as he thinks the people will side with him against you, so that his real object is to make a show if he can. (Musgrave Estate Papers, Brooke to Musgrave Jan 29, 1877: Musgrave Mss., 875–76)

As the event drew near, Brooke became increasingly anxious, and his hesitation to inform the priest about the day on which he should expect the sheriff well illustrates the perceived precariousness of his position. If he notified Magroarty as to the day, Brooke reasoned, the priest could really set the stage; if he did not, then Magroarty could later claim unfair treatment. Either way, Brooke now clearly saw that nothing less than a "show" was in the offing.

The *Derry Journal* ran the following account of the event:

EVICTIONS IN COUNTY DONEGAL.

On Wednesday the 4th inst., a number of evictions were carried out at Carrick, county Donegal. . . . There are three particular houses on this property (in Carrick) — one the residence of the Parish Priest — the Rev. John McGroarty — the other two, of Mr. Cassidy and Mr. Cannon, respectively, both sub-tenants of the Parish Priest. For the last two years there have been disagreements between the Messrs. Musgrave and this tenant, the Parish Priest, the last of these disputes being about the raising of a mud fence by the priest on a portion of his land, as a protection against trespass, which was very considerable. This fence when almost completed was objected to by Messrs. Musgrave, who ordered the priest to desist further erection, and to level what had been already built to it. The fence was of considerable length, and the priest, I understand, rather than do this, offered to pay them an increased rent, if they would allow it to remain, at the same time promising to let it crumble into its former position through time. This they refused, and the Rev. gentleman then proposed the following as a settlement of the case — that he should be allowed to sell to the best advantage; that he should be paid the tenant-right of the farm, or leave the whole to the arbitration of lawyers. But all to no purpose, as all these proposals the Messrs. Musgrave refused, and a notice to quit, shortly afterwards served upon the parish priest and his sub-tenants, was the issue, which was carried into effect by the eviction of all three on the above date. At about nine o'clock a.m. on Wednesday the Sheriff and his men, with Mr. Brooke (Messrs. Musgrave's agent), arrived here and as the day wore on the village filled with people, who had evidently heard of the matter and flocked in from the surrounding districts to be spectators of the scene, and at the same time to sympathise with those about to be evicted. There was no extra police force in the barracks up to this time, and it was thought necessary to have the usual force of the station augmented by three members of the Royal Irish Constabulary. These were obtained from the neighbouring village of Kilcar, and placed in readiness under command of Constable Gear. All went on smoothly, and one by one the articles of furniture, &c., were removed from the priest's house and placed in the street. All was soon cleared out, except a quantity of potatoes and hay, with two cows, a horse, and car. These were disposed of in a similar manner, and the house of the priest secured fast. As for Mr. Cassidy and Mr. Cannon they were allowed immediate repossession of their houses, on becoming tenants of the Messrs. Musgrave. By this time the village presented quite a holiday appearance, being crowded by spectators, all expressing sympathy for the priest. The lands, which lay some mile and a half distant in the country, had also to be taken possession of by the Sheriff, Mr. Brooke and that official having proceeded by car to the place for that purpose. They were about returning to Carrick, when those in the village marched en masse towards the chapel-yard, and with crowbar and other tools proceeded to level the stone wall described as separating the plot at the hotel from the chapel-yard. They had got about one-third through with their undertaking when Mr. Brooke and the Sheriff returned amid loud and prolonged cheering by the crowd. Mr. Brooke on alighting from the car proceeded to the scene of action and from that to the police barracks, where he at once ordered the extra force, which had a short time previously left for Kilcar, to return. These with some of our regulars were at once on the spot where the wall once reigned supreme, but for some cause best known to their commander they did nothing but obtain in writing a long list of the so-called offenders' names, and desired the men who had up to this time been busily at work throwing down the wall, to desist, which was immediately obeyed by them; but if so, it was only to give the female portion of the crowd an opportunity to display their willingness and ability to outdo their predecessors at the work, in the face of the commander and his men. A scene ensued which was at once strange and amusing. From the oldest mother present to the youngest female child able in the crowd, none were idle where work presented itself in the shape of destroying the wall; and in a shorter time than would probably be credited, it was quietly lying at their feet a victim. The skillful manner in which the women handled the tools, some of which were of no small dimensions, would have done credit to the best of Messrs. Musgrave's ironworkers. The scene wound up with three cheers for the victory won by the women of Carrick and its neighbourhood. I omitted to mention that the gate which was presented as an entrance gate to the parishoners by the Messrs. Musgrave was also taken down, and its funeral, well attended, wound its way to the green opposite the hotel, where the crowd gently deposited its remains. (*Derry Journal* Mon., April 9, 1877)

The following letter from Musgrave arrived hot on the heels of this report, correcting the "errors" therein. He explained that the land in question was commons

to which the other tenants on that townland were equally entitled. Some of the latter complained to us that they were being deprived, not only of their pasture, but that the turbary set apart for the use of the townland was included in the part enclosed by Mr. McGroarty. We at once sent a note to each of the parties, pointing out the illegality of what they were doing, and asking them to remove the fences, otherwise we would be obliged to employ such remedy as was given us by law. All except Mr. McGroarty stopped their fences, and eventually removed them; but Mr. McGroarty burned the notice, and when our own tenants refused to work at his fences, he brought a body of men from an adjoining property, and completed them in open defiance of our rights. (*Derry Journal*, Wed. April 11, 1877)

Thus Musgrave wrapped himself in the flag of the tenantry; it was he, not Magroarty, who was defending their commonage from enclosure. Musgrave then went on to explain the offers he had made to both Magroarty and Bishop MacDevitt (none of which are mentioned in Magroarty's letters).

Magroarty replied at considerable length, not only answering Musgrave's assertions and arguments but availing himself of the opportunity to hit every symbolic chord at his disposal.

Some two years ago "four neighbouring tenants" and your humble servant thought proper to fence in portions of land we held under the Messrs. Musgrave. By the legality or illegality of that act I am prepared to stand or fall. Well, the landlords gave us notice, not only to discontinue the fence, but insisted on levelling what we had erected. We contended then and there that we had a legal right to fence in what had been set aside for each farm, and had been lockspitted by Mr. Conolly's surveyor for the express purpose of taking them out of rundale. . . . It was a "serious question" whether the tenants could or could not fence in for improvements what they considered as their own. I felt it must be resolutely met, otherwise the tenant-right on the whole estate would not only be greatly depreciated (I thank the Jew for the expression) but would be substantially destroyed. . . . The other tenants submitted, and removed the fences. I need not say what terror and consternation notices to quit and evictions spread among poor, simple tenants with large families to support. If Jupiter Tonans sat on Slieve League, and scattered his thunderbolts among the villagers, he could not strike them with greater fear than their landlords can by notices to quit and evictions. I stood alone in the breach. I looked upon myself as the representative of the tenants and with their rights in my sole keeping. My position was anything but enviable. I did not like, indeed it was very much against my mind and inclination, to do "freedom's battle" against the Messrs. Musgrave, for whom I entertained none other than feelings of friendship and kindness. . . . They know, whether they were right or wrong, that the law as it stands at present enables them in a court of law to evict any tenant, whether he is right or wrong, with or without cause. They think that by this fell swoop they overawe all future resistance and indirectly do away with the tenants' other rights in their legal power to evict. . . . What was I to do?

The answer came in the shape of offers from the Messrs. Musgrave. . . . Every offer either to myself or through the bishop was nothing other than a bribe to trample principle under foot, and let the tenants be immersed one and all with the conviction that in point of law the landlords were right — that while the Hebrew people must make bricks the straw is absolutely in the giving of the Egyptians. They would not offer me anything but what my convictions, my sense of self-respect, and every manly feeling within me, forced me to reject. In and under these circumstances I am the evicted parish priest of Glencolumbkille. The cause of this eviction, my part in it, and the Messrs. Musgrave's part in it, are before the public; and both they and I stand at the bar of public opinion. — I am willing to abide by the verdict. The Messrs. Musgrave say that "some of the tenants complained that they were being deprived not only of their pasture, but the turbary, set aside for the use of the townland was included in the part enclosed by Mr. McGroarty," and that in consequence "the rights of the poorer tenants were set aside." This statement is not only utterly untrue but the people are highly indignant at its boldness. They regard it as a calumny on themselves, which they are prepared to repel upon oath. I am now some twenty years on the mission. The tenor of my entire life is more than enough to refute this charge. I appeal to those who know me — and I am not unknown in the county — did I ever invade or try "to set aside the rights of the poorer classes" of my countryman! The son of an Irish farmer myself, I should not, as I would not. As a clergyman, as an Irish priest, could I so forget myself! Could I sink so far below the noble standard of that unselfish patriotism and high morality which is the glory of the Irish priesthood! Of nothing am I so proud as of belonging to that order, and that I enjoy their confidence and esteem the which I should not nor did I ever "set aside the rights of the poorer classes" and "deprive them of their pasture and turbary." The fable of Saturn devouring his own children is not more absurd than that the priests are opposed to the interests of their people.

— Your obedient servant.

John McGroarty, P.P.,
Carrick, Co. Donegal

(*Derry Journal*, Mon. Apr. 23, 1877)

Magroarty's rhetorical flourishes convey some sense of the pastor in his pulpit. In this letter he certainly claims the moral high ground — the guardian of tenant right from the incursions of rapacious landlords — but he goes further. For the rhetorical weight of the letter is toward the end, where Magroarty uses his defense to define — once more — the Irish Catholic priest and his role as paternal pastor and protector of his otherwise defenseless flock. Such an image might be telling not only in opposition to landlords but to alternative, secular political leadership from such nationalist or tenants' rights groups as the Fenians or Land Leaguers, the latter of which was in action in this period. Most generally, this sort of rhetoric contributed to the continuing definition of religion as a sphere of activity and experience.

Magroarty makes no mention here of the £700 he *was* prepared to accept. His private correspondence with Brooke, on the other hand, made far more reference to the losses he faced than the "matter of principle" claimed here. As for Magroarty's reference to his outraged neighbors, however, corroboration of the pastor's claim, and a lesson on land tenure, arrived soon after at the editor's office:

EVICTIONS IN CARRICK, COUNTY DONEGAL — DECLARATION OF THE TENANTS

To The Editor of the Derry Journal.
Sir — I am requested by the persons whose signatures are attached to forward to you for publication the accompanying declaration in the matter in dispute between the Messrs. Musgrave and the Rev. John McGroarty. Some years ago the late Thomas Conolly thought proper to survey, map, and applot to his tenants the lands on his Glencolumbkille estate. . . . His surveyors divided the lands into three zones or belts, which were not only distinctly marked on the map but lockspitted and surface-marked on the land. The first and upper division, consisting of thousands of acres of the mountains, moors, and rugged topland was marked off for "commonage." It served as rough pasturage. . . . On this mountain "commonage" the tenants reared various kinds of stock as the source of any little wealth they possessed. . . . No tenant ever thought of appropriating or fencing in one square yard of it. The second division was the

arable farms in the lowlands, and on which such dwelling-houses as the poor people had were built. These farms were in many instances mere patches, quite inadequate to produce as much food as would support the families obliged to live on them for half the year. Hence they were always from May to August in the market for Indian meal. The third division was a small zone or stripe between the mountain "commonage" and the arable farms. This portion, though in itself considerable if reclaimed, was of comparatively little value as it stood. And inasmuch as the arable farms were miserably small, and not able to support the families living on them, Thomas Conolly, with that goodness of heart which distinguished his treatment of his tenants, applotted this inter-mediate portion and marked it off with the intention that each tenant might, as his means and his circumstances permitted him, add it to his arable farm by continuing the mearings up to but no further than the boundary line of the mountain commonage. This intermediate belt was held in common by the people alone of each townland respectively, and it was only "in common" until fenced in; and moreover it was clearly understood that all or any of the tenants might do so when convenient. It was not intended to remain permanently a "common" like the upper zone. In fact many of the tenants had already taken advantage of this privilege and fenced in the portion allotted them. . . . Now it was this intermediate stripe along that Father McGroarty fenced in, and for which he has been evicted. . . .
— Your obedient servant,

A Correspondent.

We, the undersigned, the entire tenants of the townland of Carrick Upper, and who alone are entitled to move in this matter, as we alone are interested, learning that the Messrs. Musgrave stated in the public press that we com-plained to them that the Rev. John McGroarty, our parish priest, had deprived us of the right of pasture on the "Carrick Common," and also deprived us of our turbary by building certain fences on the top line of his farm, do hereby most solemnly declare that the statement is entirely without any foundation; and we hereby give it, in every sense, the flattest denial and contradiction. (signed by ten tenants, *Derry Journal*, Wed. Apr 25, 1877)[67]

The argument seems a reasonable one, as the distinction is visible on the land itself—rough pasture versus mountain bog. But a look at the map (Figure 14) makes it difficult to see how every tenant could simply extend upwards his or her holding. Musgrave's estate record—which includes the transfer of property with all provisions and exemptions—makes no men-tion of this possibility, nor do the maps show the "lockspitted" boundaries the signatees claim were specified under Conolly. They may well have been, but if they were, it may well also be true that Musgrave and Brooke knew nothing about them; there is no such reference in their correspondence to one another.

Even more interesting than the letter is the process — though we cannot know it — that led to the letter's writing. Was it heartfelt indignation that prompted the declaration, fear of the priest, or both? Not all Upper Carrick tenants are represented; why did the others not sign?

At any rate the landcourt did meet on the issue three months after the eviction and issued a decree that Brooke, at least, found only partially satisfactory:

July 11, 1877
. . . Are you satisfied with the Judgement? On the whole I am pretty well, though I must confess I cannot understand the last part of it, where the Chairman says no evidence was given of the violation of any usage of the right of the tenantry and then immediately afterward says McGroarty's conduct was unreasonable in refusing to pull them down? Again I think he should have deducted something for Mr. McGroarty's conduct, more than merely disallowing his costs. As it is, he has given him the full value of his holding and more — it matters not that this is less than he paid, I am afraid a handle will be made of this . . . though I do not think it likely that you will ever again have to put out a tenant on the Glen estate for the same cause. There is no doubt that this part of the judgement is misty and to my mind contradictory.

Brooke was apparently correct that such a case would not come up again. If the battle over legal rights was settled more or less in the landlord's favor, however, the moral struggle was another matter, and had not awaited court action. As the newspaper (and Brooke's letters) report, on the day of the fabled event a local "mob" tore down the wall between chapel and hotel — a more symbolic piece of property would be difficult to find. Guerillas continued to fight for the priest's fallen honor; his cows were led daily by his servant onto the very pastures from which they had been driven. Meanwhile, a committee had organized itself to meet in the church and raise money for the building of a new residence for Magroarty. A frustrated Brooke found Magroarty sympathizers even within the constabulary barracks and asked Musgrave to send a band of Protestant laborers who could be trusted to act properly. Their arrival, of course, only served to reinforce the religious and ethnic definition of the antagonism. In the end, Brooke must have either wearied or shied from the battle, for the priest's new house stood. Magroarty died soon after, but his replacement, a man named Peter Kelly from whom Brooke expected a pleasant change, was soon reported to be passing petitions in church demanding fair rents. In 1888, the same Father Kelly — though by then parish priest in the north of the county —

engaged Musgrave in another newspaper battle over the latter's alleged improvements during the very harsh local conditions of the early 1880s.

*   *   *

All this is in the archives. But now, one hundred years after the event, I found myself sitting in the kitchen of Máire, a ninety-year-old retired schoolteacher and a resident of Upper Carrick, just a few doors down from Magroarty's fabled home. A few older men had come for the occasion, and Máire was clearly happy for the opportunity to tell a story she knew well.[68] As she related the struggle between agent and priest, Máire used the classic forms of the *seanchaidh* (storyteller): the formulaic beginning phrases and a tone of voice and focus that was entirely distinguishable from her conversational manner. But there were none of the antics now popular among the professional "storytellers" on the American circuit — no gesticulation, no imitation of voices. Máire, like any *seanchaidh*, let the words themselves and the informal, easy theatricality of the occasion conjure up the events and the emotions of one hundred years before. The story was told in Irish, in which language declarative sentences typically begin with the verb. When Máire had completed a key sentence — "thainig Brookes . . ." — Brookes came . . ." — her audience would often repeat the initial verb — "thainig," "he came" — their rapt attention undiminished by the fact that they knew the story well. To hear history as one knows it is to know again that it happened and that the events are still "there," in the story.

> It seems that the priest was a big, strong, confident man, and he had a hound, maybe a couple of them, and he was very fond of taking them out hunting, do you understand me? But then there was a bailiff in that place, do you know, to watch it — I think you needed a license, maybe that wasn't going at the time — but it's likely that the priest had no license to be going out hunting, but whatever happened that evening, the bailiff caught him on the hill and took him in in the name of Brookes, or whatever it was, do you know. He was in that house up there, the last house [just a few up from Máire's own], that was the place he had, and he paid rent on it. It would have belonged to the Musgraves, that place. Anyway, there was nothing done about it, until he came to pay the rent. The rent wasn't accepted from him then; he was told that he had broken the law, that he had been out in the hills hunting, and that he had to leave the place — the house.
> Well, sure enough he wasn't happy about that — but what could he do? Well, then the people of the parish heard about it: he had been the parish priest

among them a long time and they weren't a bit happy to hear what had happened. But it seems that time went on, toward the day he was to be out, and time grew short, and in the end, the last day arrived. And according to the story, there were no cars in those days, but there was just one carriage and that belonged to Brookes—I don't think there were many wheeled vehicles at all at that time.

But the priest was upstairs, and guarding the way out. And he saw then that they were coming around the corner—there were soldiers there and Brooks was in his carriage—no one hiding. And the curate that was in the place—I believe in Glen he was—he came and the people of the parish came, all of them that were in it, from all over the place. And the curate came, when the priest was at the top of the stairs, Father Magroarty, and he [the curate] went into the place, and he pulled his stole from his pocket and he put it on his shoulders and he pulled out his book and he began to read from it. . . . "Put that back" he [Magroarty] said, "into your pocket. Interfere with nothing." He did as he was told. The priest went out the door and he wasn't seen and he wasn't heard. No one saw him go out.

Well, that was fine. The intruders came but there was no priest to find, he had left. They searched and put out whatever they found of his belongings—out into the street. And when they had that done, all of it, they put the door under lock, after they had left, lest anyone else enter it after them. Whatever kind of lock it was, they had none like it in Carrick, and they had to wait till a man brought one to them and put it on the door, and then they left. And the people were in a rage.

In those days, they were very strong—men and women. And the men wouldn't start something until the women had started it first. There was no law on the women, so it didn't matter what they did, it seems. But there was one woman and she was as strong as anyone in the parish, they say that the two shoulders on her . . . she was that strong, the hands on her and the fists on her, that it didn't matter what she'd catch hold of, she could pull it down. But the women wore shawls in those days, and they took crowbars in them and up with them all to the hotel that the Musgraves had—it was very nice. And that strong woman, she took hold of her crowbar and she went at the ornaments they had out on the lawn and pulled them down. And when the men saw what she had done, they all went to help her and it wasn't long till they had the place wrecked.

Well, that was fine. But the priest was out with no house to go into. Every person—the people of the parish—got together then. Money was not plentiful in those days, and they had no money to give—but every man and every woman had two hands, and they could do whatever they needed to with them. They met together then and they started to bring stones and they went at it until they had the house built where the priest is now—in three weeks, and according to the story, the priest was living in it a couple of weeks after that. They did it together, do you know, the men and the women. And I heard my mother talking about it and she heard the old people talking about it. (Máire Ni' Cunnigean, tape recorded, 1976; my translation)

That was Máire's story. The starring role of the local women — also reported in the newspaper account — clearly delighted the storyteller. Her eyes had sparkled as she showed me her own delicate fist in order to conjure up those of the heroically strong women. Two points on which this tale diverges from both Brooke's and the newspaper account are worth noting. Whatever the historical veracity of the hunting incident, Brooke makes no mention of it and, given that he never hesitated to decry Magroarty's infractions, it's hard to imagine he would have passed up the chance in his letters. It is impossible to say whether the hunting incident was offered by Magroarty as a justification, or supplied by one generation or other of storytellers in search of an appropriate cause of eviction. In either case, it has the virtue of attributing poaching, the favorite local criminal sport, to the priest, and thus aligning his interests with those of his parishioners. Conspicuous by its absence is mention of any possible violation by Magroarty of communal grazing rights, or of any element of competition between him and his flock. In the confrontation at the house, the curate arms himself with stole and book — an important theme (as we shall see) in the genre. It is not clear to me whether or not the reason that the priest walks out of the house without being seen is that he has rendered himself invisible, though this latter reading would put the story very much in line with others of its type. Most important, Magroarty has succeeded in casting himself (as he did in his letter to the paper) as *An Sagart* — the heroic priest. The forces of good are thus dressed in priestly garb and here pitted against the ascendent forces of evil arriving in the class emblem of carriage, Protestant by implication of the narrative structure and the logic of binary opposition.

*   *   *

To Brookes's and Ni' Cunnigean's versions of the story I will add my own. To a large extent, of course, I already have: positioning myself with critical distance with respect to the actors and their behavior, sometimes echoing the mild irony of the journalists reporting the eviction, and choosing from among the countless details and events to construct a narrative. I have also widened the frame of the story in time and space — "contextualizing" the local — and thereby implying its epiphenomenal character, the degree to which its actors and actions may be understood as expressions of larger social processes. I could have done that far more extremely, however, by submerging the characters completely, speaking for them, or eliminating "speech" in that sense altogether. It makes a better story this way, of course, something I may have learned in Donegal. Imagine if Máire had lectured on the evils of landlordism and the sanctity of priests, rather than telling her tale. But there are theoretical considerations as well; the end of my story is "about" stories. For one of the larger social processes going on here is in fact the creation and competition of discourses. That theoretical view arises from and complements, rather than undermines, older social scientific "takes" on the action.

For example, a classic political anthropological reading would see the agent and the priest as "brokers" (Wolf 1956, 1966) or "mediators" (Silverman 1965) whose power as local political actors was based on their connections to external authorities: respectively, the landlord and church regimes. This status and role involved Brooke in social as well as economic management, and brought him into direct competition with the priest, who in turn represented an increasingly powerful religious regime headed by the bishop. In the context of this conflict, the eviction can be interpreted as a frontal assault by the agent on the position of the priest and/or a strategic move by the priest: political theatre aimed at defining the nature of the conflict in such a way as to ensure the support of the locals and undermine Brooke's growing influence in the parish. While the particulars of this case were—to my knowledge—unique, there were at the time quite a few confrontations between priests and landlords or agents throughout the county that could easily be accommodated in this model. The same Brooke struggled with our own Monsignor Stephens in Killybegs over control of the local school, for example, and there are many hints in the diocesan archive of conflicts throughout the county on issues of authority. The most famous case was that of Father McFadden, parish priest of Gweedore, defender of evicted tenantry and himself accused of involvement in the murder of Lord Leitrim just a few years after the Magroarty eviction.[69]

If the structural view that sees priest and agent as competing mediators is put into a historical perspective, however, then our attention is drawn to longer term social process. There is evidence of a great deal of cooperation between landlords and priests several decades earlier, as we saw in the last chapter. What had changed? Some of the change had taken place in the center, rather than on this periphery. Under the direction of Cardinal Cullen, the Church had taken an increasingly aggressive posture on a number of issues—particularly education, and the centralizing Irish Church had, not coincidentally, also been bringing the "devotional revolution" to the populace. These changes, we saw, were also effected in southwest Donegal. The shift from Conolly to the Musgraves can also be viewed as a local manifestation of the general shift from old style gentry landlords to capitalists, a transformation abetted by the Encumbered Estates Court. Yet these two processes — frequently described and debated by Irish historians — seem also perfect instances of more general processes described by Weber. The connection between political power and domination on the one hand, and devotional shifts on the other, fits well into Weber's model of the evolution of priestly domination and the institutionalization of charisma. The changing character of landlords — to keep with the Weberian model — exemplifies the replacement of patrimonial with rational/bureaucratic landed regimes. In these Weberian dramas Brooke was well cast — the "ideal type" — in the role of the rationalizing agent, as was Father Magroarty for the authoritarian priest.

There is also a Marxist take possible on the events. For Marx (1886: vol. 1, ch. 25) these same changes in relations to the land were an important aspect of his model of the development of capitalism. Ireland, from the point of view of Marx and Engels, was at once a colony and a provincial periphery of England. But unlike the case in England, rural depopulation in Ireland began only with the famine in 1845, when massive evictions and starvation eliminated much of the poorest agricultural classes. Those who survived to leave went not to Irish cities, however, but to England and, most often, to America, thus dispersing the most potentially revolutionary class.

Cattle and sheep did not, however, replace the marginal peasantry everywhere in Ireland. In the extreme west, in areas like southwest Donegal, the rural proletariat continued to grow in number even as the size of their meager leaseholds shrank. Survival depended on migratory labor and cottage industries such as linen manufacture or fishing, with marketing through local merchants. What was the class consciousness of this proletariat? Did the national political movements of Fenianism in the 1860s and the Land League in the late 1870s and 1880s succeed in fostering within these people a thoroughly class-oriented view of themselves and those around them? The evidence suggests that it did not. The question for Marxist theory is why not? What were the competing social ideologies, and why were they more successful?

Both these models, appealing as they may be, reduce local actors to ciphers, and in doing so not only render invisible what may be significant but reify and mystify the larger processes they describe. Moreover, the very questions left unanswered — concerning the source and power of the ideology, identity, and belief intrinsic to the changes they describe — bring us back to real people, their actions, and, most especially, their words. It is a question of discourse — of stories of the eviction.

And in considering the stories, the specifically religious aspect becomes clear in what might otherwise seem a purely political drama. The chief question, as we noted at the outset, was the genre of the tale. Father Magroarty acted as a farmer in enclosing some land for his cattle, but he performed — on the public stage — in a political/religious play and hoped to engender a specifically religious narrative — the story of the eviction of a priest. Brooke and the Musgraves certainly understood the symbolic potential of such a "reading" and resisted it, seeking instead to hoist other flags.

But Máire's reading of the story was not solely dependent on the behavior or rhetoric of the priest, but on the evolving categories of a folk discourse — a discourse we have seen in operation in relation to holy wells, for example, and which was contained and reproduced through the production and performance of narratives: some of them treating a dreamtime of wandering pagan heroes or early local saints, others appropriating "history" as it happened, casting events in meaningful form. Thus the "local meaning" of Máire's story can only be approached by rediscovering its place in the more general discourse, in a sub-genre of local priest legends.

In this class of narratives, the priest's power is pitted against various elements of the local Protestant ascendancy: landlord, agent, bailiff. The setting is historical — not a dream time — and the priest is often named. Several stories recorded by a local folklorist in the 1940s (O hEochaidh 1945) detail the exploits of Father Charles MacNeely, Magroarty's immediate predecessor (see above), and one celebrates Father Peter MacDevitt, parish priest from 1886 to 1905.[70] In all these stories, the priest is depicted as the defender and avenger of the unfortunate, and his weapons are supernatural. Sometimes he simply freezes his opponents with his breath, but most often he delivers a damning prophecy of great ill fortune that is to befall his enemies (a technique no doubt having deep pre-Christian roots and strongly associated with Columcille, whose prophecies are known by heart by many older locals), or "he pulls out his stole and puts it around his shoulders and pulls out his book and begins to recite,"[71] a phrase that recurs in several of O hEochaidh's stories). Those actions may be the prelude of anything from leading salmon into the bay to bringing a dead Protestant up from hell.

It is interesting, in reference to Weberian categories, that these "magical" acts are performed with the aid of the paraphernalia of the Church —

objects associated with its institutional charisma.[72] The forcefulness of the particular priest does usually play a part in his role as hero, but is not implicated in the miraculous feats performed — as other personal charismatic qualities are in another genre of priest stories that is the subject of the next chapter. This commentary on priestly power is joined by a particular construction of the social world. The Irish word for Protestant, *Protastunach*, is never used in any of these stories; as in the holy well stories discussed in Chapter Two, they are all *na gall* (the foreigners), usually in contrast with either *na bunadh an pharoiste* (the people of the parish) or *na Caitlicigh* (Catholics), though in more casual conversation the opposing pair might be *gael* versus *gall*. In all these cases, however, the effect is to identify the central conflict as one between the indigenous Irish, unified behind and led by the heroic priest, and the foreign Protestant intruders.

That idiom was not limited to the "folk." Devoid of the miracles, the discourse of heroic priests and loyal tenants "doing freedom's battle" — as Magroarty put it — in the face of English landlord evil was increasingly the norm in the popular Catholic press. Within Church discourse, however, the idiom of oppression and heroic resistance had a special role to play in conjunction with what I have called the "idiom of empire" (see Taylor 1993). Not the British empire, but the alternative, Irish Catholic empire in which Armagh and Dublin were situated, not at the periphery, but at the center of their dominions: the Irish Catholic lands of Australia and North America. The pages of the *Irish Catholic Directory*,[73] the addresses of Cardinal Cullen, the pastoral letters of bishops, are all replete with this idiom, which describes in opulent detail the building of every new Gothic church or cathedral, every magnificent installation and consecration — often in the same breath with, or on the facing page of, a harrowing account of Father So-and-so resisting, for the sake of his poor, otherwise leaderless parishioners, the English agents of evil.

For the Irish Catholic Church as a whole, then, a self-definitive discourse developed — especially in the middle decades of the nineteenth century — that combined two idioms, each of which was reactive to the authoritative ideology and discourse of the British. In the "idiom of empire" the Church defined itself as an alternative center, in the "idiom of oppression" as the heroic resistors on the periphery. From a Weberian perspective one could put it this way. As the charisma of the church was increasingly institutionalized — vested in the ever more imposing material presence of the Church as building, rite, paraphernalia, and costumed personnel — the heroic battles of priests against representatives of an alternative and still materially far more imposing authority infused the priests with a very different sort of power: the anti-structural charisma of the prophet warrior.

Thus, in the local context, the priest was not only the symbolic representative but the chief agent of an institutional authority that was increasingly successful in its "civilizing mission": not only battling folk heterodoxy with clerical censure and new devotions but subjecting the people to a bodily discipline far more subtle and effective than any such imposed by civil authorities. At the same time, however, the same priest could make himself another sort of symbol altogether, and perhaps tap some of the very same sources of power the Church itself—along with the civil authorities—repressed. One thinks, for example, of the attack on the landlord's wall in the story of Magroarty's eviction. The women surged in where the men could not—their bodies now unleashed as agents of destruction. That is how Máire described it, her own body—practically unmoving through the rest of the narrative—taut with the excitement of the moment; her two fists clenched on the imagined landlord's gate.

As Louis Althusser (1971) put it, ideologies are formed as means of domination and resistance; they are never simply free to set their own terms but are marked by what they are opposing. This was certainly the case with Irish Catholicism, whose discourse was forged in the crucible of Anglo-Irish politics.[74] There were, in fact, alternative ideologies and discourses developing in the period, such as the secular view of landlord "feudalism" associated with the Fenians and then the Land League.

Peculiarly if not uniquely Irish, the historical and political circumstances allowed the prevailing religious regime to promote middle class civility and actively oppose various forms of dangerously uncivil behavior, even while it identified itself with the oppressed peasantry. The discourse managed (and still manages) to link a comfortable clergy to the outlaw prophets of Penal times, and keeps class-conscious anti-clericalism at bay even as it revivifies the charisma of dramatic opposition in the face of routinization.

At the time of Father Magroarty's eviction, the local world was a stage on which various dramas were enacted by players representing at least three nationally based institutions: the landlord class, the Catholic Church, and the secular leaders of the Land League. Such dramas, and their narrative interpretations, made substantial contributions to the local understanding of social relations and, through time, to the continuing social construction of "history." All the players, moreover, were interested in defining the nature of social relations as well as in exercising political domination. The landlord and his agent sought to teach and enforce a contractual view of estate relations as well, no doubt, as to demonstrate authority on any number of levels. In this world the radical changes experienced over the previous decades were progress and improvement. The Land Leaguer or Fenian interpreted these social relations in the idiom of nationalism and class exploitation. The clergy, however, were in some ways as threatened by the one as by the other; the Church had its own version of social reality to construct.

Father Magroarty was a political power broker astute enough to recognize and act in his own and his institution's interest. So, too, was the agent Brooke, and both he and the priest were in positions to mediate not only between locals and external sources of power and authority but among the various elements that comprised the local social system. In this competition it seems the agent should have had the upper hand, being possessed of more influence over the worldly affairs of his tenants than was his competitor. But in the drama, the priest had the theatrical advantage, being able to demonstrate a symbolic power more definitive and, indeed, more memorable.

Hence the story: the local residue of the competing narratives of the actors, each of whom appropriated events to fit them into developing discourses. This was as true for the locals, whose story Máire told, as it was for both Magroarty and Brooke. In each case the story is engaged in the continuing task of self and world definition; each version is aware of, informed by, and reacting to the others. As Pêcheux (1982: 98) argues, ideological struggle is not "the meeting point of two distinct and pre-existing worlds." Rather, the worlds define themselves in the struggle. From this perspective, the meaning of a word does not exist "in itself" but antagonistically, from its position in the struggle. "Words . . . change their meaning according to the positions" from which they are used (Pêcheux 1982: 111).[75] Pêcheux's argument politicizes and historicizes structuralism; Lévi-Strauss's concept of binary opposition as the source of meaning is recast in terms of material opposition and political struggle. *Gael* versus *gall*. Rather than static systems of meaning expressed through narratives, the stories, letters, and newspaper accounts we have encountered in the case of the priest and the agent can be viewed as elements in what Pêcheux calls the "discursive process" in which words take on meanings rather than simply expressing them (MacDonell 1986).

But what, from this perspective, are the statuses of the various unfolding narratives? Is the story according to Brooke and the Musgraves an exemplar of the "prevailing discourse" and the priest's a subversive "disidentification"? Probably not — at least for most Catholic locals, for whom Father Magroarty's voice and idiom were likely more authoritative. Was Máire's story, then, subversive? Is it best viewed historically as a "disidentification" with Brooke and all he represents, or an "identification" — a folk embracing — of the Church discourse discussed above. To answer those questions we need to plunge deeper into the world of those narratives, which will wait until the next chapter.

*   *   *

The more I read and heard of Father Magroarty the more he reminded me of Father James McDyer, parish priest of Glencolumbkille when I arrived in that part of the world. He too had tended to the broadest possible definition of the pastorate.

My first view of Father McDyer was soon after I arrived in Teelin in 1973. He was leading his parishioners through the gorse just a few hundred feet from the ruins of the coast guard station, from the shrine to the well — Tobar na mBan Naomh — on the annual turas of June 23. That coast guard station, after a shootout with the guarders inside, had been burnt down around 1920, during the war for independence from Great Britain. So too was the Musgrave lodge near Carrick. The local Republicans wanted to destroy any building large enough to serve as a barracks for British troops. Aside from their possible military function, these two buildings were the most imposing local manifestations of the *gall*, whose colonial gaze swept the coasts and glens: the "othering Other" within. A Teelin woman remembered wandering onto the estate as a little girl. She had been picking berries and had not noticed that she had reached the lawn directly before the lodge.

> I looked up and saw the door to the house was opened. I couldn't help myself, but went up to it and looked in. I can remember the grand carpets and a great chandelier hanging down — it was so beautiful. I saw all the gleaming silver on the table and then I got frightened and I ran away. . . . My mother found out I had been there and she spanked me! I never went near the house again!

All that remains of the property is the stone wall that surrounded the grounds, and a gate house. Other buildings — the church, school, and barracks — were the staging grounds for far more penetrating forces of social control, but they had become, I think, "natural" features of the landscape by that time, the local social world in some ways inconceivable without them.

In the post-independence social world, the political position of priests had of course changed. The charisma of prophetic opposition was not so easily generated without the enemy, but new mediatory powers were accorded activist priests in the new order. The financially struggling Irish Republic had come to rely on the Church not just for moral leadership and ethnic identity but for its institutional structure. When McDyer arrived in Glen in the 1950s secondary education was still completely in the hands of the Catholic Church (excepting those few schools run by the Church of Ireland and other Protestant groups), and as for primary education, the public national schools begun under the British remained very much under the control of the parish priest, who was always the president of the local board. The government was accustomed to treat priests — particularly in the west — as the natural "representatives" and leaders of their people.

This included leading them around the holy well — for Father McDyer, who had become parish priest in 1971 after a long and famous career as the curate on the Glencolumbkille side of the parish, took some interest in that sort of folk devotional matter. He had even tried to revive the long defunct and far more demanding turas up Slieve League to the well of Aodh Mac Bricín, but without success. "If I can't get into heaven without going up that mountain," said an acerbic and arthritic neighbor of mine, "then I'll just have to go to the other place." Actually, McDyer was at least as interested in the social function of such exercises as in their possible contribution to personal salvation. He was a Durkheimian in his approach to the role of Church and priest — his mission the salvation of the local community.

The local definition of priesthood and religion — forged in such circumstances as we have been exploring — along with the structural possibilities inherent in the Republic, allowed McDyer, and other priests so inclined and talented, to take on such a mission. When he came as curate to Glencolumbkille in the early 1950s, James McDyer (himself from the town of Glenties) found himself in one of the poorest regions in the nation. Glencolumbkille, like much of the country, was gripped by a new wave of emigration, which, given the rather complete lack of local economic opportunity, threatened to empty out his parish completely. His goal was to develop the economic potential of the region and, at the same time, strengthen the social fabric.

Father McDyer agitated until first water and then electricity finally made their way to his outpost. He then turned to his more ambitious program to develop the "potential" of the region by organizing cooperatives,[76] in both the manufacturing (principally knitwear) and agricultural spheres. The knitwear he organized with some success in the Glencolumbkille end of the parish, where he served as curate. Agricultural matters proved more difficult. In curious reminiscence of Magroarty's efforts on his own behalf, McDyer hatched a scheme to improve the extensive mountain "waste" and divide it into individually owned farms.

> In 1962 I attempted to get the Land Commission to subdivide our mountain commonages to provide each smallholder with about seventy acres of mountain. This could be converted into reasonably good grassland and would give a chance to the more progressive farmers to better their lot. As it was, the sheep were so undernourished that their mortality rate and that of lambs was far too high.
>
> Officials from the Land Commission came down, but true to form, they would not subdivide if there were one or two dissenters, and each commonage had a few objectors so the officials folded their maps and went home. (McDyer 1983: 64)

Perhaps the locals were wise in resisting this idea — as they had for hundreds of years — insisting that such "improvements" ended up costing more than they were worth. Then Father McDyer veered in the other direction:

> Then it began to dawn on me that we should try to make a virtue out of a necessity. If the land for sheep-grazing were already in communes, why not endeavour to persuade as many of the smallholders as possible to communise temporarily the farms which were all too small to be economic. There would then be no question of sub-dividing the existing mountain commonages into comparatively small little strips of about seventy acres each, but instead, the mountains would be divided into two groups, one for those who wanted to communise their little farms and one for those who did not wish to do so. (McDyer 1983: 64)

According to Father McDyer, it was the government suspicion of what sounded like communism and the red tape of bureaucrats that thwarted this mission. One wonders, however, whether all the locals would have gone along with this version any more than the other. Aside from the inherent problem of agricultural potential in his far from fertile region, some of the contrast between knitting and farming lay in the difference between the priest's authority among women and men. While male church attendance and "respect for the cloth" was and is certainly far more evident than in most areas of Catholic Europe, most women were far more visibly tractable before powerful clerics.

Undeterred, Father McDyer — raising funds through local subscriptions as well as government funds — cajoled his parishioners into growing vegetables to be processed for distribution and sale in a factory built for the purpose three miles north of Carrick, in Meenaneary. Though the vegetable scheme collapsed, in fact the factory was eventually and successfully converted to the processing of local seafood.

In the long run most of Father McDyer's schemes seem not to have worked economically,[77] but the social and cultural process of their organization is certainly striking. Like Magroarty, McDyer defined his role as pastor very broadly, arguing with some reason that he could only attend to the spiritual welfare of his parishioners if they could make a living, and hence remain, in the parish. Like any power broker, he faced both up and out, toward Dublin, and down and in, toward his parishioners. In order to get things done he needed a strategy that moved in both directions. The more involved and ambitious his schemes, however, the more he emphasized the outward aspect of his role. Not only was he in Dublin arguing for development funds, but he spent much time "consulting" or fundraising elsewhere in the country or even, in the time honored tradition of priests and Fenians, in America. As the years passed, his once familiar figure — the large-framed black-suited pastor rambling among his flock — was increasingly replaced by brief encounters with his Ford Cortina as it careened around some deadly curve, heading for the Dublin road.

His procedure at home was to set up committees to achieve essentially predetermined goals, to which he recruited from the narrow band of local "elite" composed of schoolteachers and others. His reputation was for inspired but authoritarian leadership. His commanding presence, voice, and enthusiastic vision stirred people to initial action. When it came to the drudgery of actually running an enterprise, however, Father MacDyer's visionary approach was less useful, but he retained, nevertheless, a sense of his own pre-eminent competence. Those who disagreed were labeled "naysayers" and "begrudgers," and a number of his initial supporters fell off the bandwagon over the years. He also had his consistent critics, like the local merchant who had said of Father McDyer, "As a priest he's a very fine businessman, and as a businessman, he's a very fine priest."

It was not only local economic development that interested McDyer, however, but rather every aspect of local life, every one of which received comment and direction from the altar during my time in the field. The priestly control of the national school was still important. Priests are in the habit of entering the national schools weekly to instruct students,[78] and, most important, have the final say over the hiring and firing of teachers.

According to his critics, Father McDyer used that very power to punish an entire local, middle-class family, that had provided the area with schoolteachers for over a century. One of their number, an educated young woman, had dared to disagree with the priest on his proposed future use of a derelict building and, much more, had passed a petition through the community gathering names. While she was out of the region one weekend, Father McDyer "read her from the altar." This practice tends to be far more subtle and indirect than in Magroarty's day, but clerical censure is still expressed and the recipient, even if unnamed, in this little world is clearly identifiable. But times had in fact changed, for in this case the woman, having been apprised of Father McDyer's remarks, showed up at his house and asked for a copy of "last Sunday's sermon." According to some, Father McDyer's subsequent action in choosing a young and inexperienced man for schoolmaster over the brother of the young woman—a long-time teacher there—was nothing other than simple vengeance.

In a strange reversal of the Magroarty legend, this tale could be called the "eviction of the O'H——," for, disgusted with their treatment, the young woman and her family left for another Donegal town, and her brother, the teacher, for Dublin. What about the narrative? There was no public platform for the victims in this case, no newspaper exchanges, no excited defense from the neighbors—nowhere to take the moral high ground. On the other hand, Father McDyer, who died in 1989, two years after retiring from his pastorate into a local house provided by his grateful parishioners, has left countless memorials of himself, and not only in the collective memory. He wrote a widely read autobiography in which he portrayed himself struggling against footdraggers at home and in Dublin, and in the "folk village"—an outdoor museum he organized to promote local tourism—a huge portrait of his graying, heavily chiseled face looks out at the local women pouring endless cups of tea and the weary German tourists who shelter there from the rain, drinking them.

5. The Drunken Priest

We're off to Letterkenny to see Father McGinley . . . to have him say an office for my father.

It was a cool autumn morning, and Meg, a woman in her late twenties, was explaining why her family was piling into a borrowed car outside their cottage in Rinnakilla. Meg's father had been recently diagnosed with a grave illness. He was being treated by medical professionals, and would eventually be taken to the hospital. I know of no case where medical treatment was resisted in favor of religious procedures. On the other hand, most people felt that there was certainly no harm in exploring other curative paths: holy wells, saints, and in this case the prayers — "offices" — of particular priests. Particular, for despite the rite of passage that confers certain powers on all priests regardless of personal qualities, only a few were believed to have special curative powers. As politically powerful as Father McDyer was — perhaps because of it — he was not understood to have the "cure." As he told me himself, there had been a time and place when the context indicated a different reading of his powers.

> My first post in Ireland [he had been a priest in England during the War] was Tory [an island 10 miles off the northwest coast of Donegal]. Well, I wasn't long there before people were showing up asking me to read an office for toothaches and everything else. . . . The Tory people believe that any priest who is sent there is being punished by the bishop; they figured I had done something terrible, and that I had all kinds of curing power. (Personal conversation, 1987)

Whatever Father McDyer's appeal in other respects, however, he was no longer sought for cures. On the other hand, Father McGinley — the goal of my neighbors' journey — was. He had been curate in a neighboring parish some years before and had the reputation of being a quiet, scholarly, gentle man, who drank. In the end he was removed from his curacy by the bishop and eventually hospitalized for his affliction. "Father McGinley," Meg put it to me in Irish, "is a very good priest." (*Tá an t-athair Mac*

Fhionnlaoich ina Shagart an-mhaith). It was a phrase I would hear many times, not just in reference to curing priests but in explanation for the success of one saint over another, again in reference to cures. "Oh, Saint Martin is a very *good* Saint."

The contrast between Fathers McDyer and McGinley — as priests and in the powers they were believed to wield — could not have been more striking. As in the historical case of Father Magroarty, the real individuals were "read" in the context of a corpus of stories, appropriated in the continuing discursive process. The discourse of priests and their powers, as I soon discovered, was all around me as well as in the archives. In the collections of O hEochaidh there are the tales of the heroic priests who battled "na Gall," as we saw in previous chapters, but there was also another subgenre within which Father McGinley could find a place. Here's one story of that type:

> There was a priest here not long ago, and with all due respect to his cloth, he had a taste for a wee drop. He was up in the village one day, and he with a drop taken. Well, he went into a pub and asked the boy that was there behind the counter for a drink. The boy said that he wouldn't give him one, that he had had enough as it was. "Well," said the priest, "if I come in to you at this time tomorrow and ask you to give me a drink, you'll get it for me and welcome the sight of it!" He went out the door then and said not another word.
>
> That was fine. The boy went to bed that night, and on the next morning when he arose he was so blind he couldn't dress himself. Well he knew that it was the priest who had brought that upon him with the words he had spoken the evening before. He sent a messenger for the priest, who came to him in his own time. "What's kept you in your bed there?" the priest said when he went into the room. "O Priest," he said, "Whatever happened to me since I went to bed last night I am blind and I can't put on my clothes." The priest only put his two fingers on the boy's eyes and in a short while he had his sight back as good as ever before. "Now," said the priest as he was leaving, "when I come again and ask something of you that I want, you'll know not to refuse me!" (NFA, vol. 143; my translation)[79]

This cleric, and the many like him in other stories, are unlike the "heroic priests" we saw in the last chapter, who battle the evil forces of the Protestant Ascendancy in their local incarnations: landlords, agents, bailiffs, Protestant farmers, and the rare Catholic collaborator. Those priests, like Father Magroarty in Máire's story, are typically armed with the paraphernalia of the Church, like the priest who dons his stole and recites from his book in order to bring a Protestant up from Hell as an object lesson to his unregenerate family. The priest who blinds the boy belongs to another category, that of those who "have a taste for the wee drop" or, to translate the Irish euphemism, "drunken priests." These protagonists perform their magic, whether to help or harm, usually unaided by anything but their inherent charisma.

Such legends are not so often heard as in former times. However, they are still told formally and, far more often, informally, in many of the households and pubs of the region. The priest who blinds the boy in the above story, in fact, is the subject of many stories currently told (as will be clear below). We will return below to the question of performance, but suffice it to say for now that the narratives are rarely if ever presented as "fiction" and that no one laughs when such stories are told (though some may smile in apparent discomfort). Arguments sometimes ensue about whether such and such an account or version is strictly accurate, in whole or in part, but the story is "taken seriously" by all tellers and most listeners. Moreover, as we have already seen, the powers of such priests are not confined to narratives. Individuals sought, and continue to seek, such clerics for their special powers, particularly for curing.

The beliefs and stories about drunken priests constitute a reprise in our own story of the constitution of local history and religion. They reveal another aspect of what we have called the "cthonic field of religious experience," a different — though certainly related — response and appropriation of priests from that informing the story of Father Magroarty. This notion of priestly power — and of kinds of power generally — is embodied in certain behavior and in a discourse that comprises not only formal narratives but brief remarks, observations, and even gestures.

Beliefs about drinking priests are, however, first and most strikingly open to outsiders in the collection of the National Folklore Archive. For most academics who have an interest in such forms, priest stories are "legends," in some respects akin to others found throughout Europe (see Thompson 1955–1958) and in certain special features reminiscent of specifically Irish (or perhaps Celtic) traditions. As such, they may enjoy various human and social functions: for example, as occasions for moral *exempla* (O hEalai 1974–76), the celebration of communal solidarity, or artistic expression (Glassie 1983). The stories and their performance can also be read in their own context, as features of a more general discursive process that both issued from and aided in the constitution of local social worlds. As we have seen, that process, that discourse, developed in the larger context of competing discourses — competing constructions of meaning and power.

Academic talk about competing discourses — local stories as alternative, even subversive constructions or deconstructions of "hegemonic" representations — has permeated (rather than subverted) older talk about great and little traditions or orthodox and folk religion. Anthropologists, most of whom are happy to celebrate and even identify with such unthreatening acts of resistance and rebellion, have attended to talk about priests mainly under the rubric of "anti-clericalism," and have understood such verbal acts to be manifestations of the distance and hostility between "folk religion" and "orthodoxy." Following historian John Bossy's (1970) seminal treatment of the social objectives of the Catholic Counter Reformation, Joyce Reigelhaupt (1973, 1984), Caroline Brettel (1990), and Ellen Badone (1990), have seen anti-clerical remarks and stories as an expression of local resentment of and resistance to the anti-communal campaign of the Catholic Church that began with the sixteenth century Council of Trent. From this perspective, the local priest is an outsider representative of the ever-extending hegemony of the institutional Church. To this political perspective Stanley Brandes (1980) and David Gilmore (1984) add a psychological consideration of the extremely sexual form of anti-clericalism that seems to characterize at least some of the Mediterranean culture area.

While "anti-clericalism" is by no means absent in Ireland, it does not seem to play anything like the central role it does in Portugal (Cutileiro 1971, Reigelhaupt 1984), Spain (e.g., Brandes 1980, Gilmore 1984), or Italy (Silverman 1975). In my experience, Irish priests are far more typically praised than damned, and while individual clerics do run into opposition on particular issues, Irish priests are awarded a general respect and even veneration that would be the envy of their Mediterranean colleagues. As for the "stories" as such, only a tiny percentage of those O hEochaidh collected or those I heard could, by any stretch of the term, be called "anti-clerical." Yet the stories about drunken priests, as is evident from the opening example, are at least ambivalent, and the nature and roots of that ambivalence invite exploration.

It might be argued, with some cogency, that the absence of anti-clericalism in rural Ireland is a testament to the total domination achieved over the last century by the institutional Church. If that is the case, however, it has not produced a static uniformity of religious belief and practice, nor an elimination of the difference and tension between the fields of religious experience we have so far encountered. Stories about both heroic and drunken priests are certainly not expressions of "orthodox" Catholicism. Rather they are local compositions (though in many cases with much borrowing of elements from other localities). They can be understood in this light, along with other elements of so-called "folk religion," as a people's creative response to their experience of religious power — another discursive process reacting to experience and other, rival, discourses. The stories may thus express a dialectic of opposition between locals and intrusive political, cultural, and psychological forces.

The priest as sorcerer, using the sacred books and objects of the Church, is a familiar enough figure from the folklore of other parts of Catholic Europe, for example Brittany (Hélias 1976, Badone 1990). In the case of the heroic priest stories, clerics who might elsewhere in Europe be perceived as part of the problem become, in Ireland, a magical solution to Protestant domination. Although O hEochaidh's stories were of nineteenth century clerics, I was told one of a local parish priest who, with the aid of his stole, froze two Black and Tans (1920s British occupation forces) to their seats overnight. Yet the Church was never perceived as the unflinching ally of the folk, and less so of their culture. As we saw in the last chapter, local clergy were agents of another "civilizing process" (Elias 1982) aimed at purging folk Catholicism of its heterodoxy and, even more so, folk society of its unruliness. This "civilizing offensive," to use the more appropriate Dutch term (see Verrips 1987), would seem to have had a profound psychological effect. By the later nineteenth century the rural Irish seem to have internalized certain forms of religious repression so well that local resentment rarely took the form of sexual innuendo as it does elsewhere in Europe (and elsewhere in the Catholic world), though comments about clerical avarice were more usual.

Stories and beliefs about drunken priests, however, were and continue to be common. Not only did I hear stories concerning living and recently deceased priests, I have known many individuals, young and old, who sought the efficacious prayers and blessings of such clerics even, as with Father McGinley, in the sanitorium. Taken together, such beliefs, stories, and practices may be interpreted as a kind of folk commentary on priestly power in general, as well as the people's response to the increasing domination of the institutional church, and perhaps a less conscious way of handling psychological repression. All this will be apparent through a closer inspection of the stories, beliefs, and practices themselves.

*   *   *

The "heroic priest" stories, as we saw in the last chapter, show that the idiom of oppression and resistance was as important for the folk as for the hierarchy. In southwest Donegal it was "Gael (as in Gaelic or Irish) versus Gall" (foreigner), the latter term designating the substantial minority of Church of Ireland Protestants resident in the area since the seventeenth century. Moral and political issues, such as eviction and persecution, are central to these tales, in which the priest uses sacramental magic to triumph over his evil enemies.

Drunken priest legends, however, are a very different matter, as one can see from our opening example, "the priest who blinded the boy." Such narratives invariably begin with a phrase something like "there was a priest here and he was fond of a wee drop." Disclaimers, such as "with all due respect to his cloth," or "though I shouldn't say so," are sometimes inserted for apparently prophylactic purposes. The stories are never set in a church or other ecclesiastical setting; rather the drunken priest is out walking in nature or among his people. Protestants, regular characters in the heroic priest stories, rarely appear in the drunken priest narratives and almost never as enemies; when the priest faces adversaries they are his own innocent parishioners — guilty only of attempting to deprive him of drink or money.

In a story similar to that of "the priest who blinded the boy" a drunken priest falls asleep at a baptism party, at which point the man of the house hides the one remaining bottle out in the byre. Upon waking, the priest asks for a drink, only to be told there is not a drop in the house. "Go out to the byre and get the bottle you hid there," the man is told, and the poor fellow is cursed for his trouble, losing five sons to consumption. In another story a shopgirl refuses a priest a loan of a few shillings for drink and wakes up the next morning with a beard (NFA, vol. 143; 1945).

The drunken priest is not always malignant, however. There is, for example, the one who found a party of men hesitant to start the haymaking in the face of a threatening storm. "Work away," he told them, reclining against a tree with a jug of whiskey. The rains came in torrents, but not a drop fell on the field where the men labored (NFA, vol. 143). Most often the benevolent drunken priest cures — either humans or beasts. As mentioned earlier, such miracles are performed without the aid of stole or book, usually with blessings but sometimes with the further action of contagious magic. In one story, for example, a woman from Teelin, desperate over the decline of her prize sow, finally sought the miraculous Father McShane, the very same priest, as it turns out, who blinded the boy (and to whom we will be returning at length below). She saw him approaching along the road, but before she could tell him what was wrong he said, "I know what trouble has brought you to me," and with that he scraped a bit of the dirt from the sole of his boot and told her to mix it in the pig's food. A complete recovery ensued. In this case both the boot and the earth are significant. The latter is of course the very essence of a "cthonic" substance and typically sought for cures from the graves of saints. As for the boot, as we shall see below, that reappears as a full fledged relic after the priest's death.

As the two accounts concerning priest McShane illustrate, cures and curses are attributed in several cases to the same priest; it is not a case of good and bad priests, but rather priests whose power is both strong and capricious. They look into mortal minds, they control the forces of nature, and they are as likely to harm (if crossed) as they are to help. Justice doesn't come into these stories, although it is central to those of the heroic priest.

The power of such priests is further illustrated in the performance of these stories. Folklorist O hEochaidh (NFA, vol. 143; 1945) prefaces his collection with an interesting note which translates as follows:

> Stories about priests are wonderfully difficult to collect because people believe that it is neither right nor proper to be telling such stories for fear that something will befall them for the telling, especially if there is something wrong with the priest in the story. (NFA, vol. 143; 1945)

If the legends were not often told, they were heard frequently enough to be known. If warnings were included about the danger of telling such stories, then these admonitions, like the phrases "with all due respect for his cloth," only served as extensions of the protagonists' power: they could reach out of the text and blind the narrator. I suspect that such stories were less than willingly told for the collectors, not so much because they might be outsiders but because they were writing them down or, worse, recording them onto a disk and thereby concretizing the event of the telling.

While the formal context of the *seanchaidh* (storyteller) is rarely encountered in southwest Donegal today, I found that many older people knew at least some of the stories O hEochaidh recorded, and were quite willing to add others of their own. Whenever I told a story I had heard, listeners would adopt an attentive and apparently believing attitude, shaking their heads at the wonder of the priests' miracles. I was also present at discussions in pubs and homes where a small number of men or women, having raised the topic of priestly power, would relate such stories — sometimes in the "classic" narrative form discussed above, and sometimes more in the way of less apparently structured anecdotes. One such story featured a good Protestant, and the theme of reciprocity — this time delayed — was once again central.

> Did you ever hear about the priest — he was down in the North somewhere and he took a drink, do you know, and cured many people. . . . Anyway, when that priest was a boy, there was Protestant farmer up his way and it seems he was a good man, the farmer, and he was friendly to the priest's father, who worked on his farm. Anyway, that man didn't know where he'd get the money for the son's schooling. But the farmer said, "Don't you worry, I'll pay for it." And he did. Years later the farmer found himself in trouble with debts and the sheriff was going to take away his cattle. The young priest was talking with him about it over a drink, do you see, and he said, "It would be a great shame if your cattle ever strayed past the stream we used to take them to on the edge of the farm." Well, the next day nothing could get the cattle over that stream.

A more anecdotal form often related events much more recently transpired. There was a Father Heany, for example, who died only four or five years ago. He was known not only to take a drink but to see "patients" in the local bar. "Oh Father Heany was very *good*," a neighbor of mine told me. "My boss John — he's not even a Catholic — had a terrible pain in his neck. He was having a drink in the pub and he told Father Heany about the pain, and Father Heany just put his hand on John's neck and kind of rubbed it. Well, the pain just went away and it never came back. Oh, Father Heany was a very great priest."

Two other remarks concerning Heany add depth to the portrait of the curing priest. His housekeeper told me that it was his curing activities that eventually killed the priest — describing his demise in terms of physical and spiritual exhaustion, but also as intrinsic to the "conservation of illness": "He took all their illness on himself, do you see, and it killed him in the end." That view of the matter was echoed by some others who felt that the cure involved the removal of illness, which, by that logic, must go some-where — as in holy well cures. Alternatively, some thought that the priest's growing illness might be interpreted as "the price paid" for his breaking the rules, using his powers in a way the Church might not have sanctioned. Speaking of the same priest one night, a tradesman in his forties who had known Heany fairly well said:

> I use't go in to him sometimes for confession, and there was none like him for that. I can remember the feeling when you left. . . . You were that light . . . like a burden had been removed from you, do you see, and you would not feel the

same way with another priest, whatever was in it. I don't know was it something he'd say . . . but you'd just feel something terrific.

The conservation of illness and the physicality of confession speak of the
materiality of sin and the spirtuality of the material—all linked in the notion
of exchange: the drunken priest, like the holy well, gives, and hence something must be left behind.

Of all the local drunken priests, Father McShane, who blinded the boy
and cured the pig, certainly figured largest in the local repertoire, and an
extended look at McShane stories and how they are told reveals much about
the meaning of the stories for their tellers, and also about the historical
circumstances that may lie behind such legends.

I first encountered the blinded boy story in the archives in the form
presented earlier in this chapter. Returning to the region, I asked a man of
about eighty, in the midst of a general conversation about priests and their
powers, if he had ever heard anything about the powers of priests who
drink. After a pause and with some small show of discomfort with the topic,
he pointed his pipe stem up the road toward the nearby markettown.

> Sagart [priest] Condy Rua . . . he was a McShane from Carrick, from the
> house there by the post office—you know it—you know the shop there, well
> that was Johnny Condy Rua's, and Sagart Condy Rua would be his brother.
> Well he took a drink and once he went into the house [pub] that was there
> across the road—it was McShane as well—and, whatever happened, he asked
> the boy who was behind the bar there for a bottle of whiskey that was up on
> the shelf. And the boy didn't want to give it to him—maybe he owed too
> much, do you see. Anyway, he said to the priest that he couldn't see the bottle.
> The priest said to him that he would wish he could see it tomorrow. And he
> left. Well the boy woke up blind the next morning. So . . ."

Thus the story ended. "And did he ever see again?" I asked. "No."

Some time later I was asking a local school master if he knew anything
of the priest McShane.

> Aye, that would be Sagart Condy Rua, Johnny's brother. I grew up next to him
> there in Carrick. He was already dead when I was born but I often heard
> Johnny talk of him, and my mother had great faith in him.

He then proceeded to tell me a version of the blinded boy story similar to
the one above, but without specifying at what point the boy went blind.
"Did he go blind right away?" I asked. "I think it must have been maybe six
months or a year later," came the reply. At this point the teacher's wife, a

very pious woman who had married into the community from a far more anglicized region of Ireland, remarked that, of course, such a story could not be true. Her husband, like his wife college educated in Dublin, was visibly upset by her comment. He insisted with stubborn and humorless determination that the story was in fact true, that he knew the parties involved. He went on to relate another incident, closer to home, involving the miraculous Father McShane.

> My mother died last year at the age of ninety and she often told me the story her mother told her, about when my mother was born with a deformed lip and my grandmother was going to take her to the doctor to have it operated on. Well, she stopped in the McShane house there in Carrick on her way, and Sagart Condy Rua was there at home visiting. He said that he knew she was on the way to the doctor for the baby's lip but that she should not go. "I'll tell you where you will find a cure for that lip," he said, "at Cartha's well in Kilcar. Just go to the well and do the stations and put a drop of the water on the lip of the child." Well, she did that, and within days the lip was completely perfect. Now my mother often told me that.

Several months later, Alice, a neighbor woman in her fifties, came to visit my wife and me for tea. Conversation began as it almost always did with a discussion of the immediate neighbors and what they were up to. Her conversation was suggestive of her worldview — in the sequence of anecdotes as well as in their individual content. Speaking of one household she said that she had attended the "stations" (a mass held in the home with the neighbors as guests) held there by the new parish priest. With that observation she diverted herself to the topic of priests and how some of them were "holier" than others. I then told her that I had recently spoken with the housekeeper of Father Heany (the recently deceased cleric whose barroom curing is described above), who had retired to a town about fifteen miles away and whose housekeeper had told me of the hundreds of people who would line up for blessings and cures every weekend. She was apparently unfamiliar with Father Heany, however, and seemed uninterested in discussing him, but began instead to tell us of her experience with Father McLafferty, the charismatically inclined priest whose monthly "healing mass" was attended by hundreds of people from all over the county and beyond. She had taken a local mini-bus to the event the month before (see Introduction and Chapter Eight).

> I had this terrible gash in my leg I got when I fell in the house, and it wasn't healing well. And this pain I had in my side — just a terrible sort of ache that

would come and go. Well, I went to the priest and told him my trouble and he bent his head and listened, and then he put his hand on my side and kind of moved it across me here and prayed over me. And that pain just went away and it hasn't come back since!

Alice then continued, with no provocation from me, to recall the exploits of Father McShane of story fame.

He had wonderful power. He cured many a one around here. My father went to him once with a very bad eye [here her tone changed to that of serious storytelling] and Father McShane asked him why had he come to him.
"For you to cure my eye," he told him.
"And do you believe I will cure it?"
"I do."
And he told my father to kneel down by a table he had there and he pulled the cloth that was on it over my father's head and said an office [blessing] over him and then my father went home. Well that eye cleared up and never troubled him again. Oh, Father McShane was a very great priest. . . . You know Seamus; he has his boot. Ask him and he'll show it to you.

I did on the next day. I found Seamus, a successful small farmer of fifty-six, at home and told him that I had heard he knew something of the priest McShane. Seamus then proceeded to relate how, in his youth, he had come across the boot when cleaning out the byre and had almost thrown it away with the trash.

"Boys, oh boys, oh dears, where are you goin' with that boot?" me father asked me. "Many's the cures that's in that boot," he told me, and that was the boot of Father McShane. So I put it back in the byre for the cattle like.
"And I keep it shined up," his wife added.

Later on his wife produced the boot for our inspection (Figure 22) and asked those present if we "wanted to take a blessing off it" (that is, to touch the boot as one would Holy Water, blessing oneself after contact). The same man told me another story about Father McShane:

They say that Father McShane was out walking through the countryside and he came upon two carters [men who made their living transporting goods in carts to the far-flung small shopkeepers in remote regions]. He would often be out like that and he asking someone for money — I guess for drink. Anyway, he asked this one man for money and he told the priest that he hadn't enough for him. "Well, you have the money now," the priest said to him, "but you won't have money in the future." And then he came to another carter, a fellow called Boyle — he'd be a cousin of mine — and he asked him for the money and the

Figure 22. Father McShane's boot (photo by Maeve Hickey).

Boyle fellow had only half a crown, just enough to feed himself and his horse, like, but he said he'd give it to him. And he did. And the priest said he would never have empty pockets and by God it was true for him. That man never married, but he left a good packet of money to some of his relations — gave them a good start like.

Several days later I was on the other side of the parish on a remote mountain road when I spotted an interesting looking local man cajoling a donkey up the bray with a cart-load of turf. I stopped and we chatted about the place and he asked where I was staying. I told him and he asked if I knew a cousin of his who lived nearby: Seamus — the man with the priest's boot. I asked him if he knew the story of McShane and the carter.

Indeed I do, wasn't it my own uncle, there, who was in it? [He nodded toward his own home on the mountainside.] He was carting for that Haughey shop there in Meanacooley and he gave the priest money and prospered for it. The other man was from down Lougherakirk way. . . . He would give the priest nothing and he had nothing but bad luck himself out of it.

And a funny thing about that story . . . my uncle himself never told us that story — and he lived with us all his life and died when I was twenty years old [about thirty-five years earlier]. And the day he died neighbors who knew him told us what had happened with him and the priest.

These McShane stories, and the circumstances of their telling, may say much about the role of the drunken priest in local consciousness. But Father McShane was not invented "out of whole cloth," so to speak. He certainly lived, and his actual historical situation suggests some of the reasons both for his suitability for the narrative role of drunken priest and for the genesis of this narrative form.

McShane was curate, or assistant priest, under a parish priest named O'Donnell who served the parish of Kilcar from 1893 until his death in 1910. The Rev. O'Donnell is memorialized in his parish in two forms. First and foremost is the parish church in the village of Kilcar, which in ornateness is reputedly second in the diocese only to the cathedral in Letterkenny. While there is some good agricultural land in the parish, there is far more that is very poor and mountainous, and in most respects Kilcar was a typical west Donegal parish: nothing would lead one to expect the rather impressive parish church there. A local antiquarian told me that in fact the church was built through money raised in America and, what is more, that it was the curate McShane who was sent there on a number of occasions to collect funds. According to his account (a "story" itself — true or not), Father

Figure 23. Mission cross (left), Kilcar (photo by Maeve Hickey).

O'Donnell was an imperious, egotistical, and crassly materialistic man who resented and exploited the more spiritual and intellectual McShane. According to this account, McShane, exasperated with his constant travels, finally refused to go off to America, and O'Donnell had him "silenced" by the bishop, with drink the legitimating excuse.

The other memorial, which also sheds light on O'Donnell's relation to the parish, is a large concrete "mission cross" dated 1907 (Figure 23). Such crosses were erected during the Redemptorists' parish missions (see Chapter Six), when representatives of that preaching order took over a parish for several weeks of intensive sermonizing and confessions. These missions had two chief foci and effects, the introduction of Roman devotions and, especially in the West of Ireland, aiding the local clergy in their ongoing attack on uncontrolled drinking and the unsupervised socializing of "big nights" (parties held in houses). A successful mission "campaign" would be concluded with the erection of just such a memorial cross, and indeed such missions often etched themselves into local memory as powerful events. O'Donnell was for these reasons a perfect representation of the Church as oppressor of local life, a point extended in another story I was told wherein he actively opposed the local efforts in the fight for Irish independence.

Thus there is in the O'Donnell/McShane pair a perfect binary opposition between parish priest and curate in terms of politics, temperament, and their respective relationships with the people. Moreover, they have both ascribed and achieved characteristics that lend deeply resonant symbolic dimensions to the opposition. O'Donnell arrived from another part of the diocese and not only ran but actually built a most impressive church. His further association with the Redemptorist mission, memorialized in the cross, makes him the ideal personification of the increasingly successful forces of religious domination and institutional authority that so characterized local experience throughout most of the nineteenth century. On the other hand there is McShane: born locally and thus intimately associated with the sacred landscape — including the local holy well — drunk, wandering through the countryside, and especially so after being "silenced" by the bishop. There is also a wonderful inversion in the types of "begging" the priests do: O'Donnell's is for the Church, McShane's is for drink (although he himself was apparently sent to America to "beg" for O'Donnell). Clearly there are two kinds of power figured in this opposition, but equally clear is the fact that the conceptual opposition did not originate with these two historical personalities. Rather, the experiential opposition made McShane a particularly appropriate and potent magnet for beliefs about drunken priests.

* * *

Why, however, do drunken priests have such powers? I found the people with whom I discussed these matters quite willing to talk about the subject but usually unable to come up with an explicit theory; their conceptual schema was both created and embodied in narratives. Typically the response would go something like, "Somehow it's the priests that take a drink that always have the power, the old people always said that, and it's still the way it is — whatever's in it." One old woman ventured a tentative explanation: "Maybe it's because when the drink is on them they can't control themselves so much."

The theme of control is an interesting one and consonant with views often expressed concerning that other and closely related type of powerful cleric (combined, in fact, in the case of McShane): the silenced priest. A silenced priest is one who has been removed from the pulpit, in the event very often for excessive drink. Of such clerics it is said, "the *smacht* (control) of the bishop is off them." A local, and sober, priest elaborated,

> They think that the priest's miraculous power is under the control of the bishop, so that he is not allowed to work miracles. If the priest is silenced, the power is released.

This commentary on the folk theory indicates a telling reversal of the official church position conveyed by the term "silenced." Such priests, from the folk religious point of view, have voices indeed. But the uncontained power, no longer channeled into the safe conduits of the sacraments, is both stronger and more dangerous. Following Mary Douglas (1966) and Victor Turner (1969), such priests would be labeled "anomalous" and "liminal." Out of the *smacht* of the bishop — no longer part of the institutional Church — the priest is a shaman. This theme is clearly evinced in the stories of drunken priests as well, who, like McShane, are portrayed physically away from the church, wandering in Nature, and performing their miracles without aid of the symbolic implements of the institutional church. The matter of silencing, already achieved or threatened, indicates that the opposition between drunken priest and parish priest and/or bishop is more than conceptual, it is political. Although the case of McShane makes this particularly clear, it is worth noting that in every case of a historically identifiable "drunken priest," the cleric in question was a curate rather than a parish priest. In nineteenth century Ireland there was a substantial difference in the power and income of parish priests and curates (see for example O'Shea 1983: 315), and the drunken curate was unlikely to rise in the hierarchy and was hence an excellent symbol of political subordination within the authoritarian church.

The other clear theme of drunken priest stories is reciprocity — the wandering beggar who asks for drink or money for drink. Refusal brings disaster; the "gift" is rewarded with cures and luck. There is here an obvious echo of similar motifs in the holy well stories and usages (see Chapter Two). Folklorist Padraic O hEalai (1974) has noted the pervasiveness and centrality of the reciprocity theme in Irish priest stories generally, but its particular appearance in these stories in conjunction with apparently "magical" cures and punishments suggests, as Jane Schneider (1990) has pointed out in the broader European context, the need to amend the Weberian version of the historical transition from magical to religious/ethical formations. Schneider argues persuasively that such changes are better represented as the replacement (or attempted replacement) of one ethic — "equity consciousness" — with another. Certainly the ethnographic record (since Evans-Pritchard's 1936 classic account of Azande witchcraft) bears her out on the ethical dimension of such beliefs. As far as the historical, European context, the Irish case examined here exemplifies the centrality of the equity conscious ethic and its connection to the "supernatural" domains of ghosts, fairies, and wells. Before the 1830s, as we saw in previous chapters, the most important material base of that ethic was in the relationship to land. Competing ideologies issuing from both landlord/state and Church regimes accompanied attacks on those relations and/or the beliefs and symbols that supported them. In that context, the drunken priest stories might be taken as part of a continuing discursive process in and through which the people responded to that historical and contemporary experience, reasserting that ethic in the face of attack and change, through appropriating the very version of the priest that the Church rejects.

Certainly the case of McShane makes clear the real historical — as well as symbolic — character of such clerics and, potentially, of the situations portrayed in the stories. The McShane legends offer an indication of how specific persons and events are appropriated and incorporated in the ongoing construction of ideology. Following Turner (1982: 72ff.), I would argue that there is a dialectical relation between social dramas like those involving McShane and the stories told about them. The curate's confrontation with O'Donnell was probably real, but it was also particularly meaningful in a cultural sense. Thus the conflict provoked a story. But the narrative that was eventually formed no doubt selectively appropriated the event. Finally, insofar as these stories provide an ideological framework that influences behavior, they may act as both models *of* and models *for* history. The genre of drunken priest stories — appropriating "history" as it happened — is, like the heroic priest stories that are their complement, part of the local discursive process, which continues to develop and articulate an understanding of power and meaning in response to experience. That understanding is developed in the central motifs of these stories. Their representation of clerical power in relation to reciprocity and the earth, and in terms of the controlling authority of the institutional Church, are culturally interesting and resonant because they draw upon a variety of rich experiential sources and have the metaphorical potential to stand for similar themes, consciously or unconsciously understood, in their own lives.

In culturally constructing the type of the drunken priest, the people have availed themselves of a variety of potent traditions. Within the non-Christian Irish and Celtic tradition, one is reminded especially of the *file*, the poet whose words have magical efficacy to curse or help prosper. Drunkenness turns out to be one of the important ways and signs of inspiration/possession for such poets, and thus provides one line of cultural resonance for the drunken priest character (see O hOgáin 1982). Moreover, the image of drunkenness has long been a central feature of the national-ethnic stereotype, and in my field experience, it is still a highly ambivalent aspect of corporate and/or individual self-image. As such, it is related to a whole series of attributes forged in the binary opposition of "reasonable" (read dull) Anglo-Saxon with "emotional" (read creative) Celt.

There is a tradition of internal symbolic opposition within the Catholic Church as well, embodied in the dichotomy of the political/worldly versus the spiritual/natural. The latter form was of course rooted in the image of Christ and his disciples, a troop of prophetic mendicants who cured without tools or emblems of office. This charisma of poverty and anti-institutionality periodically re-emerged in the history of the Church in the shape of several religious orders, such as the Franciscans, who appropriated that sort of image and power, and who were criticized by the secular diocesan clergy for "begging" in eighteenth century Donegal (as they had been elsewhere since their inception). The drunken priests of the nineteenth and twentieth century were probably linked in popular consciousness to these monks, who as stranger/beggars embodied the power of mendicancy, which we saw voiced in the Poor Law Commission Reports of the 1830s (see Chapter Two) as well as distance from and even hostility to the institutionalizing diocesan regime under construction (see Chapter Four).

Long before that, however, Ireland (as we saw in Chapter One) was home to one of the earlier forms of this monastic tradition, and most Irish saints (and all local ones) originate in the Celtic eremetic tradition of the fifth, sixth, and seventh centuries. Although Irish monasteries were certainly important and occasionally wealthy institutions acting directly in the political world, the stories of the early saints, as we saw, form another subgenre of folk religious tales, and all feature lone, wandering figures.

These saints are clearly identified with Christ, about whom similar legends are told. They wander, they are poor, even mendicant. They are also intimately connected to the landscape, especially to the holy wells, which retain associated curing power, but also in the place names of more ordinary features of the local terrain. Their magic defies natural processes (growth, death, rain), and, though they are capable of acting divinely sweet, they also have tempers. Associating the saints with Christ in this way serves to extend the foundation myth of the Church in time, but most importantly, in space; it resists once again the desacralization of the landscape, which, as we have noted, was a central feature of the growth of the institutional Church. It asserts, using this Christian idiom, that the local landscape is in fact sacred by symbolically associating it with the Holy Land.

It is through this sacred landscape that the drunken priest wanders, and in this characteristic, as well as in his mendicant, holy, but dangerous ways, he is linked with these local saints, especially the major one, Columcille (Saint Columba), who behaves very similarly in many narratives. In this context the relic of Father McShane's boot hanging in the byre makes sense, as does his linkage with St. Cartha's Holy Well. People speak of having "great faith" in a particular priest with the same language they use to discuss devotions to saints. Priests can be associated directly with both the poetic and saintly traditions by displaying such "natural" characteristics as insanity, drunkenness, and unpredictability, and especially if they run into trouble with authority. Christ, in their stories, is more a shaman than a prophet, Columcille is both, but neither, as noted, uses the paraphernalia of the church in performing miracles, nor does he use his magic against political authorities. Further, the drunken priest begs, and punishes those who do not recognize him, as do both Columcille and even Christ, in the folk if not biblical version of his exploits.

The folk construction of the drunken priest, with the themes of reciprocity and "control and release," can be read as a commentary on the
process of becoming a priest but also on the longer historical process of the
growth of institutional Church power through priestly domination. They
are, if you will, a local response to the processes described by Weber. From
this perspective, the priest's charisma, whether natural (as some people
indicate) or achieved through the rite of passage of ordination, is not augmented through religious training. What the priest learns is self-control; his
charisma is institutionalized (see Weber 1963). The further a cleric rises in
the Church, the less sacred power he manifests. Another sort of royal charismatic power emerges at the top in the hierarchy of bishops, cardinals, and
Pope, for whom the splendor of costume and paraphernalia is increasingly
important. In ordinary circumstances, however, Irish bishops are perceived
more as politicians than as princes; no one goes to bishops for cures (except
at the moment of their consecration).

Analogously, this figuring of priestly power can also be read as a metaphor for the Church's attempt to civilize and contain the natural power of
local folk religion and, indeed, of those elements of local folk life perceived
as uncivilized. As we saw in the last chapter, mid-nineteenth-century Irish
Catholics were subject to the steadily increasing domination of the clergy.
Mass attendence became regular, and official religious objects, such as scapulars, miraculous medals, and rosary beads, provided concrete foci of sacred
power and devotion. Through the same period, the Church also represented the most active agency of general social control (see Connolly
1982). The people were not silent, however. There was and is power in the
Word as well, and if they recognized the force of priestly language, the
tellers of priest stories thereby exercised their own linguistic power—appropriating the clergy as actors in the very religious field they typically
opposed. In this sense the stories both react to and create history, not only
as event but as process. For the people, the drunken priest represented, and
to some extent still represents, a kind of natural power, less controlled or
contained than that of the ordinary clergy; a force released beyond the walls
of the church, in the mountains and stories of his parish.

There may well also be a less conscious, psychologically motivated
metaphor at work in the priest stories, though one materially connected to
the historical circumstances discussed above. As we have seen in previous
chapters, and will again see below in the next chapter on the Redemptorist
mission, it was not only—or even mainly—heterodox religious practice
that the nineteenth-century Church sought to control. Rather, powerful

religious dramatics were brought to the task of suppressing sexual and violent behavior. It is interesting in this regard that there are not in Ireland the number of sexual stories of priests that abound in other areas of the Catholic world. A Freudian addendum to our thus far historical, structural, and symbolic analysis of the drunken priest would suggest that perhaps the actual or implied opposition of drunken and ordinary priest metaphorically represents aspects of self with which that very Church and its personnel have been, and are, intimately concerned. That is, the potent but capriciously destructive drunken priest may represent, unconsciously, the libido "when the *smacht* of the Church — and its internalized aspects of the self — is off it."

This interpretation does not seem arbitrary in light of both the actual historical role of the Church in repressing sexuality and the evidence of its success in the high rate of celibacy that has long characterized the region. As noted, the rarity of sexual motifs in the Irish stories is in stark contrast with priest narratives from such regions as Spain. If the stories and beliefs do have this psychological aspect, then their telling and hearing might provide opportunities for "release," albeit in a more sublimated form than, for example, that of the sexual stories of Spanish priest discussed in this way by Brandes (1980). If so, it would make sense that these stories are both compelling and dangerous to tell.

The drunken priest, when put into historical as well as folkloric context, thus illustrates the dynamic nature of "local" religion and the particular power of narratives in constituting a field of experience, which adapts to changing conditions — political, cultural, and psychological. Indeed, the degree to which these categories, in their conscious and unconscious forms, can be linked in such stories is precisely what makes them powerful.

Finally, these beliefs continue to operate, not just in stories, but in behavior. The search for relief from affliction continues to motivate much religious behavior, and if alcoholic priests are not as popular as in the past, they are certainly still sought by individuals young and old. The reputations, in this regard, of contemporary clerics like Fathers Heaney and McGinley rise and fall like those of holy wells, saints, and particular devotions. In all cases, proof of efficacy is conveyed in narrative form, so that the power of the story is critical to the perceived power of the curer. Medicine shows no sign of obviating such needs, and even if their form shifts, such beliefs have a future. The woman who went to see the healing priest looking for a cure found herself at a Charismatic Mass, a novel religious form imported to the region from the United States, home of the "Pentecostal Catholic" or "charismatic renewal" movement (see Chapter Eight). There is a chance that her experience there may lead her, as it has others of her neighbors, to join a local prayer group. In the context of such a charismatic or pentecostal "community of affliction" she would, as in the story-telling sessions, take part in the corporate construction of experience. In such contexts, however, narrative serves a more radical enterprise. An idiom foreign to the ordinary situations of local life is adopted and the search for a cure becomes a quest for "healing," a key notion at the heart of a new discourse and a new field of religious experience.

6. The Mission

My wife and I returned to Teelin in the summer of 1986, having found a small cinder block holiday cottage to let in the townland of Aghragh, at the opposite end of Teelin from Rinnakilla, close to Carrick. Aghragh consisted of two groups of houses, about eight along the main Teelin road and about the same number above those, nestled on usually small bits of flat ground on the steepening slopes of Slieve League and accessible from an unpaved deeply trenched road that the county council had been promising to fix for several years. Our own cottage — one of two built by a local entrepreneur — was the highest in the townland. The cottage was well enough built for the summer — its intended usage — but by sometime in August the weather had already "broken," as they say there, and by late September the relentless winds of autumn were already whipping the rain under the door. We were beginning to realize why the hillock on which the cottage was perched was called *Min na gaoithe* — "the high valley of the winds" — another case of the difference between the traditional homes, always sited with shelter in mind, and the newer ones, not only tourist cottages like ours but the "bungalows" of several of the younger locals, positioned for the view.

The bad weather only encouraged more and longer visits, however, for at most a few hundred yards, and often far fewer, separated one household from another. As elsewhere in Teelin, those households varied in their composition. Along the main road the houses were more likely to contain continuing families: married couples with children; there were even a few brand new bungalows with younger families. Up above on the higher, dirt road, however, was a more varied assortment of structures and people.

There was a largish (by Teelin standards) farm run by two brothers who lived there with an invalid sister. The eldest brother, Francie Mór (big Francie) was, among his other virtues, a gifted mechanic who — with a bit of wire or even a stick — always kept my ailing Cortina on the road long enough until his cousin, whose garage in Carrick was a place of miracles, could manage to frustrate the junkman for another month or two. "Uncle Willie" lived in a small, but tidy caravan he had roped down onto his ancestral land in upper Aghragh. His restricted world—up and down the road to Carrick—was a long awaited ending after many decades of wandering and hard labor under the vast skies of the Canadian Yukon.

The last thatched house remaining in the townland belonged to Hugh. The rough whitewashed walls sheltered three generations. The county council was prepared to replace the old home with a modern bungalow, but Hugh held out for another few years. I usually found him outside: leaning his tall, thin, and bending frame against the turf rick, a pipe inevitably thrust in his mouth. Hugh told me that his family name—not a local one—came to Aghragh with an ancestor from the south "down Tipperary or Limerick way . . . in the time of the famine." The Griffith Valuations (1858) revealed a few such migrants in Aghragh and elsewhere in the area—Hugh's own ancestors, as well as Kennedys, Maloneys, and two Hickey families—all north Munster (Counties Clare, Limerick and Tipperary) names. My own wife's family were Hickeys as well, and had emigrated to America from Clare. Hugh seemed to enjoy the reappearance of the name in the townland. "How's the Hickey woman keepin'?" he would ask me—and if I were on the way home, "Now, the Hickey woman will give you some tea."

There were other households we visited, but none more often than the cottage of two women—Brigid, who appears at the end of Chapter Two as my guide to the Well of the Holy Women and her sister, Maggie Ann. The house was traditional in design; one entered into a central "kitchen" with two bedrooms off either end—one below, one above. Only a small pantry had been added beside the upper room. The larger bedroom, below, had been their parents' and was now the elder sister's. Brigid and Maggie Ann had remained in the house to take care of their aging parents, while their several sisters had married, two in Killybegs and one down a grassy path to the farm just below. Brigid had always been there, but Maggie Ann had just completed over forty years of work in Roger's Hotel—a fixture of downtown Killybegs. Inside, the house and every object in it—there were many—was immaculate. Maggie Ann, a self-confessed "terror for blue" had painted the walls and many articles a bright azure. The Stanley range set in the old hearth gleamed gray silver; every stray ash was swept up as soon as it fell. Outside, a beautiful garden of flowers and vegetables filled the space between the "little house" (outhouse), where even the paper was pink, and the nearly life-size statue of a burro. "Do you like the donkey?" Brigid asked. "We paint the eyes every year." Sure enough, this season they were bright blue. The ceramic creels on either side each held blocks of turf, also added by the sisters.

Maggie Ann and Brigid told us of the few events that promised to punctuate the dreary stretch of darkening days until Christmas. "Well, now," Brigid assured us, "there's the *fleadh ceoil* at the end of the month, but before that we have the mission." A *fleadh ceoil*, I knew, was a traditional music festival that—given the ability of local fiddlers—promised to be an effective antidote to the weather. As for the mission, Brigid explained, "The Redemptorist missioners will come to Carrick and we'll have special sermons and services and confessions for the week. . . . They come every second year, do you see, last time they were great." I was not surprised that Brigid and many others welcomed the religious occasion of the mission, but I had not expected the genuine excitement of anticipation.

A mission, as I was soon to discover first hand, is a highly structured Catholic parish revival, carried out by a team of priests from one of several religious orders specializing in such activities. Vincentians, Oblates, and most often in Ireland, Redemptorists come to such parishes as Glencolumbkille every two years or so and submit the parishioners to a one or two week religious "total immersion." The fathers visit homes, especially shut-ins, hear many hours of confessions, celebrate daily Mass, and preach special sermons every evening of their stay.

Brigid and Maggie Ann were not alone in their excitement, for missions, especially in regions like this one, are for most locals special events that break the monotony of the ordinary rounds of activity, or inactivity. Like a pilgrimage or fair, the rural mission is a social occasion, a community festival appropriately presaged by the arrival of the "missions stalls": large kiosks set up in front of the church several days before the opening of the festivities. From these stalls people will purchase from a wide selection of rosaries, statues, and other religious objects—and even a few cap guns and monster teeth for Halloween. The excitement, the air of expectation, especially among the older people, is quite palpable. The obvious theatricality of the mission, however, does nothing to detract from its religious impact. Quite the contrary. The mission is by design a dramatic religious occasion whose power and meaning in such regions depends as much on form as on content.

However, the Glen mission is only the most recent of many. The Redemptorists, and several other preaching orders, have been coming here for nearly a century. They have been active elsewhere, as we shall see below, for far longer. This particular mission is thus part of the history of the order, the history of the Catholic Church, the history of the region, and the personal histories of those who attend. These intertwining histories also inform the meaning of the event. Considered as a piece of historically dynamic, interactive religious theater, the mission offers another port of entry into the construction and texture of local Catholic religious experience. In this light, the arrival of the Redemptorist mission team in Glencolumbkille in the autumn of 1986 may be grasped as one moment in the ongoing process we have been following: the Catholic Church's penetration into Irish life and culture. Yet communities and individuals are not entirely passive in the face of this institutional advance, and the mission is a particularly good example of the real dialectical character of the interaction between so-called folk and orthodox religion. For although one would be hard-pressed to come up with a better example of a "religious occasion" that is entirely conceived, constructed, and imposed from above, the mission is also a local event, and its meanings for the people of the parish are determined not only by the intentions of the clergy but by the place the mission occupies in the audience's own religious world view(s).

   * * *

The mission as a Catholic religious form predates the foundation of the Redemptorist order, and can indeed be traced back to a very old tradition within the Church of wandering friars (such as the Franciscans and Dominicans), whose theatrical preaching attracted huge crowds beginning in the later middle ages (see Burke 1978: 101–2). Later, both Protestant and Catholic Counter-Reformation preaching drew upon this tradition. The Jesuits especially became famous in the seventeenth century for their dramatic missions; clearly the overseas experience was not wasted on them. These missions were notable for their introduction of new ritual forms, such as processions of the Stations of the Cross, where the path of Jesus is symbolically followed by means of a series of icons representing events on the way to the Crucifixion.[80] Processions as such, of course, have an ancient history in the Mediterranean, and the Jesuits should perhaps be seen as creative adaptors of the very same popular traditions they had once preached against. The most elaborate missions were those conducted in the middle of the seventeenth century by the Jesuits in the Kingdom of Naples, where dramatic sermonizing was conjoined with processional ritual (Burke 1978: 231).

  It was there in Naples, and no doubt in the context of that tradition, that the Redemptorist order was founded in 1732 by Alphonso de 'Liguori, the son of a Neapolitan gentleman who, after a brilliant career as a lawyer, the story goes, took up the religious life. His aristocratic connections as well as his piety were instrumental in the success of Liguori's order. By the end of the century the Redemptorists had houses, not only in the Kingdom of Naples but as far afield as Poland, Austria, and Switzerland. Notwithstanding struggles with various states that were not anxious to see permanent houses founded within their borders (a general difficulty among religious orders in the period) and occasional run-ins with other clerical bodies, such as the fathers displaced by the Redemptorists when they took over the shrine of the Blessed Virgin at Triberg in the Black Forest, the order spread and developed an apparently consistent approach to its task (Stebbing 1924, Anonymous 1933). Considered from the perspective of Church as political regime, that task was one of a series of strategies through which the Catholic Church sought to regain, extend, or consolidate its control over the people of Europe. Within this general campaign, the Redemptorist mission in particular was initially directed at the relatively peripheral peasantry.

Liguori adapted the florid Neapolitan tradition in which he was raised to eighteenth-century conditions as he saw them. He continued the preaching of the already established missionary groups, but at once strengthened and simplified the language. He also introduced the *vita divota*, in which "the last few days of the mission were devoted to building a popular piety through the teaching of a simple method of meditation and a basic "rule of life" designed to safeguard the fruits of the mission," (McConvery, personal communication). Contained amid Saint Alphonso's many writings are not only religious texts for every occasion but many directives concerning how missions should operate and why they are effective. We can, following Liguori's own implicit categories, understand missions as combining elements of text, theater, and ritual, and distinguish three interrelated elements: text, performance, and symbolics.

The texts of the sermons, extensive enough to fill four weeks of mission, amounted to an "intensive course" in the orthodox Catholicism of the Counter Reformation. The language of these sermons, according to Liguori's directive (Liguori 1867), was to be above all simple and direct, "avoiding not only the flowery idiom of pedantic ecclesiastics, but intellectual musings, novel observations, and even jokes that leave the people remembering the witicism but not the word of God." He called instead for a simple and coherent argument that established the nature of sin, the listeners' sinful state, the awfulness of the hell that awaited the sinner, the salvation of Jesus Christ, and finally, the Church's possession of the sacraments, through which, and only through which, that salvation could be achieved.

The argument sought to convince the listener of the absolute necessity of immediate and authentic participation in the sacraments of the Church. This authentic as opposed to mechanical participation could only be achieved through a genuine act of contrition — the "general confession," which involved a thorough examination of conscience and confession of a lifetime's mortal sins. Ideally, this act amounted to more than a spiritual renewal; according to Saint Alphonso himself, the experience sought was "conversion." Thus the mission discourse sought to engender among the congregants a "rite de passage" of life-crisis proportion.

Finally, the miraculous or official priestly sacramental "magic" (as an external perspective might see it) was by no means eschewed in the symbolics of the mission. The miracle of the Eucharist was imbued with new life through the ritual of the Exposition and Adoration of the Blessed Sacrament, and the special powers of Marian iconography were fully availed of, particularly in the nineteenth century. The Redemptorists even succeeded, by the middle of that century, in literally capturing from the Augustinians in Rome their very own miraculous icon with a reputation for curing — "Our Lady of Perpetual Succour" (Buckley 1948). Thus, the power of the Word and rational argument was always accompanied by displays of other sorts of power capable of triggering strong associations in the psyche and culture of the "folk." The continued efficacy of the mission was ideally assured by the Confraternities of the Holy Family the Redemptorists organized in the parishes they visited, which sought to institutionalize the devotions introduced by the mission.

As noted earlier, Max Weber argues that the domination of priests over people was achieved historically through a shift from "magical" to "ethical" religious forms. From that perspective, it might be argued that the discursive element of the mission, rationally argued as it was, and coupled with the final ethical self-searching of the general confession, helped achieve this very transformation. What better way to ensure the domination of the confessor-priest? However, the other elements of the mission and the mission priest's behavior — the immensely theatrical, visual, even sensual elements of the mission experience — fit less neatly into the Weberian model. Although Weber was certainly aware of the variation within his "ideal type," "priest," he has little to say specifically about missionary priests of the type discussed here. In some ways the Redemptorist was the epitome of the priest type. He arrived in the full panoply of the institutional Church, a man of great learning and a master of sacramental power. But, the performance element of the mission brought a vital emotionalism to the text, symbols, and sacraments — conjuring the "reality" of hell and evoking equally strong emotional reactions from the listeners. In his emotional performance and presentation of self as "carried away," the missioner seems to partake of certain elements of another Weberian type — "the prophet." That characterization may have been most apt when missions were highly unusual affairs, but the difference between the local priest and the missionary may have been great. The missionary's otherworldly severity typically contrasted with the more comfortable mien of the local clergy, thus lending the Redemptorist something of the oppositional charisma of the prophet. Certainly Saint Alphonso himself was well aware of the special impact of the religious/stranger, a type that could play upon the folk traditions of prophetic charismatics.

*   *   *

Where successful, the mission certainly augmented priestly domination, in the Weberian sense, but of *which* priests depended on the Church's political situation. As Bax (1987a) points out, in areas like Belgium where a weakened diocesan clergy allowed for the permanent settlement of the Redemptorists and their undertaking of regular pastoral duties, the order could pose a competitive threat. In Ireland, to which the Redemptorists came in 1851, the situation, as we have seen in earlier chapters, was very different. Though the country was reeling under the blow of the recent famine, the Church was making headway. Hundreds of new churches had been built throughout the country and a better-trained company of parish priests, now often assisted by curates, were bringing constant pastoral attention to even the most remote mountain parishes. This attention was further augmented through the new national school system, which, as we saw, although state supported, was once again under the control of the Church.

The religious orders, on the other hand, crippled by British persecution during the eighteenth century, were in a sorry state, and the well-organized national diocesan clergy were now strongly led by the papal legate, Archbishop (later Cardinal) Paul Cullen (see Larkin 1980). It was Cullen who had invited the Redemptorists to Ireland, no doubt confident that they imposed no threat but rather would serve him, much as they served the Pope on the continent, as "shock troops" in the spread of Roman devotionalism. They did.

Father Prost (Hosp 1960), the Austrian leader of the first mission team, left an account of his efforts that conveys something of the impact of the early Redemptorist efforts in Ireland. The first missions were held in the cathedrals of Limerick, Waterford, and Raphoe, and Prost's description of the huge and apparently highly charged crowds reminds one of the great tent meetings of the Methodists. Thousands gathered in and around the churches, weeping and fainting through the marathon sessions. The Catholic mission, like the Protestant tent meeting, delivered The Word in a highly dramatic form and format, encouraging emotional conversion experiences among the listeners. The preachers in both cases would have appeared, in some measure, possessed by the Holy Spirit.

There were, however, some salient differences between such Catholic missions and evangelical Protestant assemblies. Both mission priest and Protestant preacher would have appeared to be wandering charismatic prophet/strangers in direct and powerful contact with divinity. The Redemptorists, however, had "wandered" into the cathedral, a setting that would have conveyed a rather different symbolic message from the tents or open air meetings of the Methodists. The emotional power of the missionary, in the Redemptorists' case, was thus framed in the physical as well as conceptual structure of the Church, their preaching always conjoined with the richest symbology and rituals. Some of the more dramatic of these rituals were yet more impressive and forceful by virtue of their apparent novelty to at least the western Irish peasantry. Prost reports, for example, the introduction to the people of Galway and Donegal of the Procession of the Stations of the Cross and the Exposition of the Blessed Sacrament (where the sacrament, encased in an ornate stand called a monstrance, is placed on the altar and addressed through a series of prayers). The icon of Our Lady of Perpetual Succour was displayed and Marian devotions encouraged.[81]

While he thought the religious orders constituted no threat to his regime, Cardinal Cullen was wary of some of his own "Gallican" bishops — as clergy were called who supported national, over Vatican, control and ritual. Their Catholicism, like their politics, was too Irish, and Cullen no doubt hoped that the Redemptorists would aid in correcting their deviations. In the staging of the events themselves, however, it was possible for these same bishops to bask in the imported charisma of the mission. Archbishop McHale of Tuam, for example, having witnessed the Redemptorist procession of the Stations of the Cross, encouraged the missionaries to do an elaborate version of it for the multitudes, but with himself leading the procession (Hosp 1960). In such cases the Redemptorists promised to revivify the ritual power of the local clergy — if the diocesan priests could rise to the occasion — rather than threaten them with an alternative regime. Only in the cities of Limerick and Belfast, especially the former, were the Redemptorists able to establish a permanent base for the growth of their own pastoral regime, drawing congregants away from parish clergy and establishing Confraternities of the Holy Family whose membership cut across urban parish boundaries. Elsewhere the Redemptorist mission may have brought a "foreign" piety to the people, but in doing so it seems to have reinforced and extended native diocesan clerical domination.

These early Irish missions were extraordinary events and generated a particular kind of fervor appropriate to the life crisis they sought to engender. Later missions, however, reached most parishes regularly, which would have changed their impact; it is emotionally difficult to be born again every few years. But when contrasted with ordinary religious life the mission still had the aura of the unusual and perhaps even extraordinary religious experience. This power, if religious in origin, was brought to bear in an apparently more and more systematic fashion on the social control of the peasants and laboring classes. Reconciliation of "faction-fighters" (feuding kin groups), an early focus, gave way to an unremitting assault on the evils of drink and of unsupervised and potentially uproarious social occasions that might involve its use. This policy, as Sean Connolly (1982) has observed with regard to the pre-famine diocesan clergy, and as we saw in previous chapters, was a central concern of the nineteenth-century Irish Church in general.

Sociologist Tom Inglis (1987) applies Norbert Elias's notion of the "civilizing process" to these and other Church strategies, but neither historians nor sociologists have paid much attention to the specific role of the missions in this endeavor in Ireland, bringing as they did a particular power and authority to the task of transforming the peasantry. In fact, the missions seem clear instances of the civilizing offensive (Verrips 1987), rather than process. A distinction is necessary to appreciate the respective roles of parish priest and Redemptorist missionary. The parish priest — as we saw in earlier chapters — might well have represented a role model of civility for the aspiring rural middle classes, and thus performed a civilizing function in Elias's sense of the term. The conscious effort of individuals and groups like the Redemptorists to stamp out unwanted behavior through dramatic manifestations of power and authority is another matter altogether — an "offensive" in the full military sense of the term. In such cases most of the congregants were hardly encouraged to see the missionary as a model of anything they could hope to emulate.

This distinction between parish priest and missionary priest, in terms of their respective civilizing efforts, adds another dimension to our discussion of the place of the missionary priest in the dichotomy of priest/ prophet. The perception of the missionary in such cases can only be understood in the context of structural oppositions. The parish priest was often a "stranger" in Georg Simmel's (1950) sense of the term—"the person who comes today and stays tomorrow"—and thus, within the local context, in opposition to the secular mundanity of daily life. However, when juxtaposed with the Redemptorist—the true wanderer who not only comes and goes more quickly but who never sinks into secular life—that same local priest appears in a different light. With the missionary, the ritual of confession assumes a more purely religious force, as do the elements of social control linked to that sacrament.

The effectiveness of the social control must, however, have rested finally on the power of the mission, and of the "story" it told, for Redemptorist discourse was wrapped up in narratives that competed to some extent with stories of wells, saints, and priests.

> What voice of God is this? Is it the voice of the Eternal Judge, who sentences you to be thrown into the abyss of hell, thus to depart from him for evermore? No! It is the voice of your merciful Saviour, who visits you today, who invites you to make your peace with him—who offers you the great, extraordinary, rare grace of a mission—"Come," he says "depart not from me—Come to me." Before the commencement of the Mass you witnessed the opening ceremony —"This is the acceptable time." ("Mission Sermons")

The textual qualities of this opening mission sermon, especially when considered in light of their performance, are both powerful and strikingly different from those of any of the local stories we have so far encountered. Is it a narrative? The Redemptorists, like other preachers, had frequent recourse to narrative *exempla* to illustrate an argument. As performed and heard, however, the opening sermon of the mission also had less obvious, but arguably compelling, narrative qualities. The task of this opening sermon was to narrate the mission itself, to draw attention to the dramatic structure of the event—indeed to make it "an event." What is crucial is the quality of time, and that is the theme of the sermon—the "acceptable time." The mission was portrayed as a potentially transforming experience, an event in the story of your life and the life of your community. This was, of course, the literal truth. Parish missions lasted for at least two weeks, and in rural hinterlands were certainly "events" in all senses of the word. Moreover, the sermons that stretched over the time were a series of dramatically linked texts that told the story of salvation and how to achieve it. Thus, to the degree that it succeeded, the sermon promised to be its own story, to narrate itself and the lives of the parishioners. This made the listener, of course, a character in the story. What the missioner hoped and called for was a self-narration, a conversion story that, if told at some future date, would make of the mission the climax, the critical moment in the plot.

For the listeners, there were of course other things going on in and around this text. Like folk narratives of holy wells, for example, it was concerned with describing the characteristics of supernatural power and representing the ways in which that power is mediated. Thus it portrayed holy space as well as holy time, but in the sermon that space was decidedly vertical rather than horizontal, as it was in the stories of wells. Heaven was above and hell below, as the listener would be reminded throughout the mission. Moreover, mediation was to be found not in the landscape but in the Church, in the sacraments, and in the person of the missioner himself. If the mission was an "acceptable time," it was also an "acceptable place." Finally, this verticality was communicated not only through the content of the sermons but in the performance. Rather than simply reflecting a pre-existing social order, as Durkheim might expect, the mission sermon helped produce as well as reproduce a social mirror of the sacred universe it de-scribed. The missioner demonstrated priesthood as domination and, more generally, the overwhelming cultural power of the encroaching institutional world. In the process, of course, the specific language of the sermon — a particularly inflamed and romanized version of institutional church dis-course — was empowered, including such key notions as Heaven, hell, pur-gatory, sin, grace, penance. By all accounts, this performance quality, as well as the texts themselves, made mission sermons very different things from ordinary Sunday homilies.[82]

Finally, however, the cultural force of the missions can only be grasped by turning to the people at whom they were directed.[83] We have seen what was said, but what was heard? Something of their impact on the "folk" is conveyed by the stories that have found their way into the National Folk-lore Archives.[84] There are only a handful catalogued as "mission stories." Most were collected from elderly men and women in the 1930s, relating stories of the missions of their youth or that of their parents. The emphasis in these short narratives is on the forceful, and fearful, power of the occa-sion. Several speak of miraculous feats, such as keeping candles lit in high winds and, in maritime communities, bringing fish into local waters. Others stress the conversion of an especially inveterate sinner, typically involving the renunciation of drink. No doubt the "poitín [illicitly distilled whiskey] missions" of the twentieth century, which reached a peak in the 1920s and 1930s, in which the theatrical conclusion involved the burning of stills around a mission cross, left a vivid impression, but the folk narratives focus on the miraculous.

What is striking in all these tales is the lack of separation between ethical/behavioral transformations and so-called magical power. The general confession, which was for the Redemptorists the point of the mission, figures in the folk memory mainly in terms of extraordinary penance, which for them only naturally accompanied a transforming religious experience. The mission was a powerful and penitential event on the order of, for example, a pilgrimage to a holy site like Station Island in Lough Derg. These local interpretations, it must be noted, would still have done nothing to detract from the efficacy of clerical domination.

An examination of Irish Redemptorist mission sermon texts from the late nineteenth through the mid-twentieth century reveals little change throughout this period. Popular wisdom has it that the real modernization of Irish society only began in the 1960s and coincided with the religious transformations of Vatican II. Rural depopulation from immigration in the fifties and from movement to the city later on no doubt also contributed to some weakening of the clergy in these areas. Although Irish Catholics continued to be among the most observant communicants in the world, the Irish Church began to share that loss of confidence in the "traditional" structures and rhetoric that seemed to characterize the world Church in that period. The Irish Redemptorists apparently also felt the need for a new relevance and accordingly convened in Dublin in 1971 to reassess the mission. The result was a document that recommended a radical shift in the character of the mission, calling for an egalitarian, personalistic, even intimate set of encounters.[85] While such a model has apparently made headway in suburban Dublin, it has had little impact on the rural missions of southwest Donegal.[86]

*   *   *

The 1986 Glencolumbkille mission team was composed of three priests who, because of the dispersed nature of the parish, were forced to act independently, one preaching to each of the three parish congregations. The senior Redemptorist presided in the parish church of Carrick, where the newly installed parish priest turned his congregation over at Sunday's second Mass. The masterful manner of the Redemptorist and his striking costume — his floor-length black soutain, his distinctive white collar, and, most of all, the large crucifix slung in his belt — rather suggested a takeover by elite troops of some carelessly run regular army camp. Nothing in the next week detracted from this initial impression. Humorous and homey though he might occasionally be, the Redemptorist never ceased to cut a dramatic and powerful figure in church, shop, or parish road.

That first morning was a typical Mass, followed by good natured salutations from the Redemptorist and exhortations to come to the mission and to bring family and neighbors. The mood was upbeat and the mission was presented as both a duty and a potentially enjoyable occasion, a proposition made somewhat convincing by the presence, and rhetorical flair, of the preacher.

The first full mission session began that evening with a degree of pomp and an apparently heightened sense among the parishioners of ritual occasion. The preacher led a recital of one decade of the rosary in Irish, establishing his Gaeltacht credentials, and then spoke briefly of prayer to God and Mary, the Queen of Heaven: "She's everybody's mother, so she's all love, and she's the Mother of God, so she's all power." The sermon, which like the mission in general was conducted in English, began with a text drawn from an inspirational book about the British prisoners of war on the river Kwai and their spiritual survival through prayer and the discovery of the saving power of Jesus. Although the example might have suggested that salvation could be achieved by the sincere efforts of any group of believing Christians, the story was immediately followed by a more material commentary on the meaning of salvation, which involved being saved only through "remaining in the Body of Jesus" — that is, through the sacraments of the Catholic Church. The sermon was followed by the Exposition and Adoration of the Divine Sacrament, solemnly performed with the accompaniment of incense.

The following days of the mission followed this pattern. Morning Masses were further elaborations of central themes, though often pointed particularly at the National School children who were brought by their teachers every morning. On one such occasion, the preacher spoke of the multifarious character of prayer — any sort of prayer, whatever suited your inclinations. "You might have seen charismatics on TV waving their arms and singing away and you might have thought, 'Sure, I don't know how to pray at all.' Well, you just pray the way you're able. That's fine for them; they have a beautiful way of praying—for them." Having said that, however, the mission priest proceeded to instruct the children in the specific times, places, and appropriate manner of praying, leading them in the recital of a traditional Irish prayer (though in English).

The morning and evening sessions continued in this manner over the ensuing week, with a combination of sermon and sacramental ritual interspersed with the recitation of numerous prayers and the singing of songs mostly unfamiliar to the locals. The greatest break in this pattern was a slide projection sermon on the Shroud of Turin, to which we will return below. Between and after the formal mission sessions, the missionaries conducted visits to the sick and many hours of confession.

Through all these sessions it was clear that mission discourse, though not the "personalistic" one recommended in the 1971 Redemptorist Conference Manual cited above (this chapter, notes 6 and 7) had in some measure changed over recent years. The word "hell," for example, was not mentioned or even directly alluded to. Purgatory was similarly unnamed, as was limbo—although that has now officially dropped from Church discourse. Sin, confession, and salvation were still, however, the central themes, though their order of presentation was significantly altered. The Carrick mission began not by conjuring the reality of hell and sin but by describing salvation as something we all naturally yearn for.[87] The preacher then turned, in subsequent sessions, to the various sacramental means through which—and only through which—salvation was to be achieved. Sin stood in the way, and the nature of sin, as elaborated over the week, was never a failure to "be in touch with oneself," as implied in the 1971 document. Rather, it was the breaking of a rule of God or Church, whether that rule was ethically connected to social life, as in the cases of dishonesty, theft, slander, and so on, or simply a rule—so the presentation implied—as in sexual violations.

Throughout the sermons, as in the first one described above, the preacher would begin with a general "truth," whether folksy or spiritual and often with a contemporary ring to it, but then turn, as if compelled by the logic of the argument, to the necessary sacramental structure of the Church. As the week progressed, and the character of sin was made clearer, the missioner also built upon the concrete imagery of the Crucifixion, which stands, of course, at the center of Catholic ritual pratice. The sufferings of Jesus were vividly described—the pain endured by both Him and His Mother to assure salvation. If the verbal imagery of the preacher were not sufficient to evoke the sufferings of the Savior, then the slide show of the

Shroud of Turin certainly served the purpose. The missioner presented and commented on the slides in a manner that can only be described as forensic. Every wound of Christ was illustrated in close-up detail, and the preacher even went so far as to "correct" the traditional representation of the Crucifixion in a number of points, such as the placement of the nails, which, "science shows," could not have been put through the palms, since the body could not be supported in that manner. Instead, we were told, the nails must have gone through the wrists, precisely in the manner shown on the Shroud of Turin. The crown of thorns was instead a "helmet of thorns," which, one could and should imagine, "caused Our Lord horrible pain as they penetrated not just the skin but probably the skull and into the brain."

Thus this missionary added the authority and language of science to the task of conjuring a very corporeal Christ, whose physical pain and suffering added a concrete reality to what otherwise might have been metaphorical notions. The head missionary returned again and again, over the course of the week, to the imagery of Christ's blood, which evoked both the guilt of the listener, whose sins "added to the suffering of Christ," and the cleansing of the Church: "Come under the Cross and let the blood of Christ wash over you."

Some sense of the performance aspect of the mission can be had from the preceding description. Although outright shouting and pulpit thumping were not in the missioner's repertoire, he did make effective use of theatrical shifts in tone and volume. Typically, a sermon would begin in a seductively easy, even folksy and humorous manner, the missioner, a Mayo man, making it clear that he was, like everyone in the congregation, a country man with good common sense and a lively sense of humor. He was one of them, an age-mate of anyone over thirty, wryly remembering the changes of the last few decades. "Remember when we were young the only sin was sex (tentative chuckles from the audience). Then in the sixties and seventies, sex wasn't a sin at all anymore!" By now the congregation relaxes and smiles along with this easygoing preacher. Suddenly, the tone shifts dramatically and the listener is caught, "Wrong! People don't think sex is a sin at all—but I tell you, the fornicators and adulterers will not get into heaven!" This style of alternating tone and relationship—from peer to authority—characterized the entire mission. In both form and content, this mission, once again, seems to have little to do with anything suggested by the "new mission" document. To judge from their reactions, it was apparently effective in holding the audience's interest and emotional involvement.

As should be apparent from the preceding account, the manipulation of material symbols was as vital an element of the performance as was the language; each added force to the other. Beyond the Redemptorist costume — the crucifix was occasionally removed from the belt and held overhead in dramatic emphasis — and the regular symbolic features of the Mass, a number of special ritual acts such as the Exposition of the Blessed Sacrament served not only to enhance the religious experience but to make the constant point that the sacramental "magic" necessary to salvation was in the possession of the Church.

There were also many specifically Marian rituals, which were given added force by the display throughout the mission of a large rendition of Our Lady of Perpetual Succour. The feminine forgiving mediator was thus a constant presence beside the increasingly stern figures of the Crucified Christ and the Redemptorist himself. The identification of these latter two was rhetorically achieved in descriptions of the act of confession, in which the priest acts for Christ, but was more dramatically acted out in the culminating ritual moment of the mission — a mime of the Last Supper. The apostles were silently played by a dozen local youths while the parish priest read the gospel and the missionary, with grand gestures, took the leading role.

These rituals, some special to the occasion and some not, added force to the verbal message, the discourse of the mission, but their use in the event also succeeded — to judge from the reaction of participants — in recharging the literal potency of the symbols themselves. For the locals, the mission was not only a powerful occasion, it was an occasion of power. It was one of those points in time and space when the transforming power necessary in healing, for example, is released or accessible, and they accordingly brought in for blessing their own religious articles — rosaries, scapulars, and salt, which when blessed is considered in much of Donegal to have curing power (as we remember from the last chapter). This seeking after power as well as "graces" is, as have already seen, a common feature of local religious behavior at other points — such as holy wells or apparition sites — where divine power is felt to be more immediately present than elsewhere or at other, more ordinary times.

Indeed, an appreciation of the meaning of the mission for locals requires a consideration of their observable behavior both during and after the event. As much as the missionaries might seek to define the nature of the occasion, it was up to the people to place it in their own "fields of religious experience." The church was well filled each night, and the morning Masses (there were two to choose from) were attended by the great majority of the local populace. A few of the unmarried young men would come less regularly or, more rarely, not at all. Otherwise, the attendance equaled or surpassed that of Sunday Mass (nearly universally attended), drawing a few from the neighboring parish as well. The mood, especially at the evening sermons, was palpably more excited and expectant than at weekly Mass. Most people clearly looked forward to the mission and a performance that would, in some sense, entertain as well as edify them. They never seemed dissappointed in this expectation.

That is not to say that the congregation were either passive or non-religious in their attitude. Far from it. Weeping and fainting are no longer aspects of congregational behavior as they were in the nineteenth century missions, and might well be seen now as inappropriately excessive responses. However, many listeners were clearly moved by the exhortations and the rituals, whose critical moments were met with a silence and intensity of attention perceptibly different from that typical at regular church rituals. Most took advantage of the unusual privilege of taking communion twice in one day. Tears were more than occasionally visible in the eyes of the congregants, and especially those who remained in the rear pews after the mission each night, awaiting confession.

Locals also talked about the mission, and about former missions, memories of which were evoked by the occasion. Many people spoke, before and after the mission had begun, of how today's missions were very different from those that prevailed up until ten or fifteen years ago. In the "old days," they reminisced, it was all hell and brimstone, with the "missioners" intent on frightening the congregation as badly as possible. The current mission was perceived, by contrast, as absolutely benign. When the missioner did lash out at the dishonest big farmer or craven adulterer, nearly all listeners could rest in the assurance that they themselves were not under discussion, but rather the one or two neighbors that sorely deserved the chastisement. A few of the older people told stories, of the sort that are contained in the National Folklore Archive, about former local missions.

I remember my father telling me about the mission in the next parish there, back in the early years of the century, and there was a young woman there who was maybe distracted, you know, and anyway she was watching a bird fly around the ceiling of the chapel—a bird had flown into the chapel—and the missioner was going on about the Devil, and he saw the girl and he thundered out, "The Devil can take any shape to fool us, even the form of an innocent bird!" And the girl heard that and she fainted dead away from fright—and they took her away from there to a mental hospital.

This sort of tale stresses the emotional power of the mission and although the point was made that contemporary missions were not as tough as those of former days, neither were they being presented as the complete opposite. As the mission progressed and the rhetoric became increasingly forceful, the people began to associate the experience more directly with the missions of memory and story, maintaining an ambivalence rooted in the simultaneous contrast·(the contemporary missioners still seemed relatively benign) and resemblance between the missions of memory and story and the present occasion.

By contrast with evangelical Protestant occasions, the emotional expression of the congregants can only be described as extremely restrained. When the mission ended each evening, people poured into the main street and gaily went about their business in shop and pub. Conversations in public places afterward, if they mentioned the mission at all, did so by comparing it favorably with former missions, as discussed above, or else with a simple acknowledgment of its quality: "Isn't it a good mission!" The one element that aroused some criticism was the slide sermon on the Shroud of Turin, which, as noted above, queried the traditional representation of the Crucifixion. "What about all those stigmata?" one reflective shopkeeper reasonably mused. His assistant added that she certainly wasn't going to confuse her children with such novel views. Perhaps the scientific idiom also clashed with their expectations and detracted from, rather than added to, the force of the occasion. There was also a little critical speculation on the cost of the mission (which is partially financed by the parish), but the overwhelming view seemed positive.

The performance character of the mission for the congregants is also indicated by their aesthetic evaluations. "Wasn't that a beautiful mission" was a frequent, typically female comment. "Are you enjoying the mission?" Once again, it must be noted that such an appreciation does not indicate a lack of specifically religious interest. However, in marked contrast to Protestant revival meetings in Pentecostal communities, there was very little demonstration, verbal or behavioral, of a conversion experience. As stated above, a few parishioners, again mainly women — both young and old — demonstrated a strong degree of emotional involvement, their eyes frequently tear filled during the services and their mien withdrawn and serious between them. As for the others, most displayed a generally serious demeanor during the services, and in other settings a happy appreciation of the fact that a show was playing on the local stage.

Such was the public discourse, but more private occasions yielded a far deeper interest on the part of several parishoners, one of whom said that her "life had changed." The missioner spoke to me of his own more personal contacts with the people. Many came to see him over the week, but home visits are also a central part of the mission. Many, especially the old, were concerned with "illness, loneliness, and 'nerves'" (mental or emotional difficulties). Thus the mission takes its place in the local "quest for therapy," as one of many religious and non-religious avenues to be followed in the search for a cure.

*   *   *

The mission exists at the juncture of power and meaning. In the history of the Catholic Church, it played a role not only in the strengthening of the Church as a whole but in the competition of regimes within the Church. It was not enough for the Counter Reformation to attack heterodoxy or to make war, as Bossy (1970) and other historians have argued, on local, communally focused ritual forms. Such orders as the Jesuits and Redemptorists apparently felt the need for new ritual forms of their own. Thus, even if they sought to refocus religious energy on individual salvation, and thus bring about the sort of domination that Weber described as appropriate to an ethically based religion, they were also interested in building up their own power and influence within the Church. These goals were not mutually exclusive, and, in the service of both, such orders staged theatrical productions calculated to generate true "ritual effervescence." In elaborating these occasions, men like Alphonso de' Liguori were conscious of the possible impact of symbol, ritual, and, perhaps in particular, the missionary himself, on the audiences they would face.

However, both the political and devotional consequences of these missions, in Ireland and elsewhere, were contextually determined. Politically, the mission's impact was a function not only of church/state relations but of the power relations within the church. In Ireland, the curious combination of antagonism and hidden support that characterized the relation of Protestant state and Catholic Church probably served to disguise from the people the degree to which missions, like other Church institutional forms, served the state interests of social control—domesticating, if not civilizing, the "wild Irish." As far as relations with other Church institutions and groups are concerned, the dominance of the Irish diocesan and parochial structure left room for rival Redemptorist institution building principally in the cities of Limerick and Belfast. In such settings, the confraternities organized by the missions constituted voluntary associations that may well have served (and continue to serve) social and cultural functions for which there was and is little need in more rural areas. Elsewhere, the missions seemed mainly to reinforce the dominance of the local clergy and the social boundaries of the local community.

Whatever the goals of those who promulgated such occasions as missions, they acted in the realm of meaning, devising theatrical performances whose efficacy depended on their dramatic and symbolic structure. As the writings of Saint Alphonso show, he was not only a creator of texts, but also a self-conscious devisor of symbolic strategies. Although he would not have known the term, he certainly seems to have understood the potential psychological power of a rite of passage, perhaps even of that great emotional release implicit in the "liminal" moment of general confession. He certainly knew of the possible impact of the "stranger," and advised his missionaries to take full advantage of that powerful role. Indeed, if the missionary partakes of prophet — as well as priest-like attributes, perhaps he is not only a conceptually intermediate type but rather a real historical construction based on a conscious appreciation of the resonance of both types and the advantages of linking them in one person.

Ironically, the historical contribution of missions to the achievement of priestly domination may lie in their having left room — creative space — for a local construction of the meaning of the event, wherein the mission resonates with associations of the extraordinary.

Local reaction to the mission suggests that although a dramatic personal conversion is probably not the typical outcome, the mission is still an important and powerful religious occasion. For individuals, it is an opportunity not only to "change one's life" — which I suspect is rather unusual — but to capture the divine power loosed at particular points of time and space. They seek cures or at least a means of coming to terms with personal difficulties. Not that the mission does this job alone. Rather it is one of several settings and occasions that act together to maintain the field of religious experience that includes visits to holy wells and perhaps drunken priests and even story telling sessions that reiterate idealized experiences with the divine. While many such rituals and occasions have their respective origins elsewhere, they acquire a particular local significance by virtue of the place they take in the local field of religious experience. That field is thus created by those people who, together, participate in and interpret such events, sharing a discourse that establishes the meanings from which the individual, in her or his need, may draw.

＊　＊　＊

Our neighbors, Maggie Ann and Brigid, were among the most devoted and happiest of mission attenders. We often went together, talking and joking on our way to or back, and in the years that have since elapsed we never see one another without reminiscing. Brigid will always say, "Remember the mission? Wasn't it great?" The mission left material traces as well. Maggie Ann is something of a *bricoleur*. Proudly displayed in her house there is a large model sailing ship (given to her in memory of her years with Roger's Hotel), to which she likes to add odds and ends—human figures, for example. She was looking for tiny tires that might be suspended from its sides "like the trawlers have to protect them from the docks." Something of the same aesthetic impulse seems to be at work in her religious assemblage. On a shelf in another corner of the kitchen, Maggie Ann has a continuing shrine—a collection of statuary chosen for their religious potential and potency and their pleasing appearance. The arrival of the mission is always a good opportunity to expand this collection, to change or add to the household shrine, and to materialize the memory of the mission itself.

This time it was Saint Martin she was seeking at the mission stall. Saint Martin de Porres, canonized in 1962, has been very popular in Ireland. To judge by appearances, he is an odd saint to have found such a following in this corner of the world. Martin was born in 1579 in Lima, Peru, the illegitimate son of a Spanish nobleman and a black woman. His life's work— "trying to reconcile a multi-racial society to itself" (Coulson 1957: 516) might have been stretched to encompass Irish ethnic conflict, but I've never heard the claim made. Anyway, the statues of the saint are of a black man— or of a standard European-featured saint painted black—and that is his clearest mark, and one with only strangeness as a local referent. I heard a story about a famous local character who, having seen a Nigerian sailor walk past him on the streets of Killybegs, exclaimed, "Dear God, I've just seen Saint Martin!"

Saint Martin was popular in Ireland, however, not because he was black, or a symbol of racial reconciliation, but because during his "cause" in the 1950s he was vigorously promoted by the Dominicans and others. Blessed Martin [the stage preceding sainthood], in the form of widely distributed statues and pamphlets, left so indelible a mark that now, thirty years after his canonization, most older people still call him "Blessed" rather than "Saint Martin." In order to reach sainthood, a candidate must have miracles attributed to him or her and verified by Vatican inquiry. Most such miracles are cures, and those promoting the cause of a prospective saint must not only tell the story of his or her life, but present evidence of curing prowess. That evidence comes in the form of testimonials, letters acclaiming the cure. Such letters can be published in local newspapers (as they are elsewhere in the world) but play the strongest role in promulgating a cult when included in the little booklets that are so ubiquitous in Roman Catholicism. At the same time, statues are provided to and through which "favors" can be directed to the ascending object of the devotion. "Ascending," for the path to sanctity is through the recognized preceding stages, venerable and blessed. When a cause is underway, prospective devotees are naturally attracted to this saint-in-the-making in whose process of canonization they can take a direct hand, personally contributing to the rise. The newness of the saint also adds to his or her curing potential—like newly ordained priests still glowing with holy chrism. Finally, in the face of desperate illness, which is often the subject of such letters, a new saint is like any new possible cure—raising hopes and excitement. The role of saint-in-the-making now belongs to Padre Pio, the Italian Franciscan who died only in the 1960s. During his life his devotees witnessed his stigmata and enjoyed his cures, which now continue after his death. A young woman we knew was wearing a Padre Pio relic: "I feel guilty," she told us. "I haven't prayed enough for his cause."

The first such regularly published devotional literature to reach the area—according to local memory, early in this century—was probably *The Sacred Heart*, a Jesuit publication to which a number of statues and pictorial representations are linked. Most ubiquitous is the Sacred Heart shrine with a perpetual light to be found in nearly every local household. The monthly booklets of the Sacred Heart, Saint Martin, and many others are now displayed at the back of most churches, where any devotee can pick them up and drop some coins into the slot provided. But they are also given a special promotion during missions—the devotional revolution continues—and some locals subscribe at such occasions, and enjoy the excitement of home delivery.

> Oh Blessed Martin's very good. I get his book, and when I'm done with it I pass it on to Margaret, and she then gives it to Mary, do you see. It was

Margaret first used Martin, and she got a cure for the daughter — and so then I tried him. . . . Oh he's very good altogether.

There are other such distribution networks elsewhere formed in a similar manner. One woman subscribes to "Martin's book" and then passes it on through a regular connubium of readers, all of whom chip in to the modest cost of the publication. While the "book" contain narratives about the life and deeds of Saint Martin, the women I spoke with seemed generally unfamiliar with the black saint's biography and were far more practically oriented toward the testimonial letters, to which they would draw each other's attention.

Having thus become a devotee of the cult of Saint Martin, Maggie Ann was happy to find a variety of renditions of the black-faced statue in the mission stall. Although much taken with a large one, she settled on a mid-sized Martin who would find a place on the kitchen shelf. Such household shrines — as they developed and filled with statues and lithographs through the later nineteenth and first six decades of the twentieth century, represented the penetration of the church into the domestic world, a continuing thrust of the process that had at the time only just brought such decorations to the churches themselves. In this enterprise, missions played a leading role, bringing the imagery as well as the discourse of the Church into the intimate domestic domain. Ironically, in the wake of Vatican II iconoclasm, one encounters more objects of this genre in homes than in churches, where — while they certainly serve the objectives of the missionaries — they are also put to personal use by women like Maggie Ann: elements in an aesthetic as well as religious collage, and tokens in the continuing formation of local social relations.

7. Pilgrimage: Lough Derg, Lourdes, and Medjugorje

These days, the holy wells do not attract great numbers, but the people of southwest Donegal, like the Irish everywhere, still go on pilgrimage. The oldest of these, and the one most like the holy well turas, is Lough Derg — the quintessential penintential pilgrimage. More than 15,000 still come to an island in this southeast Donegal lake every year, some of them from southwest Donegal. Far more people — perhaps three quarters of a million per year — go to the much younger Marian shrine at Knock, in County Mayo — a day's outing by bus. In the last several decades, cheaper and easier access has brought Lourdes — the French Marian apparition site that attracts the largest European Catholic pilgrimage — within the reach of many Irish. Quite a number of our neighbors had been among the four and a half million that go there annually, some several times. Finally, there is Medjugorje in Bosnia in the former Yugoslavia, where the Virgin Mary appeared to a number of Croatian Catholic children in June of 1981. A few locals — most of them from Killybegs — had already made the voyage there in the early 1980s.

These destinations are different in many ways. They vary greatly in historical depth, and each provides pilgrims with a distinct structure — place, objects, activities — in and through which they will construct their experience. There is also great diversity among the pilgrims and in their manner of approach and expectations. In the interaction of place and pilgrim, experience is constructed and so too, sometimes, history.

Lough Derg

> Oh, Lough Derg is very hard. You go over on a boat to Station Island and you don't eat that whole day — from when you set out in the morning — and then they take you over and you eat nothing that whole day and you don't sleep that night. There's a priest there that'll give you the elbow if you fall asleep — and

the second day you don't eat—but you can take a little dry toast and Lough Derg "wine"—that's black tea made from the lake water! And on the the third day you leave, and you should have nothing to eat till you get home. And while you're there you do the stations, so many times around the stones that are there. And you do it barefoot. Oh, it's very hard. But Lough Derg is wonderful, you feel great when you've done it. I us't do it when I was younger.

So Maggie Ann described the famous pilgrimage to Lough Derg. The lough itself is about forty miles to the east of Carrick, in the rolling brown inland Donegal bogs near the Fermanagh border. "Station Island" is in the center of the lake, the scene of an important pilgrimage to St. Patrick's Purgatory since the twelfth century—when the Anglo-Norman Augustinians took over the site—and probably of a more ancient turas, if Harbison (1991; see Chapter Two) is correct, to the shrine of the local saint, Dabheoc, and before him possibly to the place of a pagan deity.

In one sense, the anthropologists Victor and Edith Turner (1978) were thus certainly correct in calling Lough Derg an "archaic pilgrimage." On the other hand, it has clearly changed over the centuries in several significant ways. Presuming the pre-Augustinian turas was of the standard local saint type, the innovations of that order—as we saw in Chapter Two—amounted to a rather ingenious appropriation of the site. They retained the basic structure of the pilgrimage, but added two more "generalized" religious foci: Patrick (whom the Anglo-Norman monks may have aided in his rise to national saint status) and purgatory, into which Patrick entered by means of a cave located on the island. It was in this very period, according to historian Jacques le Goff (1984), that the idea of purgatory was being preached in Europe, particularly by religious orders, and very much in connection with the promotion of pilgrimage. That undertaking offered a means through which individuals might gather indulgences: time off their sentences in purgatory. Such journeys, however, took the pilgrim not to caves or mountains, but to ecclesiastical structures where art, architecture, and the clergy sought to conjure up the awfulness of purgatory and hell, even as they offered the sacramental means of avoiding or mitigating that fate.

Lough Derg was different. If every pilgrimage is in some sense a rite of passage, as Victor Turner put it, in which the pilgrim leaves the world, experiences the liminal, and then rejoins the world at the end, then St. Patrick's Purgatory was a rather more forceful version of the passage. According to medieval accounts, the pilgrim was led into Patrick's cave and there left alone for three days. During that time he underwent the presumably psychic torments of purgatory. On the third day the monks opened the door and, if he had survived, led out the pilgrim, who had paid his purgatorial debt in advance. The efficacy of this rite of passage lay in its direct confrontation with the horrors of the other side—a "real" experience of death and rebirth.

At least that's the story as told by the Englishman Sir Henry of Saltrey in his twelfth-century Latin account of the knight Owein's pilgrimage. To what extent it represents the actual rites performed in that remote corner of Christendom is impossible to say. One thing is certain: given the popularity of his book there is no question that the "idea" of St. Patrick's Purgatory was a powerful one in Europe. That narrative joined the artistic renditions of purgatorial horrors to locate and concretize the concept and place in the European imagination, as well no doubt as contributing to the Augustinian coffers and bolstering their reputation. The place itself, however, could only have attracted a small stream of hardy and unusually well-heeled pilgrims from outside Ireland, in dire need of extreme purgation. We read, for example, of patricidic knights. Of the local, Irish sense of the place in these years we know much less.

Late in the fifteenth century things began to change. The first enemy of the pilgrimage was not the Protestants, but the Pope, Alexander V, who ordered the cave filled in (Harbison 1991: 59). The Vatican was evidently concerned with "abuses" there, and perhaps interested in weakening the Franciscans, who by then had wrested control of the place. The order also coincides with the continued growth of Marian devotion on the continent, however, and this rite of descent and re-emergence in a cave certainly speaks a different language from that of the mediatory intercession of the Virgin Mary. It was another instance of the historical dialectic of Catholicism: Vatican center versus religious orders on the edge; the image of a vertically structured Church that mirrors a similarly constituted Heaven with a strong monarch—Christ—and the merciful mediatrix, His Mother, versus a more "horizontal" notion of powerful places on the "edge," of a journey across a landscape. But Lough Derg was far from Rome, and the wrong cave was filled in.

A much more thorough job was in fact done by the Protestants—for the seventeenth-century Puritans were rather exercised by the "the great folly," as the Rev. John Richardson (Harbison 1991: 59) called it. The Protestant bishop of Clogher, in which diocese Lough Derg was situated, demolished all the buildings there in 1632. But by that time, the purgatorial rite of the cave had apparently disappeared and ecclesiastical material culture had attempted to take the stage. In 1630 a visitor described the church on the island: Above the altar was a statue of a Pièta, a picture of the Adoration of the Magi, and a depiction of the Crucifixion. There were also three wooden statues — from their condition probably far older — of Saints Patrick, Dabheoc, and an obscure "Voluscius." There was also a house for hearing confessions and walls dedicated to various Irish saints as well as Saint Catherine, who, as we saw in Chapter Two, was an Augustinian introduction to the area (Harbison 1991: 59–60). Such representations bespeak a layering of devotional foci and a general movement away from the cave and into the Church, from a rite of passage based on descent into a cave to a confrontation with purgatory through fasting and devotional exercises carried out under the gaze of Christ, the Virgin, and a variety of saints. As Harbison points out, there is a considerable contrast between such "pious penitential practices" and the emphasis on visions in the accounts of pilgrims during the first few centuries after Henry of Saltrey's account in the 1140s.

> The knights of late Romanesque and early Gothic era, intent on purging themselves of sins acquired through heinous crimes, did so by encountering the horrors of the other-world, and by talking to those who had already passed through the doors of death. . . . These knight-errants were silent about the beds and the minutiae of the prayers to be said in doing the rounds. But so too were the Irish. (Harbison 1991:63)

The pilgrimage continued through the ensuing centuries, despite interference, fines, and censure. The form has not much changed in the last five hundred years. What has changed is the way one gets to Lough Derg and, of course, the character of everyday life in relation to which the special experience of the pilgrimage necessarily takes on its meaning. The Turners (1978) note that the meaning of a pilgrimage needs to be sought in the "field" of pilgrimages made. While this is certainly the case, we need also to consider the general cultural field in which the pilgrimage is experienced. Even among local Irish men and women, the structured *communitas* of Lough Derg may take different shapes for those who live, respectively, on and in the land, in the civil world of the town, or in a more secular, even somewhat alienated, life-world.

There may also be a difference of gender. Pilgrimages like Lough Derg — though attracting both men and women — have been among those most interesting to local men, while others, like Knock and Lourdes, have been far more central to women.

We us't go in a group, do you see. A gang of us [men] would decide to go to Lough Derg and we'd set out early in the morning with our boots slung over our shoulders and we'd walk all the way there, and, then, of course, we'd have the three days of fasting and no sleep. And in the end we'd walk back. Oh we often did that turas in the old days. (seventy-five-year-old farmer/fisherman)

The walk was something over forty miles each way. Up until the 1930s or so, the practice of going everywhere — even great distances — on foot was common for both women and men. Every autobiographical account of those days (see, for example, MacGabhann 1959, and Patrick Gallagher 1979) tells of seasonal "tramps" across dozens of miles of mountain and bog to hiring fairs or ports of embarkation. Such journeys were usually made in the company of a group of friends or siblings, and the pilgrimage to Lough Derg followed that pattern. There are still some that make that trip, but most people now arrive by bus or car.

Once there, pilgrims go through a great series of repetitive and physically demanding rounds — stations — of the sort that characterize holy well pilgrimages (see Chapter Two). They trudge in endless circles, still mostly barefoot, kneeling in the often inclement weather (even though the site is only open in summer), saying the requisite "Our Fathers," "Hail Marys," and so on, before the worn and scattered remains of earlier religious occupants. Through the two days and nights (always described as three, since one arrives on the "first day" and leaves about the same time two days later, on the "third day"), the pilgrim goes without food (except for some black tea and toast on the second day) and sleep. When not outside doing stations the pilgrim is in the large basilica built in 1931, which is replete with ecclesiastical imagery, of the Virgin Mary as well as Patrick. Thus the pilgrimage, in one way, seems to impose a powerfully shared structure and experience on all pilgrims regardless of their respective points of view upon arrival and seek to associate that experience with some of the central symbols of the Church.

In fact, whatever differences may separate them, pilgrims from this part of Ireland at least do seem to share some central sense of the experience. For one thing, none seem to much associate the site with any sacred personage. For some, it is still in the realm of sacred geography. The place, though east of this corner of Ireland, is still "out" on another edge. This is especially so for those who walked over hills and wild bogs and were then ferried across the water to the island. The journey was at once redolent of ancient Irish movements across the landscape and perhaps of more widely, and even more deeply, rooted notions of crossing. One thinks of Gilgamesh or Charon.

Rather than Patrick, Our Lady, or indeed any church image, almost all pilgrims talk about the journey, the stations, the fasting, and the sleeplessness: the "discipline of the body." Often their idiom combines physical and spiritual catharsis. For some, it is the fasting that is most difficult — two days with nothing but a few pieces of dry toast and black tea. Others talk of going two nights without sleep.

Of course, bodily discipline is also a key practice in the Church in general. We have seen in our discussion of early Irish pilgrimage the development of an entire tradition of ascetic religion. The control of the body involves a view of sexuality that others are prone to describe as puritanical, which has certainly been — over the last hundred and fifty years or so — a key element in the domination of priests in the local community. In reply to my question concerning his road to the priesthood, a man who came of age in the parish of Glencolumbkille in the early 1950s said:

> To tell you the truth, when I was a lad here in the fifties I didn't really feel there was a choice in the matter. We heard so much about the evils of sex — do you see — that I thought — many of us felt — that there was nothing for it but the priesthood. I mean they told you that it was all right among married couples, but if it were that bad — how could it be OK even for them? Anyway, I felt the only safe way to avoid hell was to become a priest.

But the talk of sexuality was combined with a physical discipline of the body, a self control, of the sort that Talal Asad (1983) — and of course Foucault — have seen as critical to the effectiveness of any discourse. Allen Feldman (1991) has written about the ways in which the State, in Northern Ireland, is "inscribed on the body" of the captured Irish Republican paramilitary in the process of "interrogation" and imprisonment. Feldman also shows, however, the degree to which those encounters may be occasions of appropriation, wherein the "subject" or victim seizes the moment and the experience as one of self-construction in resistance to these forces. If they are capable of so using the body, it may be that their experience of Irish Catholicism has prepared them for the task — although Feldman does not much explore that possiblity. For if anything has been "inscribed" on their bodies through life it is the Church — much more than any state. Bodily control is, from the earliest days, an absolutely central feature of any Irish Catholic's life and the conceptual, discursive realms of religion are encountered in the context of that very physical experience.

In that regard, it is tempting simply to note, in the experience of the Lough Derg pilgrimage, another episode of domination, another case in which the body is subjected to the power of the Church and in which the Church, as it were, comes to exist in and for the victim through the foot-numbing rounds of the stations, hallucinatory sleeplessness, or rumbling stomach. One might further presume that such discipline lays the subject open to the "discourse" of the Church—to the hours of devotional and moral lessons with which some of the time is filled there.

Yet something else may be going on—if not instead, at least in addition. For locals who walked there, what is remembered and talked about, at least, is the comradeship of the road, the great "feeling" of physical—and hence spiritual—lightness and the accomplishment of having undergone the physical ordeal. "Triumph" would be too strong, too assertive a term to capture the very quiet way in which such an accomplishment is talked about. But there is an undeniable sense of a self discovered in the process, perhaps recovered through the very body that has been so subjected. The fact that the individual chooses to go, and goes without ecclesiastical accompaniment, makes it his or her choice, journey, and success.

Some men in their forties from the brown hills some miles north of Carrick spoke to me of their annual walk to Lough Derg, in the context of which local pilgrimages they "do." These same men not only made such religious journeys, they also hiked through their hills after sheep through the year. They seemed to offer their account as evidence of both personal piety and masculine achievement, and most of all of their intimate connection with the land in which they lived—through which they moved.

The experience is different among those for whom religious life comes mainly in the form of Sunday Mass and other easily accessed, Church-housed events. For these too—many more of them women—the physical experience is at the core, and if the event resonates with memories of other devotional exercises—it is still seen, and talked about, as primarily in the context of other holy well visits. The emphasis, however, is not as much on the power of the place in terms of the traditional sacred geography, as with the inner experience of penance and the confrontation with one's own weakness and, perhaps, strength. No doubt there is a less conscious resonance as well with the physical tests, controls, and deprivations that are so much a feature of the local Catholic experience.

On the other hand, some of the more middle-class folks from the region, particularly those who are educated and immersed in an altogether different quotidian life, frequently speak of the unusual character of the experience, of the dramatic break it makes with ordinary life. In speaking of their time there, they are likely to dwell on precisely this contrast, and the different perspective on life that it may engender. For them, perhaps more than the others, Lough Derg takes the form of the "rite of passage" and generates the *communitas* of which the Turners wrote.

Lourdes

In 1858, a poor girl of twelve named Bernadette began to see and speak with the Virgin Mary in a grotto near her home in the French Pyrennean town of Lourdes. The pilgrimage that ensued was a key element in a general expansion of the Marian cult in that period. By the time Our Lady appeared to Bernadette she had already visited Catherine Labouré, a young nun in Paris, in 1830 and 1831, and the young boy and girl shepherds in the French alps at LaSalette in 1846. In 1879, the Irish had their own apparition in Knock, County Mayo.[88] Though in the Irish case Mary did not communicate with any of those who saw her,[89] in the French cases she did — and in fact spoke on issues of doctrine important to the growth of the Marian cult. Catherine Labouré was instructed by Our Lady in the design of the Miraculous Medal, Bernadette received confirmation of the essentially divine status of Mary from the lips of the Virgin herself: "I am the Immaculate Conception." These nineteenth-century apparitions contributed to another "counter-reformation," which in the France of that day was more concerned with the threat of Republicanism than of Protestantism. When apparitions were seized upon by the Church, or organizations within it, they were used to promote not just pilgrimage but a general devotion to Mary which in these instances was always politically and socially — as well as religiously — conservative.

Objects have always figured centrally in the spread of Marian devotion. The two items most important in popular Marian devotion had long been the Brown Scapular of Our Lady of Mt. Carmel and the rosary. These were both introduced by medieval religious orders, offering the laity a material connection to the Blessed Virgin, from whom they claimed to have received it. The Miraculous Medal given to Catherine Labouré thus represented a return to that tradition, wherein a particular religious object is said to come directly from the divine, so that reproductions of it — however mundanely manufactured — can participate in that divine origin. Reproduction in the mid-nineteenth century was of course industrialized, and "representations" of any such object could be made for everyone — and were. By the time Bernadette's apparition was officially recognized and Lourdes the site of massive pilgrimage (the 1870s), versions of the grotto in which Mary appeared were being built everywhere in Catholic Europe.

The Irish have long been devotees of Lourdes. In southwest Donegal the earliest references I can find are in letters to the bishop in the 1870s from a diocesan priest who had made the pilgrimage. By the late 1870s there were Lourdes grottos being built all over Ireland, and in the early 1880s Father Francis Gallagher, parish priest of Glencolumbkille, added the "Our Lady of Lourdes apse" to the Carrick church. In the Irish context, the developing Marian cult had a different sense from that in France. Here the dichotomy was clearly gael versus gall again, and the apparition at Knock was interpreted as the reassuring appearance of Mary at a time of great suffering. It also reinforced the authority of the Church as institution and physical setting — where statues and candles increasingly attracted devotional focus — in the face of alternative places, people, and social movements — such as the Land League.[90]

The Marian apparitions were also the occasion for launching lay Catholic movements, perhaps an even more effective way of spreading Church discipline and political ideology than objects, though clearly one reinforces the other. With the Miraculous Medal came the Children of Mary, a sodality founded to promote devotion to the Medal, but also a source of general identity construction for Catholic children.[91] The Blue Army is another, and now probably the largest, lay organization associated with Marian devotion, claiming a membership in excess of twenty-five million (Geisendorfer 1977: 46). That society was formed by an Irish American lay devotee of the Marian Apparition at Fatima in 1917, which, as William Christian (1984) has noted, was the first of the "cold war apparitions" and came through the ensuing decades to be particularly associated with anti-Communist politics.

These lay groups are present and active in Ireland, as are others of more recent derivation to be discussed later on, but they are far more evident in large towns than in places like southwest Donegal, where formal lay organizations — beyond the ladies' altar society — do not play much of a part in religious or social life. The church suffices. The objects of Marian devotion and the special devotional exercises — the May devotions", for example — are very much a feature of the annual cycle. When elaborate Church devotions were introduced in the 1840s (we remember, for example, Father Drummond of Killybegs bringing the Feast of the Assumption to southwest Donegal in 1842, above, Chapter Three), the people were already accustomed to a less ecclesiastically formal Marian devotion. There are many Irish language prayers to Mary that were no doubt popular long before the days of the Rev. Dr. Drummond.[92] These verbal formulas, along with the long popular rosaries and brown scapulars were used by people to ward off illness and calamity, most especially in the face of death.

That folk use of Mary had long been promoted by Church groups as well, for the original rise of Marian popularity in the twelfth century seems not coincidentally related to the rising cult of purgatory and pilgrimage all over Catholic Europe. As purgatory and hell became more fixed and inevitable, Mary as mediator, to whom one turned in the "hour of one's death," became an increasingly necessary and popular figure. Judging from the inevitably fragmentary evidence, this was also the case in Ireland. One reason why such a relation to Mary may be particularly deeply rooted in the folk religious field in Ireland is the continuous emphasis on Mary in the eighteenth century, when on the continent diocesan regimes seem to have been downplaying Marian cults and devotions, which were associated with religious orders. In Donegal, as we have seen, the Franciscans continued to play an important role through much of the century, and their use of the brown scapular and devotion to Mary was legendary. On the other hand, the most influential diocesan figure of the day, Bishop James Gallagher (see Chapters Two and Three) was also inclined to give Mary a fairly prominent position in his sermons and writings. All of it came together in "the Moment of Death." As we remember, the folk stories talk about "penal days" priests arriving in time for the last rites, and on the side of the dying there is the preparatory "Hail Mary" of the Rosary,

> Hail Mary, full of Grace, Blessed art thou among women
> And Blessed is the fruit of thy womb, Jesus
>
> Holy Mary, Mother of God, pray for us sinners now
> And at the Hour of our Death, Amen

It was such a prayer that provided the dying Spaniard of chapter Two with a priest at "the hour of his death" — the one thing he had faithfully done, because he had sworn to do it. Such crucial prayers are perfect incidences of the ironic dialectic between Church and popular piety. The Church instructs the people on the power and significance of such prayers, or rituals like Extreme Unction, as part of a more general plan that includes strict adherence to a moral law and observance of all sacramental duties. But the more powerful such single acts are believed to be, the more they can be used on their own — for cures, or as talismans against misfortune and even damnation.

The Mary of local folk stories in southwest Donegal (and presumably elsewhere) is a familiar character: she walks around, as does the "Savior," like the early Irish saints, often in the company of Saint Brigid. The Virgin was in this way localized and made part of the landscape like the other saints. It is impossible to know how far back that folk Marian idiom goes, but it seems clear from the archaeological and historical evidence that no holy wells were dedicated to Mary before the arrival of the Normans in the twelfth century. Perhaps it was at that time that Mary was brought fully into the landscape through such narratives.

Beginning with such displays as the Rev. Drummond's celebration of the Feast of the Assumption, however, the local populace increasingly encountered Mary in the form of ecclesiastical pomp and material object, two- or three-dimensional representations. The apparition at Lourdes may have fused the two idioms. Here was a story of a peasant girl who encounters the Virgin by a stream in a cave, and then the entire scene — cave, Mary, and the girl, Bernadette — are reproduced in stone, ceramic, or concrete and placed inside, or just outside, the church, and, eventually, on the kitchen wall. The Wandering Mary of the folk stories had come to light in the Church and household shrine. But if She was there — in the statue, in the grotto, in the lithograph — she was more powerfully present, more accessible, where she had come to earth most recently, in Lourdes.

But Lourdes was far away, and for many decades very few people from places like southwest Donegal could afford to make the voyage. If a middle class person did succeed in making the trip, it was usually only once. In recent decades this has changed. An entire religious tour industry has developed in Ireland and even as incomes rose in the 1960s and 1970s, so did the price of such a trip fall. For something like $500 a person can now fly round trip to Lourdes and stay for one week in a nicely equipped hotel, all meals included. And while the French and Italians certainly outnumber them, the Irish are very well represented in Lourdes. Most commonly they come as part of an official annual diocesan tour. They travel from Donegal to Dublin by bus, and then fly to the airport near Lourdes, which, in fact, was built in the 1960s to accommodate Aer Lingus, for the Irish are the most numerous of the airborne pilgrims.

When I first met her, Maggie Ann had already made several trips there.

It's lovely. Annie [a friend from down the road] and I have gone together three times, in the diocesan pilgrimage. Bishop Seamus came the last time. . . . It was so beautiful. I try to go every third year.

The regularity of the Lourdes pilgrimage is an important feature for many local devotees. While some certainly go seeking cures, that motive is still incorporated into a pattern of visitation: people will very often mention how many times and/or how frequently the pilgrimage is made. That sense of the experience seems to conform to the traditional Church teaching regarding the need for indulgences for purgatory or, more generally, the overall requirement for repetitive, regular observance — a feature of household prayer (particularly the rosary), Mass attendance, and such occasions as pilgrimages or devotions. Though the Church is nervous about declining observance in Ireland, with weekly Mass attendance nationally at well over 80 per cent, that regularity is clearly still a strong feature of religious practice. In places like southwest Donegal the figure is much higher.

Unlike several other regions of Catholic Europe, men are regular Mass attenders in rural Ireland. When I first visited the area, in the early 1970s, many country churches were still divided into "men's" (to the right of the altar) and "women's and children's" sides. Today, almost all married men will still be found sitting inside, but now increasingly with their families. Bachelors seem to drift toward one extreme or another. I found the quiet, shy bachelors among my neighbors to be, often, quite overtly religious. Led by loneliness or reflection to this state, they carried rosary beads and not only attended Mass regularly but might even show up during the week at Masses or special devotional exercises that were predominantly attended by women. The other bachelors — jokers and characters on the communal stage — tended to do the minimum. They were to be found at the back of the church on a Sunday, usually just outside or just inside the open door. They might talk quietly together through some part of the service, but always fell to their knees at the required moment — observing the solemn moment of the Consecration of the Host. For most men, the Church-centered devotions — as opposed to the turas or pilgrimage to Lough Derg — were duties to be faithfully undergone when necessary, and this included not only weekly Mass but such events as the mission we described earlier.

The myriad special devotions on offer, however, were much more the province of women, as were the bus trips to the Irish Marian shrine at Knock, about one hundred miles to the south, and that most important of all Marian destinations: Lourdes. Men might accompany their wives to any of these destinations, but it was almost always the woman who was represented as the instigator. "I asked himself for a trip to Lourdes for our anniversary." The more local excursions, to nightly devotions during May, or a bustrip to Knock, are not only mainly populated by women, they are so much women's occasions that one frequently hears—from the cynically urbane—that the popularity of such events has to do more with the fact that they offer a "night out" to otherwise immobile women than with the religiosity of the participants. It always seemed to me, however, that both things were true and that each aspect of the experience reinforced the other. As with the village fête atmosphere of the mission, or the typically male trek of the old style Lough Derg pilgrimage, the religious experience of these devotions and visits to shrines was constituted as an experience among women—an experience of being a woman "released" from other aspects of that identity. At the same time, as noted above, the regularity—the repetitiveness—of the event is a central feature. Both senses are visible during the journeys and the occasions themselves, when pilgrims alternate between recitations of the rosary and excited chatter about social relations, as we saw in the bus trip with which this book began.

The trip to Lourdes is, for the people from southwest Donegal, almost always made in the company of others they already know. The most typical format is the diocesan pilgrimage, organized from the bishop's office and promoted in every church in the diocese. Several dozen people sign up each year, and in a diocese like Raphoe (which mainly corresponds to the county of Donegal) the pilgrims will either know each other or quickly find the one "missing" connection that will link them. "You'd be kin to the O'Donnells in Ards." Some may well hope for a cure, and a particularly afflicted child might be included as a result of a diocese-wide fund drive to "send little James to Lourdes," but the overall character of the voyage in such groups is holiday-like. The sociability of the pilgrimage can be even more like that at home in the occasional bus tour that leaves from Donegal and takes the roads and ferries all the way to Lourdes.

*   *   *

I was standing in front of a shop window in Lourdes, trying to get my bearings. The town, especially in the summer, is a chaotic whirl of activity. In the course of the year over four million people pass through, and on a summer day the streets are jammed not only with strolling visitors but with a heart gripping parade of the grievously afflicted. Thousands of wheelchairs roll past the cafés, and one sees in one place a nearly unique array of human suffering. These souls have come in search of a cure, but others, like Maggie Ann, simply come "regularly." I was surveying the shop's offerings—the usual array of blue capped plastic bottles of the Blessed Virgin

Mother (for transporting Lourdes water, which is itself free) sized from several inches to perhaps three feet tall, rosaries, scapulars, holy pictures, and a thousand other tin and plastic trinkets—when I heard the unmistakable accent of west Donegal behind me. There were a couple of women there, from The Rosses—the region just north of the southwest peninsula—who, as they had told me, had come on a tour organized by Anthony McGinley of Anagry. Anthony and his family run a private bus service on which many people—including myself—had come to depend. His coaches provided a very economical weekend round trip to Dublin as well as local transportation within Donegal. He also offered an occasional vacation excursion to the continent—a bus trip from Donegal to Lourdes.

> Oh, we've had a lovely time. We came on the ferry to England and then to France and then we went to Paris to the shrine of Labouré—the Miraculous Medal, you know—and then we went to Nevers [the "s" pronounced] to see Bernadette, and we arrived here yesterday. We're all staying at the Tara. Now, you should come by tonight. . . . We'll have a big night, maybe a bit of a singsong. . . . You never know!"

The women were excitedly happy about their trip. They had been especially impressed by Nevers, where the body of Bernadette lies in a glass casket in the convent of the Sisters of Charity, whom she had joined there at age of twenty-two, in 1866, eight years after her encounter with divinity. She died there in 1879 at the age of thirty-five and was, of course, a serious candidate for sainthood. At the time of her death, her apparition had already been accepted as legitimate and was the scene of an ever-growing pilgrimage. In the official discourse of the Church, "When the ritual exhumation took place, thirty years after her death, her body was found to be incorrupt" (Ball 1983: 77). Canonization did not come until 1933, however, and the ritual exhumation was repeated. In fact, the body displayed in that casket was entirely covered by clothing, and more tellingly, by beautiful white wax hands and face. According to some there, the bishop had ordered the actual remains covered because they frightened pilgrims unused to such sights.[93]

> When you saw her there—how beautiful she was and still is—you cried. . . . And it makes the experience here so much more—do you see—I've been here before, but I never saw Bernadette before, like, and it really makes you understand this place, do you see?

She may not have realized that the face she beheld was a wax mask, or did not want to know, or understood it to be a "representation" of a less narrowly physical beauty.[94] At any rate the presentation of Bernadette, in the golden, glass-walled coffin, worked as an orientation to Lourdes, perhaps enabling these women to sense the simple young woman in the midst of the swirling chaos of religious supermarkets and brigades of wheelchairs.

Once in Lourdes, Irish pilgrims need not penetrate very far into France. There are several large Irish-run hotels in which guests are protected from French food, the French language, and indeed everything foreign. Although individuals wander off to one secular or religious activity or another on their own, the entire diocesan group will typically take part in the various processions together, arranged with their clergy and carrying their banner. If they so wish, such a tour can hire a video-cameraman to follow them around for the week, producing a video which can be purchased and brought home. Diocesan pilgrimages also tend to pool funds to purchase as large a candle as possible (up to several feet in circumference), which, emblazoned with a ribbon bearing the name of the diocese, is burned near the grotto.

I visited the group from the Rosses I had met by the shop window that same night at the Tara Hotel. As promised, it was a "big night." Indeed, one could easily have been at a wedding, say, in the Abbey Hotel in Donegal Town. Not only were all the guests occupying the bar and lobby from the "home place," so too were the employees: the bartender was from Mayo, and not a visible worker was anything but Irish. True to their word, the pilgrims provided a singsong and plenty of "crack" — that is, fun. Conversation was about home, for although the tour members were from the same region, they were not all from the same settlement — the ideal situation for the exchange of information. Clearly, they had had a good time on their journey together. When people from that part of the world travel together they seem always to develop an immediate joking rapport, in this case much aided by the garrulous driver. There was talk of home and of their accommodations and activities in Lourdes, but no mention of miracles.

At other times through the week there was talk of the religious events and sites on offer:

> Did you do the stations yet? I did the stations yesterday and I was in the Eucharistic procession. Tonight we're going to the candlelight procession — that's very beautiful.

There were in fact a number of very specific things to do. The stations, were not of a turas but Stations of the Cross (see Chapter Six, n.1), which were arrayed through a kind of park on high ground beside the town. But the religious "center" of Lourdes, and the scene of most prescribed activities, was the grotto itself and the huge basilica and immense empty courtyard before it, in which the multitudes could gather, or through which they could stream in one of the two processions mentioned above. The grotto contains statues of both Mary and Bernadette — the prototype for the thousands of Lourdes grottos built all over the Catholic world. Pilgrims wait on line to go quickly through the grotto, often touching it. The grotto was, until recently, adorned with dozens of crutches left by those cured as testaments to the Virgin's power. They have been cleared out now. The stream no longer flows through the grotto, as in Bernadette's day, but is instead enclosed, and pilgrims fill their plastic Marian bottles at a row of taps projecting from a concrete wall. Within the basilica Masses and devotional exercises are celebrated, and before it, on the great open plaza, thousands gather to listen or process.

Many are moved by the experience. Back in Donegal, veterans of Lourdes were apt to describe the candlelight procession as the thing that most impressed them:

> It gave me a great feeling, seeing so many faithful people. . . . It strengthened my faith, to see that there were so many. . . . It was very beautiful, most impressive. (seventy-year-old male schoolteacher)

This emphasis on the collectivity is very much a part of the Lourdes experience. One is surrounded either by one's compatriots or by a sea of strangers, and everywhere there are crowds. Outside the basilica grounds there are dozens of shops, crammed with religious objects and prospective buyers.

There is, however, one brief, but striking, individual experience on offer: immersion in the stream that flows through Mary's grotto. This "bath" is also, for many at least, the most physical, most bodily experience in Lourdes. None of the other prescribed activities necessarily involve penitential action, and the holiday atmosphere — despite the number of ill — often seems to prevail. The "baths" — one for women and the other for men — like the stream itself, are hidden behind a structure, before which there are rows of chairs for those waiting. The pilgrim strips down and is helped into and out of the cold water by attendants and then dresses again and leaves. The entire process takes only a moment. The men, being always few, need only wait minutes for their turn; the women must often wait more than an hour.

Just outside the baths a woman suddenly began to weep. I asked if she were all right.

Thank you. . . . I always have this reaction to the bath. . . . I've been coming here every year for four years now. My daughter—she was seventeen—was killed in a car accident four years ago. I was so stricken that I couldn't deal with it: I just kept to myself . . . with my grief. Anyway, there were some friends who wanted me to come with them to Lourdes. Well, I was never very religious, and I didn't see the point, but anyway they insisted that it might do me some good, and in the end I came with them. I didn't have any particular feeling from it until I came here [the bath], and when I went into the cold water— whatever it was—I was overcome and started to bawl. I cried for the first time since my daughter died. I was terribly sad, but at the same time it was a wonderful feeling of letting go. . . . I couldn't tell you what it is—whether it's God or Mary or whatever. But it had that effect on me, and it still does. I've come back now each year, and each time the bath makes me cry.

By her appearance and language, this woman, who came from near Dublin, was decidedly middle class. Places of pilgrimage delight in such stories of the not very religious—even the atheist—who has an overwhelming experience in the place. Perhaps it is not very surprising, though, that someone for whom there is the possibility of the greatest contrast with ordinary life succeeds in finding the most powerful potential of the occasion.

Whatever their private "intentions" and motivations, most Irish pilgrims come to Lourdes, undergo its events, and leave in the company of others in organized tours of the type described above. And when they leave they always take with them Lourdes water—usually in the blue-topped plastic Marian bottles—and any number of religious objects—Miraculous Medals, rosaries, and of course representations of the apparition itself, two or three dimensional depictions of a kneeling Bernadette looking up at the floating Virgin. These items are taken home and find their way onto the kitchen and bedroom walls. Two dimensional renditions are more likely to assume a decorative function over the sofa, but a statue may well find a place on a little household shrine, next to Maggie Ann's Saint Martin for example, or otherwise provide a focus for actual prayer to the Virgin.

As for the water, that—at least among the "folk"—has powerful uses. My wife and I were visited by Sean, a quiet sixty-year-old bachelor from down the road, who asked anxiously what we had thought of Lourdes—a place he himself could not afford to visit. We told him about our trip and offered him a bottle of the water we had brought back with us. He seemed absolutely dumb-struck with gratitude at the gift, and immediately unscrewed the cap and took a quick swallow of the precious contents. Some months later—after a fierce storm—we were chatting with Maggie Ann

and Brigid. "Wasn't it a terrible wind last night. . . . I woke up with it and
went and got the Lourdes water and splashed a bit of it in each corner of the
house."

Medjugorje

> I went to Medjugorje on a holiday really, filling in for someone who had
> canceled. . . . I saw the cross on the hill illuminated — all lit up — but then I
> discovered it was only a concrete cross. . . . There was a group of English
> people there staring at the sun and yet it wasn't bothering their eyes. We
> looked too and I could see the rays separated from the sun itself, and the sun
> was a disc with a "V" [wedge] out of it, and a friend of mine saw the rays
> touching the mountain. No one was dazzled by the sun like you would be; you
> didn't see spots when you looked away. Then the sun seemed to turn blood red
> and go behind the cross. When I saw the sun with the little piece missing I
> thought it meant that a small portion of the world would be saved. . . . I
> didn't really believe in the presence of Christ in the Eucharist before going to
> Medugorje, and about six months after returning I went to a funeral in Frosses
> [Donegal] and Father Michael performed the Mass, and suddenly I saw, when
> he held up the Host, the image of the sun at Medjugorje and I really believed in
> the presence of Christ — the sun had been the Host with the piece missing like
> when the priest breaks off a piece — and I was overcome and cried.

These words came from Margaret, the fortyish wife of a local grocer in
Killybegs. She and two of her friends had just returned from Medjugorje,
the current Marian apparition site in the former Yugoslavia, now Bosnia,
where they had all been transfigured by the experience. The apparition
began on June 26, 1981, when a group of suitably ordinary boys and girls on
their way through the countryside saw the Virgin Mary and spoke with her.
Under the protection and with the encouragement of the local Franciscan
priest, the children continued to be so visited, every night at 6:40. Their
language and manner were, to use the American Protestant idiom, "born
again." My wife and I were greeted with "kisses of peace," God bless you's,
and beatific smiles all around: to judge from my experience in the region,
decidedly atypical behavior. They took turns telling their Medjugorje stories,
each replete with the miraculous, but stressing a powerful moment, if not of
conversion or rebirth, then at least of direct and ecstatic contact with the
numinous. Two of them spoke of feeling "an electric shock" from touching
the hand of one of the visionaries who communes nightly with Our Lady,
and all of them remarked on the mystical feeling of peace and oneness that

dominated the scene there. "The three hours of the service go so fast. . . . Even though it was in Croatian, you paid attention and you could nearly follow it" — an interesting twist on Vatican II: here the non-intelligibility of the service augmented its religious power. All their stories testified not only to the special character of the initial experience but to the permanent transformation it engendered. For them the most important evidence of that rebirth was their subsequent founding of, and continued weekly participation in, a charismatic prayer group, which had been meeting for about a year in Margaret's basement family room.

In southwest Donegal, Medjugorje pilgrims are different from Lourdes pilgrims. Margaret claims to have gone by "accident," but, as we will see in the next chapter, there is no room in her worldview for that concept; the apparently accidental only evinces God's hand. The group that she had gone with was organized by a charismatic prayer group in Ballyshannon (see Figure 1), a more cosmopolitan town in Donegal's fertile eastern corridor. The cost of the pilgrimage was comparable to that of the one to Lourdes, now that a number of travel agencies that specialized in religious voyages had organized package tours. Thus individuals might embark by joining groups being put together by a travel agent, or through a charismatic group. Clergy sometimes accompanied such trips — sometimes as one pilgrim among the others, occasionally as "spiritual advisors," but never as official representatives of the diocese. The Vatican had neither approved nor censured the apparition yet, and the bishop knew that any move on his part that looked even vaguely like approval would be taken as an official imprimatur. A few priests were personally intrigued by the "miracles of Medjugorje," and, as at any religious site, nuns ventured over in some numbers. Even with the occasional cleric, however, these pilgrimage groups were radically different from those who went to Lourdes. They did not reproduce the local social world, nor sail under diocesan colors. They were groups of individuals on quests — sometimes for physical cures, but much more often, it seemed, for psychical or spiritual therapy. Those who were members of charismatic groups had already found an "idiom of distress" and cure in and through which to form their pilgrimage experience. Those not so "trained" would certainly hear that idiom on the way there or at the site itself. But the openness of Medjugorje, its lack of clear ecclesiastical definition, reached back into the pilgrimage experience. Unlike pilgrims on their way to Lourdes, those heading for Medjugorje expected the unexpected. They were acutely conscious of participating in the formative stage of the place, of witnessing not only miracles but history. That is not to say that everyone was convinced of the truth of the apparition—that Our Lady came every night and spoke with "the children"—but they were all curious and hopeful and, most important, talked a lot about the place they were going to and about what others had seen, or not seen, there.

Like other western pilgrims, the Irish groups flew into Dubrovnik and after a brief view of what was then still a vital and fabulous walled city, they were bused into the interior of Bosnia, to Medjugorje. Although much of the surrounding country is beautiful, Medjugorje itself—to my eyes—was not. There was no "village" there, but rather—by the summer of 1988, when I arrived—a scattering of hastily constructed or expanded houses in which the locals lodged the pilgrims. Such accommodations had been arranged by the tour agency for most Irish pilgrims, but those arriving on their own could go to a government run tourist office and be placed in a bed and breakfast arrangement. The houses were dispersed across a flat valley floor, surrounded by low mountains. A wide dirt road led to the large, modern, newly constructed church. As it neared the church, the road was flanked by stands and shacks selling religious objects and snacks, and a couple of open air restaurants stood very near the church. Pilgrims always spoke of the "peace of Medjugorje," but at that time at least the "peace" was often rent by the sounds of jackhammers and bulldozers as the locals and government endeavored to keep up with, and cash in on, the escalating demand for housing. Clouds of dry dust choked the burning July air. Drinking water was in short supply, and ice cream was selling briskly.

The "children," as they were still called, although then in their twenties, still dropped to their knees every evening at 6:40 and moved their lips in silent conversation with the Madonna, who each week gave them a short message for the world. None of these messages is surprising; they warn of impending tragedy in the world, but also advise that such misfortunes as we have earned can be avoided through prayer and fasting. The apparition site, at first a hilltop outside a small village, is now inside the new Franciscan church in Medjugorje, and the entire business is the subject of much controversy, particularly between the Franciscans and the diocesan clergy, who have been bitter rivals in the region since the evacuation of the Ottoman Turks. But these local matters are of little interest to the millions of pilgrims who sought the transforming power of the site. Depending on their nationality and class, as well as their particular experience, these pilgrims approached the site differently, but one of the distinguishing characteristics of Medjugorje as compared, for example, to Lourdes is the presence at the former of many Americans, most of whom come through the auspices of various local arms of the charismatic Catholic renewal. Many Irish Catholics come here as well, and a good proportion of them also under the auspices of charismatic networks and organizations. There is also evidence of the involvement of some of the local Franciscans with the charismatic renewal; so the entire event is colored by that religious form. This fact, combined with the textual character of the apparition itself — a series of weekly messages — makes discourse a central element of the whole show.

If they were unaware of or uninterested in the regular versus secular clergy disputes, both Irish and American pilgrims were certainly interested in the secular-communist versus Catholic opposition. The communist regime had opposed the pilgrimage, in fact incarcerating a Franciscan priest for a year. They may well have feared that the apparition would become a focus for Croatian Catholic nationalism, and this was certainly the view of some Serbians I met elsewhere in the country who remembered (whether they were alive at the time or not) Catholic/fascist associations from the second world war. Subsequent events in that corner of the world could only have augmented this interpretation.

This opposition may well have resonated with the Irish — a return to the penal days of persecuted priests. For Americans, of course, the idiom of communist atheist oppression was familiar enough. I was even told by a group of earnest American pilgrims that the people of the little valley that included Medjugorje were the last remaining Catholics in the country — an island of belief threatened by a churning sea of communism. These people were completely unaware of the millions of devout Catholics elsewhere in the country.

There were a number of things to do at Medjugorje, religious activities that all, or nearly all, pilgrims from the United States or Western Europe had on their agenda. The central event was the apparition itself, every evening in the church. The punctuality of Our Lady allowed for a properly prepared audience. Hundreds of people filled the church at six and began the rosary. The remaining seers — there were only two who were not otherwise engaged in the summer of 1988 — were alone in the choir balcony and hence not much visible to the crowd below. At twenty to seven they dropped to their knees and the crowd "witnessed" their interaction with the Virgin Mary. A light was lit in the choir so that those outside the church would know that the apparition was in progress.

There were also Masses at various hours through the day, conducted by visiting clergy in their own tongues — though the two central languages of Medjugorje were certainly Serbo-Croatian and English. Outside the church was a large water fountain, and although pilgrims did fill bottles, there was certainly not the focus on that medium one found at Lourdes. More attractive were the outdoor confessions often in progress just outside the church — their setting and style in vivid contrast to what was still normal in rural Ireland. Priests sat on folding chairs, their backs against the church wall, each with a handwritten cardboard sign indicating the language spoken. People lined up before them. The English language lines — and there were usually several — were always the longest. Each person confessing knelt on the grass in plain view of the world and held a quiet conversation with the priest, who would often put his hand on the man's or woman's shoulder. Priest and person, not separated by grill and formula, faced one another and conversed.

Beyond the church area, pilgrims could hike up the "mountain," on top of which the Franciscans had erected a large concrete cross. They could also walk a bit over a mile through the home village of the seers: modest stone houses on the flank of the hillside, and on up a dirt path to the site of the original apparition. There a large wooden cross erected since that time provided a focus for prayer. Having spent some usually silent, apparently contemplative time at that site, the pilgrims would then return through the village, pausing for a soda at a café, which had no doubt grown to accomodate the new trade. If they were very fortunate, pilgrims could stop at the house of Vicka — one of the seers. Her appearances would be foretold by tour leaders — "come with the group tomorrow at one o'clock; Vicka has told us she will talk with us." The seer would come out on the porch of her modest home and converse, through an interpreter, with the crowd. Her mood was always relaxed, almost casual, but beatific. All the pilgrims wanted to see her — for they could not hope to see Our Lady, who appeared only to the seers. They also wanted to touch her, and she was always happy to shake every proffered hand. Interviews consisted of questions asked by pilgrims and Vicka's answers. Most of what she said was familiar: "Our Lady wants us to fast and pray. . . . Pray the rosary." She had, however, begun to venture into more circumscribed territory, telling one inquisitive woman the color of purgatory, for example.

Pilgrims from Ireland, like those from the United States, were there for one week, and these activities could only take up so much of that time. The shopping potential of the shacks was also quickly exhausted, and very few seemed interested in making their way further afield in the country. That left a lot of time for talk, in which the Irish and the Americans at least freely indulged. Very much unlike Lourdes — where, among Irish pilgrims,

religious experience is usually treated as more or less private—at Medjugorje the conversation was about the apparition, about miracles, and
most of all about personal transformation.

The self-centered character of the talk is interesting given the commu-
nist/Catholic conflict mentioned above. While corporate ethnic and religious identity might well have played an important part for the more local
pilgrims, this was not the case for the Irish or American pilgrims. Although
the opposition with a communist government would seem to make Medjugorje fit perfectly into the genre of "cold war apparitions" (Christian
1984), which began with Fatima in 1917, the discourse of Medjugorje is not
predominantly angry, apocalyptic, confrontational, or crusading. Rather it
is about personal transformation and world peace in a very loose and vague
sense of the term.

American pilgrims needed to fit the rather unfamiliar idea of pilgrimage into their worldview. This they do by talking in a largely therapeutic
idiom about, for example, how "open" they felt after two trips to the magical spot. Their sense of sacred geography seemed decidely "New Age";
Medjugorje was a kind of Catholic Mount Shasta. The Irish too engaged in
such conversation, though typically in a less psychotherapeutic vein. Many
of those I spoke with, however, were on what one could call a quest for
psychological therapy—attempting to come to terms with loss, fighting
depression, more often seeking a new beginning than a cure for a biological
disease. Accordingly, besides hoping to witness miracles, they watched
their own emotional state closely. In fact, the two were often seen as related.
There were two common "miracles" in Medjugorje—seeing the sun whirl
and being able to look at it without being blinded, and having one's rosary
turn gold. Most of the Irish pilgrims I spoke with interpreted the presence
or absence of these miracles not simply as evidence—one way or the other
—of the power of the place but as a personal sign of their own religious
state: a message from God, who "for some reason does not want or need me
to see the sun this way yet." The religious alchemy to which rosaries were
subject was open to an even more complex personal hermeneutic. Margaret
showed me the rosary which she had brought with her to Medjugorje.

> Do you see, when I got back home I looked at it and I saw that most of it had
> turned gold. . . . All the beads are gold and the links; only the crucifix here
> stayed silver. Well I didn't know what that meant—why had just the cross
> stayed silver—until I realized that I used to pray a lot for vocations [that
> young men might be called to the priesthood] and I had sort of dropped away

from that and this was Christ reminding me to go back to praying for voca-
tions. You see the crucifix [which had the figure of Christ on it] stands for
priests.

There was also a lot of talk about the experience of Mass among Irish
charismatics, for a renewal of the significance and power of that sacrament
was very much part of the general charismatic discourse. The emphasis was
very much on the personal emotional experience, even conversion, in Mass
— as we saw in Margaret's opening account. Confession too fell into this
idiom, and there was much talk of deeply cathartic, transforming confessions on the grass outside the church. If the experience was individual,
however, the constant conversation made for "interpretive communities"
who corporately processed the texts, signs, and portents of the place.

To judge by their behavior, the locally originating pilgrims — predominantly black-kerchiefed older women — were mainly concerned with gaining cures and favors. The hill of the apparition was littered with notes to the
Virgin, and at nightly Mass the front of the church was crowded with these
same women jostling for proximity to the altar, and not unwilling to use
their elbows in the process. Interestingly, Margaret recognized but found
inappropriate this sort of behavior. Speaking of the "hill of the apparition"
she said,

> When I first went there it was very beautiful — now, the local people leave bits
> of rag and papers all over the hill: it's getting like Doon Well. (See Chapter
> One and Figure 24)

*   *   *

To be in Medjugorje is to see, once again, the ancient dialectic — the
reassertion of the "edge" as opposed to the "center." Peripheral discourse —
speaking of miracles — is possible because the sacred geography of Medjugorje is still "open" in way that apparition sites like Lourdes no longer are.
The Franciscans were certainly "orchestrating" the experience of the pilgrims, but compared to Lourdes, Medjugorje remained very much less
"defined"; it still left much room for independent movement, exploration,
and talk.

All apparitions have begun that way. Though not typically a literal
attack on the authority of the Catholic Church, apparitions are in several
respects charismatic, in the Weberian sense of anti-structural. By happening

Figure 24. Doon Well, County Donegal, 1987 (photo by Maeve Hickey).

where and to whom they do, apparitions may indirectly and symbolically challenge the institution as such. The important and successful apparitions have been in Nature, typically in mountainous peripheries such as Fatima, Lourdes, La Salette, and now Medjugorje. The visionaries—who are also auditors—have been children. While their messages have not condemned the Church, the apparitions do serve to demonstrate that the word of God, or at least of Mary, not only *can be* but *is* most powerfully enunciated outside the institutional context. Thus apparitions are, for the Church, potentially dangerous events—an unleashed charisma that must be contained. The thousands of pilgrims that flock to apparition sites seeking direct contact with divine power represent a potential religious movement unless the Church can either persuade them that nothing is really happening there or else "capture" the event by institutionalizing it. This is accomplished through discourse and ritual. The prophetic messages of Our Lady are interpreted as either reassertions of the role of the Church and sacraments or instructions for new devotions—such as the wearing of the Miraculous Medal. Most of all, the place itself is encompassed by Church structure and ritual, so that in going to the periphery one encounters again the center—in the form of basilica, procession, and so on.

In Medjugorje the charisma had not yet been routinized. As I write, the war in Bosnia has greatly reduced the number of pilgrims but not extinguished the pilgrimage, whose charisma for those who still go must be anything but routine. As in many of the other modern Marian apparitions, the Virgin has appeared in Medjugorje as a prophet in the Weberian sense of the term; the message she bears promises salvation through a radical reformation of both self and society. The character of these messages is of course subject to interpretation, but one of the interesting aspects of Medjugorje is the degree to which this interpretation is still in the hands of the pilgrims. The as yet unofficial character of the apparition limits the institutional Church's ability to encompass the pilgrimage experience, and so a variety of potentials exist. The centrality of the sacrament of Mass and confession might strengthen diocesan regimes in Ireland and elsewhere—the sort of "renewal" promised by the charismatic movement within the church. The reappearance of Mary, on the other hand, could give renewed vigor to the Marian cult generally, a cult that both defines Catholicism vis-a-vis Protestantism and that has played a central role in mobilizing Catholic laity in conservative social and political movements. Finally, the direct, personal experience of divine power and the habit of personal interpretation may undermine the authority of the Church.

In fact, I have witnessed all these developments, depending at least partially on the general context to which the pilgrims returned. In the United States there have been a series of Medjugorje "spin-off" apparitions. In congregations in Pennsylvania, Alabama, and Texas — all with charismatically inclined priests and a history of local pilgrimage to Medjugorje — there have been reports of Marian apparitions attracting thousands. In Marlboro township, New Jersey, a Medjugorje veteran began reporting in 1991 that Mary came to him on the first Sunday of every month. Despite an official report from the bishop stating that nothing miraculous could be discovered by his investigative team, crowds, sometimes in the thousands, filled the visionary's backyard and a neighboring lawn, praying, looking, and taking photos in the hopes of capturing an image of the elusive Virgin. On the other hand, the experience of Medjugorje seems not to lead pilgrims into the reactionary movements within the church — the most politically and religiously right wing of which has its own apparation since 1970, at Bayside, Queens, in New York. "Our Lady of the Roses" — as she called by her devotees — has told her followers, many of them women in scarfs and mantillas and long skirts who demand that the Church return to pre-Vatican II orthodoxy, to beware of other apparitions.

In Ireland there are far fewer apparitions, although in the summer of 1985 a "moving statue" in a Lourdes grotto outside Ballinspittle, Cork set off a whole summer of such phenomena. Perhaps the more routinized religious life and the far greater control of bishop and parish priest limit the possibilities. The cult of Mary continues to be very strong, and in fact enjoys a renewed prominence in national conflicts over abortion and the secularization of Ireland. In a striking example of wholesale appropriation, the Right to Life movement has taken the Mexican aspect of Mary — "Guadeloupe" — as a symbol, claiming her as the protectress of the unborn. But the experience and discourse of Medjugorje, even its potentially subversive view of the possibility of direct contact with divinity, does sometimes find a home in the protected context of the charismatic prayer meeting, where people like Margaret continue, though home in Ireland, to speak of miracles.

8. Speaking of Miracles:
The Prayer Meeting

The Prayer Group

The Killybegs Prayer Group had been meeting weekly in Maragaret He-garty's home for about a year when I began attending in March 1987. A friend in Killybegs had given me Margaret's name, and I had gone to her home to meet her and two friends. It was on that occasion that I heard the Medjugorje accounts related in the last chapter. Though all three women felt themselves changed by the experience, there were some interesting differences among them and in their reading of and reaction to the pilgrimage.

Margaret was the wife of a local grocer and herself came from a merchant-class family in another market town about fifteen miles away. At the time she was in her early forties, a slim, attractive woman with teenaged and younger children. Her account, as we heard in the last chapter, stressed the wonder of her conversion and the meaning of the transformation of her rosary to gold. She was wide-eyed and determined, apparently the leader of the group but strongly focused on her own personal, continuing path to enlightenment.

The second woman, Mary, was about ten years older, a nurse who had come with her husband from the south of Ireland some years earlier. She had been to Medjugorje twice and, of the core members, seemed most to straddle the divide between charismatic fervor and a more "old fashioned" Catholicism built around a familarity with, and devotion to, the "Blessed Virgin Mother." In fact, it was precisely there — on that potential fault line — that tension was to develop, not just for Mary but for much of the group.

Medjugorje had renewed and strengthened Mary's "devotion" to the Virgin; she seemed happy and comforted to rediscover in Bosnia the protective penumbra of one side of her own childhood, as she explained to me some months later, on the eve of another pilgrimage there.

I am getting very excited about going to Medjugorje. You know the way I feel ... this is the only way I can explain it to you ... thinking about going home on vacation when I was away at school. Now, I was at other shrines and other places, but I haven't the same fierce sort of homing instinct for it as I do for Medjugorje and I'll tell you why. When I was a small child I would go out to my aunt's in Clare — now I'm going back a long way — I didn't feel any love in my own family but my aunty was very fond of me, and my aunty lived up in the hills of Clare in a place very like Medjugorje, a very isolated place. They were hard working farmers, self-supporting in every way, and they lived in a very simple way. Now ... everything related to God. They prayed. ... There was family prayer and everything was "with the help of God" ... and they really meant it. The child will never be fooled. I knew they believed what they said and it was a *genuine* devotion, *genuine* faith ... and they didn't bother about the outside world. They didn't get the newspaper, television, or even the radio. They only listened to the news when they got it. . . . I was dying for a bit of news, but no, no [she laughed]. And we were very close to nature ... like in Medjugorje ... and yet I was always happy there; I felt very secure, I felt always well in the world when I was out at my aunty's. I used to cry when I went home. I hated going back to the city and the feeling of being ouside and not wanted. The atmosphere in my home, they just tolerated me, barely, as a child. ... I felt very much out, but I knew that with my aunty I felt very complete and nothing would keep me from Clare, and I used to tell my pals that I was really a Clare person, that really Clare was my home, and that the local people would make a great fuss over me when I used to go on my hols [holidays], making tea and scones and cakes and I lapped that up. It was a lovely rural life ... no mod cons [conveniences] ... , the wonderful bread and other foods..., simple but wonderful. ... Very little meat, there was very little meat. ... Everything was natural. It was terribly like Medjugorje and the people were the same too. Something told me that I would get back my values if I went there ...; my Christian values I lost down the years. I got very cynical about relationships; I was very distrustful, I couldn't form relationships ...; I was often let down and got a kick in the pants. But up in Medjugorje I felt it was very *genuine* and I could feel that *this is the real thing*. Now I want to go back and reinforce that, because I have a feeling that it won't be the same, it's getting very materialistic now, not the local people, but the authorities. There are kiosks, etc. ... mod cons, introducing our western ideas. Now I hope the good ones are [being introduced], but in another house they were tellin' us how the girls were sayin' about the lovely clothes of the tourists. ... There were no such concerns in Clare, we went to bed after prayer, prayed for everything, the people, the cattle, everything was prayer. (emphasis in the original)

Such an account makes utterly clear the connection among personal psychology and experience, local cultural formation, and world historical process. Intimate childhood experience resonates with Church structure: the aunt in the Marian role of kind mediator vis-à-vis the distant, punishing parent (in this case, mother), and that opposition framed with all the others: sacred/secular, rural/urban, past/present, Medjugorje/Killybegs? A lifetime of personal devotion to the Virgin might well be nourished by such a childhood and joyously rediscovered in a romantically primitive "Clare" no longer to be found in Ireland but still thriving in Bosnia. And the fears of the return—you can never go home again. One also notes the mix of idioms, most of her speech is just what one would expect from an Irish woman of her age, but the business about "forming relationships" is decidedly not—an idiom of American provenance likely learned in the charismatic context.

Fiona was different again. Where Mary might be described by her neighbors as "devout" and within the normal range of religiosity expected of women of her age and circumstances, Fiona was always said to be "holy." Her dark eyes and hair framed a face whose pallor often seemed sickly. Although she was only in her twenties, her demeanor was consistently— and for the place, uncharacteristically—serious. Fiona might joke a bit now and again, but she did not seem to share in the typical Irish banter indulged in by even the most religious of the others. If Mary's relation to the Virgin of Medjugorje can be described as that of a child to the Mother she wished she had, both Fiona and Margaret seemed to have established the more novel, and characteristically charismatic, direct connection, through the Virgin, to Christ. They had heeded "Our Lady's Messages" to "fast and pray," and had therefore begun the weekly prayer group.[95] But since then, they had adopted—and would, increasingly—a Christocentric idiom.

I explained that I was writing a book on Catholicism in the region and that I was interested in seeing the full range of religious activity—from holy wells to their own prayer meeting. I was graciously invited to attend their next meeting. I did attend that meeting and every one thereafter for about six months. I was always made welcome, and although the members were aware of my academic intentions, they had trouble imagining, I think, that anyone would so involve himself without a religious motivation. They were also confident enough in the power of the occasion to hope for and expect my conversion.

On Tuesday evenings several of what can be called the "core" members of the group began to arrive in the Hegarty kitchen a half hour or so before the actual meeting. Michael, Margaret's husband, who had joined his wife on her second trip to Medjugorje, was by this time not only a true believer but in his comportment clearly part of the core. He was a talkative, cheerful man, but wide eyed with devotional energy now and, like his wife, skilled at impromptu religious interpretations of everyday life. There was also John, a bachelor in his early forties. He lived with his mother, whom he sometimes drove with him from a community about fifteen miles to the east. Like most of the group, he was always dressed in a casual and middle-class fashion. Heavy-set and somewhat imposing in figure and voice, John's one walleye, as I was to discover, only added to a look of intense preoccupation when he read and interpreted biblical passages during meetings. Mary and Fiona also might drop in at this point, and hosts and guests would take a mug of tea and some biscuits, chatting informally with few direct religious references, until the appointed hour. After all, standard Irish sociability required that "business" be preceded by precisely such casual social exchange.

At eight we went downstairs into the large basement, which, after two years of meetings, was fitted in all respects for its function. The room had been a family "den" — certainly not a standard domestic space for any but the most middle class and forward looking families — and while some of that decor and feel had survived, it was now reminiscent (for me as an American) of many Protestant evangelical home- or store-front churches. Several dozen folding chairs arranged in concentric circles were surrounded by walls decorated with posters displaying waving fields of grain or blue skies with superimposed script messages about Christ's love. Some children's drawings, with similar themes, filled in the blank spaces.

About thirty people filed in, most of them clearly familiar with the surroundings and each other, but a few of them more tentative and awkward. They were overwhelmingly female — the male population varying, from meeting to meeting, between three and eight. The differences among "novices" and "adepts," the apparently regular attenders, and the "core" members were noticeable on entry, and were much accentuated over the course of the meeting. Despite the egalitarian circle, the seating pattern was clear: novices always took chairs in the back circle and closest to the door, adepts gravitated toward the inside of the circle or toward the end of the room opposite the door, and the core members would take seats against the wall furthest from the door, their backs to the wall and thus facing everyone. From these few leaders would issue the cues that took the meeting from one stage to another. It was only Michael, Margaret's husband, who sometimes broke this pattern, often sitting across the room from the other core members, his voice booming out from among the novices, having the effect of closing the circle.

The music would begin as people were still arriving, Ron picking out some chords on his guitar or Mary rattling the tambourine. By the time the room was filled, everyone would be joining in a full-throated rendition of "How Great Thou Art." The meeting would be informally, but always officially, called to order by a dedicatory prayer from either Margaret or Fiona. "Please Lord bless this meeting. ... We ask the Holy Spirit to descend on us."

Everyone was then invited to pray, and it was at this point—in that first meeting—that I was most struck by the "otherness," from a standard Irish Catholic point of view, of the activity I was witnessing. Within seconds the room hummed, droned, and sometimes nearly shook with a cacophany of speech: a kind of freestyle prayer. But the din was not random, and in fact the statuses I had noted at the very beginning of the meeting were clearly reflected in the type of prayer offered. The true novices—there were one or two first time attenders at the meeting—seemed as stunned as I was. Most novices appeared either to remain silent (possibly praying) or to mumble very quietly. Adepts prayed aloud in a style I knew well from Protestant pentecostals in America: "Thank you Jesus. . . . Christ help us." The most advanced of these, and most of those I have called core members, began with loud and enthusiastic renditions of such prayerful phrasing, but then, having worked up to a tongue tripping speed, erupted into "tongues": "Shebalala ... oh ... shebalala ... shebacha" and so forth. As in other Pentecostal groups—Protestant and Catholic—this behavior was interpreted as literal possession by the Holy Spirit speaking a "biblical" language unknown to the person so possessed. The particular meaning of these words, much less the specific language, was never an object of discussion, although the occurence was deemed highly significant as a sign of true and immediate contact with divinity. Among the core members, Mary, for whom Medjugorje was like her childhood Clare, was one who did not perform in this manner. Instead, she spoke aloud what perhaps other women were quietly intoning—the familar Marian prayers that are the staple of devotional life: "Holy Mary, Mother of God ..." In fact, she would pass seamlessly back and forth between these formulaic prayers and a freeform praising and pleading, but always addressed to Mary rather than Christ.

After only two or three minutes the praying trailed off and the next stage of the meeting would begin: individual readings or thoughts followed by interpretation. These would come almost always from the core members, and if anyone else did offer a "text" it was a brief thought or observation. At my first meeting it was Margaret who spoke—as she often did. Her voice was clear and self-confident, but had also a dreamy quality. "I was walking by the water and I suddenly felt like writing in my notebook." She proceeded to read the entry, "It is so easy to take God for granted, but when you look at all his creation and think about all he has given us — the sea, the beautiful beach, the setting sun — and I realized that God wants all of us to love Him and He has given us all this to remind us of His love." All fairly tame and rather non-sectarian. In fact, Margaret usually read similar texts taken from her diary.

Other core members had a different style. John always read and interpreted substantial biblical passages. A cleric manqué, one would think, he read slowly and easily with strong interest and feeling. His glosses were translations into the local idiom. "What Jesus is saying here ..." Such a procedure always took longer than Margaret's, Fiona's, or Michael's brief homilies, and I wondered whether patience was being taxed. In fact there was occasionally a disagreement within the core (though never during the meeting itself) over whether too much time was taken up with music (an activity strongly supported by Ron and Mary especially), leaving too little for exegesis (for John the raison d'être of the session). He was never interrupted in process, however, and I myself found John to be no worse than the average trained cleric at his new vocation. Others might offer testimonials of cures. This sort of communication is of course typical of the Protestant pentecostal form, but was thoroughly unfamiliar to all but one or two of the prayer group members.

One of these exceptions was the adept, nearly core member, Angus, a middle-aged Scot who had met his Irish wife in Glasgow and eventually followed her back to southwest Donegal. His wife, Una, whom we met in Chapter Two on her way back from the turas in Glencolumbkille, had been born and raised in one of the *iargculta* (farback) corners of Glencolumbkille, a native Irish speaker from a mountainy farm and no doubt at home in the folk or cthonic "field of religious experience." She had followed the Donegal emigrant trail to Glasgow and had there met Angus, who had worked in a hospital. Perhaps his work had given him an interest in illness and healing, but it was no doubt Angus's experience as a Baptist — as he told me himself — that enabled him to bring a rather different "tradition" to his own style of Catholicism when he converted. In any case, Angus was particularly concerned with healing. Among the adept members, others might offer a testimonial of the efficacy of prayer on their own illness or tell how they prayed to God to make their husbands stop drinking so much and that their prayers were in the process of being answered. Angus, however, told of *his* own powers, of how a neighbor had come to him with one malady or another: "I told him to kneel down and to pray for God's help and I put my hand on him and I prayed to God and then I was suddenly speaking in tongues." The story always ended with recovery or signs of the possibility.

When no further text or testimonial was forthcoming, everyone rose for more singing — an activity not to be underestimated. Musical performance is certainly a very familiar feature of Irish sociability. Any weekend evening in a pub, even if there were a featured fiddler provided by the owner, would also involve contributions from the floor.[96] And in the religious context this was certainly true as well. Folklorist Tomás O Madagáin has written extensively about the critical role of song in the structuring of traditional mentalité and of its particular significance in what I have called the "folk or cthonic field of religious experience." The Irish language folk prayers intoned for protection or favors daily, and especially at crucial, life crisis occasions, were always sung (see especially Hyde 1972).

But that musical religiosity was *not* part of Church experience; the choral singing of hymns is a very recent introduction in most rural Irish churches and is still mainly restricted to a choir. The rest of the congregation often does not join in. Prayer meeting singing thus represented a departure from the normal, or perhaps the fusing of forms to produce a particularly powerful experience. The leaders of the group had handwritten and then photocopied a book of songs — the standard repertoire of hymns favored by the charismatic renewal — so that all had the words before them. Accompanied by guitar, tambourine, and occasionally accordian, and led by a few very strong voices — several of the adepts were in fact quite talented singers — the others would join in. Singing in this way, a group of thirty facing one another in the small basement space, was perhaps the most physically powerful aspect of the meeting. But normal comportment was further transcended, for hands were held and bodies swayed. I had been listening to the words — a natural academic bias toward texts — but eventually I saw just how central the body was in all that I was witnessing. The movement, the touching, the full-throated singing, even the loud, freeform, free-associated prayer, were all very sensual. One was at once keenly aware — in a very pleasurable way — of one's own body and of the group as a whole, physical, surrounding thing. Many of those who went, whatever their particular interpretive slant on the events (which, as we'll see below, varied), seemed to find these sensual dimensions of the meeting very pleasing and powerful.

The meeting closed, as it had opened, with singing, but crucial interactions were to follow. Almost everyone took a moment to greet friends and neighbors and chat normally for a moment before leaving, but several would take the opportunity for more pointedly religious exchanges. One of the adepts, for example, might offer a new discovery to another member, as in the following exchange between two adepts, a man and a woman, which shows one interesting feature of the fully formed charismatic "field of experience."

> "Did you ever see this book, it's the visions of Saint Brigit of Sweden [a medieval nun whose prophecies are very popular among charismatics] ... it's fantastic what she says here ... [He reads from an apocalyptic prophecy.]
> "I have that book myself! And do you know I was reading that same prophecy sometime recently. ... I got the book from a friend. ... It was a present, she gave it to me and I wanted to pay her for it, but she said no; she wouldn't take any money for it ... that it was a gift. ...
> "I got mine from a friend too!!

They went on to explore the clearly miraculous character of these events. There is no place for coincidence in the charismatic worldview.

But the most important and visible events after the meeting were healings. Individuals, including first-time novices, would approach Margaret, Fiona, or Angus, and having mumbled in his or her ear the nature of their problem, would then sit in one of the chairs and bow her head. The healer would place a hand on the patient's head and pray aloud, and then, as in the prayer stage of the meeting, launch into "tongues."

The idea that secular individuals could have cures is in fact a "traditional" possibility, and thus part of what we have defined as the "cthonic or folk field of experience." But the specifically "religious" character of these charismatic practitioners is another matter. "Lay" curers are not rare in Donegal, but they are understood to cure through having acquired and/or inherited the "knowledge" (certain movements and formulaic phrases, which may well be prayers) and/or because of individual status or character traits. Men might be seventh sons of seventh sons; so called wise women seem more often to have personal peculiarities which set them apart. Traditionally, these curers refuse money, but will accept gifts, such as cigarettes or chocolates. While most of these practitioners are simply ordinary folk to whom one might be referred by a neighbor, occasionally one goes commercial.

For example, one day my Teelin neighbor Maggie Ann told me that she'd love to go see Danny Gallagher, a healer who was making advertised appearances at the Glenties Hotel, about twenty miles to the north. I drove, and we both underwent the treatment. A large room was fitted out with several dozen folding chairs, all of them occupied — about three-quarters by women, most of whom were middle-aged or older. A row of curtained booths was set up, and as in any busy American doctor's practice, patients were sent into the booths as they emptied, so that no time was lost. Gallagher himself was a young man — in his thirties, dressed in a suit with uncharacteristic shoulder length hair. His mode of treatment differed from that of the local seventh son I had seen for the same ailment. The seventh son, a local farmer in his seventies, had touched me and the ground repeatly while mumbling what he later told me were Marian prayers he was not allowed to name. Gallagher sat facing me, asked me the nature of my problem, and listened with wide-eyed attention. With eyes now closed he made the sign of the cross on my forehead and held my head in his palms. While the sign of the cross would seem to indicate a religious "cure," there was no mention of God, prayer, or "faith" healing in the advertisements or Gallagher's talk. Nor did Maggie Ann or the others I chatted with in the "waiting room" see it that way. This was another man who may have inherited "the cure," and his actions and words were not seen as invoking God's direct action any more than those of the seventh son farmer. However, the difference in their respective comportments did matter. The seventh son, though incorporating mumbled prayers (and in that way no different from any other lay person), clearly operated in the "cthonic" idiom — literally, since his cure involved a constant touching of body and the earth. As he explained it to me — though he was rarely if ever called upon to do so — his movements established a kind of flow that took the goodness of the earth into the person and the disease out. Gallagher, on the other hand — one suspects consciously — had adopted the idiom of the priest in a confessional. One entered the curtained booth, told of one's pain, and received the blessing. The similarity may have been responsible for producing the unease Maggie Ann clearly experienced in the encounter. As we drove home she said, "I wonder would Father McGettigan be angry with me if he knew I had gone to the healer?"[97]

Some of this same anxiety may have affected novices untrained in charismatic discourse who came to a prayer meeting seeking the healing touch of Fiona, Margaret, or Angus. It was a "quest for therapy" that brought these individuals to the meeting; particular physical or emotional problems (as an outsider might label them) were here treated in the context of a "community of affliction."

Victor Turner's (1968) notion of a *community of affliction* is appropriate, for the religious idiom of these meetings and the individual motivations of those attending were certainly therapeutic. Affliction—in the broad sense of the term—was the point of entry of all the individuals I spoke to, though the type of problem seemed to vary in a predictable way. There were some women, never many, who had come from the surrounding hinterland with very specific, somatic complaints—from arthritis to cancer. They had come here having heard that particular individuals—Fiona or Margaret or Angus—had "the cure." Typically, such a woman would be brought in by a friend or relation who had been attending the meeting and knew of the afflicted person's problem. While this sort of person might attend a few meetings—having either succeeded or failed to find a cure by that time—she was unlikely to become a long term member. The townswomen, on the other hand, were also brought in by friends, but were more likely to express other sorts of problems, involving family relationships or psychological malaise. Though they might also seek the direct physical intervention of the healers, they were far more likely to become regular attenders and to undergo healing through the conversion process that was the raison d'être of the prayer group. The process was visible, and audible, though not necessarily uniform.

There was, however, a more public, and officially sanctioned, religious occasion that provided the entrée into the local prayer group for both categories of afflicted described above: the Healing Mass of Donneyloop, the bus trip to which opened this book.

The Healing Mass

The return trip from the Healing Mass was, if anything, more exuberant than our voyage there. Less time was taken up with the rosary and more was devoted to animated conversation about the event—who had been there and whether, perhaps, someone might have found a cure. Among the prayer group members, however, there tended to be more talk of the aesthetic and spiritual quality of the Mass and the holiness of the priest who presided, Father McLafferty.

I had gone along to the Mass on the invitation of Margaret and the other prayer group members, the only male on a minibus filled with twenty-four women ranging in age from mid-twenties to sixties, most of them from the town of Killybegs and a few from the outlying countryside. On other occasions two or three other males would also be on the bus.

The Healing Mass had been going for about a year, held on the first

Wednesday of the month by parish priest Father McLafferty in the Donneyloop parish church, about fifty miles northeast of Killybegs. Inside the church we joined the other bus loads that had come from many points in the surrounding countryside and from the city of Derry about twenty miles north. About two hundred and fifty people gathered that night, something like 90 percent of them women. While a majority were between forty and sixty, a full age range was present. People milled around the church in a more relaxed manner than usual for Mass. The priest was hearing confessions, and several young people were setting up microphones for their instruments in the front of the church.

The priest turned the congregation over to "Donny," the young leader of the local prayer group who asked us to stand up and "praise Jesus in your own way." Donny proceeded to give out a fairly fluent though restrained stream of pentecostal style "praise," including a few moments of apparent "tongues." To judge by the halting, half whispered, half-mumbled "praising" from the pews, however, it appeared that many of the congregation were neither familiar nor comfortable with the form. This impression was reinforced by the priest's message that "those of you who want to learn how to pray like Donny should join your local prayer group. . . . It takes about one year to pray like that." A curious description of conversion by the Holy Spirit. The Mass itself proceeded in the usual manner, though the reading (Christ and the lepers) and sermon dealt with the theme of healing. Live music and much singing of a more or less evangelical nature—the same repertoire as the prayer group—once again clashed with the typical Donegal church experience. More extraordinary business was to follow.

The priest stepped down from the altar before the congregation and asked if there were any there who wanted to tell of how the power of prayer had healed them or their loved ones. Several came up, one at a time, and "testified," relating stories of family members in hospital, close to death. These testimonies were delivered nervously and, by contrast with American Protestant pentecostals at least, amateurishly. There was no well-worn phrasing—the "praise the Lord"s that punctuate witnessing or testifying in, for example, the Holy Ghost churches of the American South.

With the completion of the witnessing, the service proper came to an end. Most of the congregants rose to chat with one another at the back of the church, or to repair to the community center next door for tea and biscuits. Several dozen remained in the first few rows of pews, however, for what was the most unorthodox aspect of the occasion. Members of the prayer group arranged themselves in four groups of three along the dais, one of them including Father McLafferty. These were healing groups, and the congregants remaining in the pews were prospective patients. Several other prayer group members acted as ushers, sending the congregants up to one group or another as vacancies occurred. Each "patient" was warmly greeted and, having seated her- or himself with the group of choice, commenced to talk of problems and pains, after which the prayer group members would "lay hands" on the afflicted and pray silently but with visible fervor.

Two women in their fifties, by their dress and speech from the west of the county, sat near me through the Mass. Their behavior throughout betrayed an uncertainty with the entire event. "Well," said one to the other at the conclusion, "what did you think of all that?" "It was different." replied her friend unsteadily. "It's what they call Chris-matic," the first related, by way of information. What had brought these two, or the many others who come for the first time (regulars estimated newcomers to be something like a third of the congregation), to this religious occasion?

Brigid, the neighbor of mine back in Teelin who had instructed me in the proper use of holy wells (Chapter Two), had attended the Healing Mass some weeks before, on a local "mission." The brother of a severely disturbed woman in the townland had come to her to ask if she would take his sister to see Father McLafferty, to see if he might cure her. The priest was understood to be "odd" and not altogether in favor with the conservative bishop, and hence fit into the tradition of "curing priests" (see Chapter Five). Brigid, like most of my neighbors, would concomitantly seek cures from medical and religious sources — including holy wells, pilgrimage sites, and prayers directed to images and relics of saints. Thus it was natural for her to embark on such a journey, but she was as surprised as most from the western region would be by the format of the Healing Mass. "Lots of singing—, lots of music—, and then you wait your turn to see the priest." She had seen no point in consulting prayer group members who could not, in her view, have had any curing power.

Other men and women from the mountainy end of the region shared, in varying degrees, this perception. Conal, a fifty-year-old father of three young children and a small farmer without a car, jumped at the chance to take a vacant spot in the minibus from his parish. "See if you can get a cure for that back of yours," his wife earnestly directed. I spoke with him on several later occasions. Although he reported no relief of his ailment, he did say that he had enjoyed the Mass. Interestingly, his description of the event focused only on the singing and on the activities of the priest. He did not mention the prayer group or any specifically charismatic behavior. When I asked him about those elements, he seemed confused as to what to make of them. His wife's sister, Kate, chimed in at this point, for she had gone as well:

> I couldn't get up to see the priest — the queue was too long — but I got the salt. There were two young priests there: one was from the South African missions. There was a terrible crowd in it — hundreds and hundreds of people — and there was a crowd for cures and queues for confession — another priest heard them too — but there wasn't enough time. . . . Four people told their stories [earlier in the service], I think; anyway I mind [remember] two of them. One was a woman from the west somewhere who had a brother who didn't speak and she mixed in a little salt in the water for him without saying anything and then he just started talkin' away. Another woman from the North [meaning Northern Ireland, probably Derry] spoke of her nervous condition — she was depressed — but when she saw the priest, she was cured.

Kate interpreted these miraculous cures, none of which she questioned, as due to the action of the priest.

A conversation with Kathleen, a sixty-year-old woman and another neighbor of mine, makes the interpretive field at work in these perceptions even clearer. We were talking about miraculous healing priests of days gone by when she said, "It's like that Father McLafferty up in Donneyloop — I believe he is very 'good.'" It turned out that she had gone on yet another minibus excursion.

For people like Maggie Ann, Conal, Kate, and Kathleen, all of whom represent what we have been calling a cthonic field of religious experience, the trip to the Healing Mass was like a special pilgrimage to a distant holy well or curing priest. It was a journey motivated by the quest for a particular cure, a search for another point at which religious power is accessible to those in need. The specifically charismatic elements impressed them only in their peculiarity. They were not at all moved to form or join a local prayer group or attend regularly at the Donneyloop Mass. The special symbols and discourse of the event were not yet part of their religious framework.

In fact, both "cthonic" and "charismatic" were accommodated by Father McLafferty; he managed to conform to both expectations of the "healing priest." "Those of you who would like to take home some salt blessed by Father McLafferty [the salt referred to by Kate above]," the public address system announced, "can pick up a packet at the community center after Mass." The two kerchiefed women who had discussed the "Chris-matics" wasted no time trundling off for their salt. Some like them might attend a prayer meeting, to continue the curing process — perhaps coming to see lay people like Margaret, Fiona, or Angus as having special gifts and powers. But they were unlikely, in my experience, to move to the status of adepts which is to say, change their field of religious experience. Those drawn into the meeting by more psychological or spiritual needs, however, who were in a sense already in a liminal state socially and/or personally, were much more likely to move visibly into a new way of acting, speaking and, one supposes from this, experiencing.

Most of the prayer group members from Killybegs with whom I traveled were not seeking a particular cure; the Healing Mass was now a regular feature of their religious lives. Along with the weekly prayer meetings where members sought intimate contact with the Holy Spirit, the Healing Mass was an occasion for the formal and informal expression of charismatic discourse — or at least some aspects of it. "Healing," in this context has a different meaning from the miraculous cure that Brigid sought for the mentally ill neighbor. The testimony of the healed at the Mass was meant not only to evince momentary access to the miraculous but to demonstrate the power of the occasion and of the religious field with which it was most closely linked, the charismatic.

*   *   *

Specifically charismatic events, though central, were not at first the only religious occasions for prayer group members. In fact, the leaders and adepts could only be characterized as "super-Catholics." There was not a devotion or service on offer they missed: daily Mass, Novenas, Expositions of the Blessed Sacrament, Stations of the Cross, and so on. In church they were to be found in the front rows, rapt at all times, palms often held open above in transported prayer. Other new Catholic activities were also popular among the charismatic adepts. From Spain, a principal source of orthodox Catholic innovation, several forms had been introduced into the area, including intensive immersion weekends called Cursillo and Search (for teenagers). These group-therapeutic activities brought weeping and bonding to many — especially the teenagers of Killybegs — whose traumatic conversions, however, were in most cases short lived. The adult Cursillo form did not spread as widely, but was favored by the core prayer group members.

I had wondered about the extreme observance of the core members given the inherent possibilities of the charismatic experience. Having achieved direct contact with divinity — even to the point of possession by the Holy Spirit manifest in "tongues" — why go to church? The traditional, central, mediatory role of the priest would seem redundant. But this was clearly not the case, at least at first. Rather, their life in the prayer group seemed only to give Margaret, Fiona, and the others a more intimate experience of the standard Catholic devotional exercises. As we heard in Margaret's description of her experience of Mass after Medjugorje, her sense of being among the chosen personalized the Eucharist, and such seemed to be the case for the others as well. For them the regular devotional exercises had been, as it were, de-routinized.

There had been early signs of trouble, however. The prayer group had been founded in response to the Virgin Mary's call to pray and fast. That provenance had no doubt appealed enough to some of older local women with strong Marian leanings, women like Mary, who always called upon the Blessed Virgin in her freestyle prayers. On the other hand, Margaret and the other core members were increasingly drawn to the sole figure of Christ, developing what could only be called an intimate — at times sensual — relation with Him that required no mediation. Their habit of reading the Bible also resulted in an intensifying focus on Christ and a diminishing interest in Mary, who receives very little attention in the Gospels.

This division was I think accentuated at one particular meeting when a special guest, "Sandy," dominated the proceedings. Even in the context of the prayer group, Sandy's comportment was unusual and unfamiliar to most of the members, for he was an evangelical Protestant recruited by the prayer group leaders through friends in Ballyshannon where Protestant pentecostals also had a prayer meeting. Apparently he was making a circuit of such meetings to speak and heal. Though a Protestant, Sandy was astute enough to accommodate his style to the local idiom. He told the meeting that he had brought a bottle of holy oil blessed by a priest in the Holy Land, where he himself had also labored for the Lord. After the customary singing and freestyle prayer, Sandy rose and told of his work in the vineyards of the Lord, of the perfidy of Arabs, and the miracles of conversion and healing he had performed. He then stood before the meeting and pulled out his vial of blessed holy oil. Many of the attenders lined up before him, each kneeling and receiving a cross of holy oil on the forehead while Sandy spoke in rapid tongues.

That meeting seemed to mark the beginning of a more extreme turn in the idiom, and the more traditionally Catholic members began to feel — and express — discomfort. "Why don't we hear anything about Our Lady any more?" one woman asked. She was told, so she said, that the meetings were "not about Our Lady." Within a few weeks, that woman and a number of other regular attenders stopped coming. The remaining group—smaller and increasingly intense and unified in their language and experience—continued to meet in Margaret's and Michael's basement room while rumors began to circulate around town about the "over the top" behavior of the group.

It was at that point that my fieldwork period came to an end, but when I returned for the summer in 1989, two years later, I learned that a more thorough schism had split the group, this time right through the core leadership. I went to see Fiona—the holy one—who was one of those who had left. Rather than describe the split in terms of differences over the prayer meeting, she explained that she and a number of others had decided to give their time to other religious activities, in particular the Cursillo movement. As it turned out, nearly all the core members had made similar decisions, leaving Margaret, her husband, and a number of her relations from another market town at the center of the meeting. While careful not to express direct criticism of the meeting, Fiona clearly indicated that she wanted to retain a Catholic orthodoxy from which the prayer group was drifting. Cursillo answered such needs. Though a lay movement in origin, and seen as such in the United States particularly as it spread among non-Catholics, Cursillo was here introduced by and under the control of ordered clergy. It was increasingly becoming a part of the diocesan routine. The bishop not only approved of the Cursillo form, but did what he could to promote it, much as the diocesan clergy had promoted the Redemptorist missions. In fact, the Cursillo weekend retreats were much more like the "new mission" we read of in Chapter Six—the one designed for the Dublin middle class—and quite unlike the actual missions conducted in Glencolumbkille. The Cursillo weekend combined devotionalism with group therapeutic techniques and experience—confession of powerful secrets and emotional catharsis. It was a personalized, powerful rite of passage that produced group bonding, but all in the presence, and under the control, of clergy. So Fiona, Mary, and many others had apparently grown to feel that a choice needed to be made between this form and the prayer meeting, and had opted for the former.

There may well have been a more social structural aspect to their withdrawal—although separating religious from social or political causes and motivations is misleading. The "religious" experience of the prayer meeting took shape in the context of social and power relations. There were clearly leaders and followers, and both roles may have been crucial to the appeal of the group for various members. The informal structure of the meeting allowed for covert competition for leadership, and particularly at critical moments, when the overall idiom might be contested, the voice that was heard most and clearest was crucial in deciding which way things would go. Whether or not competition with Margaret had influenced Fiona and the others in deciding to leave, their departure had certainly left a vacuum, the entirety of which Margaret had succeeded in filling. That along with the now total absence of competing idioms had given the prayer meeting a new form, as I discovered one night.

The meeting began in the usual way, but after the freestyle prayer, which was now a cacophany of "tongues," Margaret rose to her feet (the old style had been to remain seated while addressing the group) and opened her notebook on a small lectern perched on a chair. She had the undivided attention of the members, who now included a number of individuals I did not know, most of them from the other market town in which Margaret had been raised and where her relations still lived. They were clearly accustomed to the format. Indeed, among the twenty or so people there, none seemed like novices.

> Last night Christ spoke to me and told me to tell you what He said. . . .
> My children, I am pleased that you gather in My name and pray together. This is very good . . . but there are those among you who do not truly believe, who haven't yet accepted me into your lives. This makes me sad. There is one among you who needs to be healed but hasn't truly accepted my love.

She continued in that fashion for a few minutes, speaking *as* Christ—in the first person. The prayer meeting had become a possession cult, a group of followers who were now contacted by Christ through a medium. The prayer group members were still among the most faithful attenders of Church devotional exercises, but their oddity was perceived by clergy and parishioners alike as more and more troublesome and extreme. But the logical, if not inevitable, end of the process came about a year later. In 1991 I returned again for a brief visit and heard from friends that the prayer group was now "on its own." There were rumors of strange goings-on, that the group were baptizing their own babies and preparing to bury their own dead in a hidden cemetery. That rumor was a particularly telling sign of perceived distance from church and community, but one denied with laughter by Margaret and Michael when I went to visit them.

I found them, as usual, having a mug of tea in their kitchen on a Tuesday evening, this time with only one other guest, Jean, a young woman from Derry. I was warmly welcomed and offered tea, but the usual social chatter was not much forthcoming. Instead, my hosts turned immediately to the subject of their new status, for some months before they had, in fact, "withdrawn from the Church." An unheard-of extremity, but Margaret needed no coaxing to tell me why:

> It's all man-made religion. . . . I realized that one day while doing the Stations of the Cross. I was kneeling before one of the Stations and Christ told me that there was no reason for me to be there. There is nothing about that in the Bible —, nothing about all the other things in the Church; it's just made up, all made up by man, and we want a religion made by God.

Margaret went on in this vein, giving a pentecostal Protestant version of religious reality — perhaps one learned directly from contact with individuals of that persuasion, perhaps one she had been led to it by the logic of the prayer group experience, but most likely a combination of the two. At any rate, when I asked her and Michael in what way their new faith was different from such Protestant sects, they were not very interested in the question. I also asked them how it is they could be so sure of their current convictions when they had been equally so of the apparition of Mary, of the miraculous alchemy of the rosary — all of which they now saw as illusion. Of course, they had no trouble accommodating these events to their developing worldview. The devil had tested their faith with such magical tricks, and now they understood that all that had been necessary steps in their journey to Truth.

Their new friend, Jean, had been watching me over her tea mug through Margaret's account of the evolution of the group, her large brown eyes intent on every word. Then she turned the tables on me, interrogating the interrogator:

> Have *you* accepted Christ? Have you let Him into your heart? *He's* ready for you right now, all you have to do is decide to let Him in. All the education in the world won't answer your questions — won't save you. You have only to decide right now to let Him enter your heart.

I tried to stall such a decision, but she knew her customer. No amount of education *was* going to answer my questions. I made polite apologies for my inadequacies, which were kindly accepted, and left.

*   *   *

The Killybegs prayer group is at the geographic and cultural verge of the "western world" of southwest Donegal. Women like Margaret and

Fiona can, in local terms, be called middle class, but their roots are very much in the surrounding peasant culture. Though a century earlier and in very different circumstances, the case of Thomas C. McGinley (Chapter Three) is in some ways analogous. The same religious and cultural geography applies. Innovation arrives from the east and, when it reaches the "border" towns, begins to draw from the west. Though the impetus clearly issued from outside, the charismatic world Margaret and the others made was in many ways their own, rising from and appropriating local forms and social circumstances.[98]

In going to Bosnia, they were making a pilgrimage as Irish Catholics had been doing for a millennium and a half. Medjugorje, however, is a current apparition site; Our Lady appears to the visionaries every evening. To go there is to seek not just more indulgences but a religious experience. For these women, that experience could not be sustained within either the cthonic field of religious experience, which recognizes the miraculous, but from an essentially peasant cultural perspective, or within the routinized and now too demystified field of post-Vatican II middle class Catholicism. The charismatic renewal, locally aided by the periodic Healing Mass, offers an attractive alternative.

Within that movement they not only redefine religious geography; they have also learned a new and powerful language, a way of speaking of miracles. There are two theoretical notions that may be usefully applied to this sort of religious discourse: Victor Turner's "liminality" and Weber's "charisma." Each defines an anti-structural power that is unleashed in certain types of persons, places, or moments, but whose destiny it is to be contained. In Turner's schema (following van Gennep), liminal anti-structure happens in the ritual context, in which the tribal community allows creative chaos into the world because it will be followed by a reassertion of cultural order. For Weber, the temporal sequence is not premeditated but rather historical. Traditional authority is disrupted by the charismatic prophet who unleashes an anti-structural force that is, by its nature, fleeting, and so eventually another, more persistent order, traditional or bureaucratic, takes shape. This is the routinization or institutionalization of charisma. In both cases order precedes and follows creative disorder, but Turner's model is meant to account for tribal society's reproduction of itself, while Weber's addresses issues of historical change. Thus, while liminality is subsumed and contained, charisma is potentially subversive. Since charisma is fleeting and unstable, it is the ensuing path of institutionalization that determines whether true subversion has taken place. That is, the charisma can be appropriated by previously existing structures or can be the originating point of new ones.

For Margaret and many others, the apparition at Medjugorje was, in this sense, a charismatic event and thus destined, if Weber was correct, to dissolve. One way in which charisma is routinized is through its incorporation and containment, as a liminal phase, within a ritual structure. Perhaps this is the case with prayer meetings, where charismatic language suffers precisely this fate. What begins as anti-structural transforming speech, subversive in the most fundamental sense of the term, is contained in the verbal ritual context of the prayer meeting as a moment of liminality that still possesses transformative power — but the transformative power of a rite of passage rather than of true charisma, in the historical sense.

The founders, and even less so the followers, did not see the prayer group as a radical departure from normal Catholicism, as an anti-structural moment. By forming a prayer group they could "follow Our Lady's directions to pray and fast" and thus remain very much within the Irish Catholic tradition. The predominantly female character of these meetings (though several of the few men achieved prominent roles) also followed the typical pattern of devotional activity. And if the format of the meeting was highly unusual in local terms, the Healing Mass offered a very useful bridge, as it began like any such special occasion (the Vigil at Knock, for example) and the strange elements (tongues and testimonials) were encountered in the familiar context of Mass, priest, and Church. Instructed by the priest to join a prayer group, the novice could then take the next step.

Once in Margaret's basement, however, the novice found the group aspect quite novel, in its freeflowing format, with occasional "speaking in tongues" and much testifying. Perhaps most unsettling, however, was the leadership of such laypersons as Margaret. Vatican II had only brought lay distributors of Communion wafers a few years earlier, and to have women like Fiona and Margaret clearly running the religious occasion amounted to a dramatic innovation.

For the adepts and leaders, the meeting was clearly an opportunity for leadership and cultural authority unavailable outside. It was not a coincidence, I think, that the leadership was composed of women and socially peripheral men (with the exception of Michael, who I think was drawn in with his wife). Two of the male leaders were foreigners and converts to Catholicism (one English and one Scottish) and none of the others could be described as locally prominent men. This access to a kind of social power was experienced through charismatic conversion — a process that began for some at Medjugorje, but that could be sustained through the prayer meeting with unmediated contact with the numinous. These meetings were also opportunities, aided by a constant flow of textual materials supplied by the Dublin-based Charismatic Renewal Information Services, for the generation and expression of a discourse that maintained their new field of religious experience. That discourse was an amalgam of liberal, person-centered therapeutics and revivified appreciations of the miraculous character of the Catholic sacraments.

Though the group and its language were thus loosely connected to the World Charismatic Renewal, the books and pamphlets associated with the movement were read by only a few of the members. As in the case of the other intrusions of external idioms we have been exploring, such language was selectively appropriated by the group and wedded to other idioms to create a serviceable religious discourse — a way to speak of miracles in their own world.

However, the language of the group was also "charismatic" in the Weberian sense; individual members gave evidence, through their speech, of direct contact with divine power, unmediated by the Church. Not only was the language of the group charismatic in content, their way of speaking made speech as such charismatic. That is to say, the prayer group provided its members with direct and indirect evidence of the transforming power of their own language. Moreover, that power may be — less consciously — related to its contrast with normal Catholic discourse and authority. As we remember from Chapter Five, in speaking of the powers of alcoholic priests — whose cures and curses are understood to be very efficacious — locals say "the *smacht* of the bishop is off them." *Smacht* in this context means controlling power, and the statement implies that the miraculous, charismatic power of the priest is released when such authoritarian containment is released. In a similar vein, it might be said of the charismatic movement as a whole, and of such prayer groups in particular, that the *smacht* of the Church is off them, and with similar results. Here again, as with the wandering drunken priest, is uncontrolled liminality and a language with shamanic power. Indeed, language is so plainly powerful and creative at such "speech occasions," that one might wonder if it is a case of the triumph of authentic personal speech over cultural text? My answer is no — but a qualified no that recognizes the truly creative character, in a literary as well as cultural sense, of such performances.

That powerful language has a central role to play insofar as the prayer group constitutes a "community of affliction." For those who join prayer

groups, whether or not they are driven or attracted by their relative depriva-
tion, as many sociologists would have it, certainly do proceed to define
themselves as afflicted and in need not just of salvation but of rebirth or
renewal here and now. The African communities of affliction with which
Turner and other anthropologists have been concerned typically accomplish such rebirth through special rites of passage. Prayer groups — though
they do avail themselves of certain more patently ritual forms in the case of
curing — spend most of their time reconstructing their members through
speech. The rite of passage form nevertheless applies. The admission or
assertion of affliction is the first stage — a ritual separation that propels the
member into the liminal world of "she who has begun to leave worldliness"
but who must now proceed to seek God and painfully reconstruct a self too
easily drawn by the Devil — either inside or outside — into old sinful ways.
However, in some ways these temptations are never thought to be finally
overcome and thus members may see themselves and each other as permanently in the liminal state. At the same time, however, there is an implicit
recognition of the special status of a few leaders that discounts their pro-
testations of imperfection. Such adept prayer group members act as if they
have "arrived," and are viewed in that light by most members. They achieve
a kind of saintly status that is both created by, and manifest in, their linguistic skills. They tell more stories, and their stories are more clearly heard;
they achieve a cultural authority within the group.

Thus the prayer meetings can be understood to constitute a rite of
passage in which novices are slowly turned into adepts. But the critical role
of discourse in this process — of learning to speak of miracles and of oneself
in a particular way — and the protracted character of the liminal stage make
this process different from most rites of passage studied by anthropologists.
Salvatore Cucchiari's 1988 analysis of a pentecostal Protestant group in
Sicily gives a good account of the creative character of the process in terms
of individual self-construction. The Irish Catholic case is very different in
regard to the external context, but some of the intra-group and personal
dynamics are similar. In Killybegs, the prayer meeting controls and contains
the charisma of the apparition/pilgrimage experience through a peculiar
sort of institutionalization. The charismatic experience and language of
Medjugorje are brought home and domesticated, finding their place in a
ritual structure — a rite of passage through which locals reorient their understanding of themselves and others. The anti-structure of charisma has
become the anti-structure of liminality; the unstable power of the historical
moment is preserved through its incorporation in a structure that allows for

its occasional release. It might be argued that this process is not so different from the usual path of routinization of charisma in the Catholic Church; the power is cathected into symbols and acts that are incorporated into ritual devotions. However, the special character of the prayer meeting reinvigorates not only the material symbols of the Church — Margaret, we remember, spoke of the Eucharist — but also the religious power of the individual and of speech as such.

Insofar as the process we have just described *is* a rite of passage, however, is the speech thus ritualized and the charisma routinized? Yes, but the rite of passage form in a sense protects and preserves the anti-structural qualities of discourse and experience in the form of ritual liminality. The power of language thus re-emerges on these occasions and continues to act forcefully on speakers and listeners.

But what of the politically "subversive" possibilities of such prayer groups? Can the power described above be harnessed in the service of Church or a rival religious regime — the charismatic renewal? Does the charismatic renewal represent an alternative Church and the Healing Mass, with its constellation of prayer groups, an alternative diocese?

The charismatic renewal movement began in the late 1960s among a group of U.S. Catholics and came to Ireland in the early 1970s, where it was embraced with enthusiasm by a number of mainly middle-class Dubliners and other townsfolk. The height of this stage of the movement was reached when an international charismatic conference was held in Dublin in 1977. Interest and membership began to slip after that, but seems to have been boosted by the Medjugorje apparition not only in numbers of adherents but, more importantly perhaps, in religious enthusiasm: the renewal was renewed.

The Healing Mass itself seems to have also come from the United States, where a number of similar, popular occasions are regular features for charismatically inclined populations. Donneyloop, though located in County Donegal, is part of the diocese of Derry, which tends to import such relgious novelties far more readily than Raphoe. The flow of religious innovations, along with other cultural novelties, follows the well worn path down the eastern corridor from Derry to Letterkenny, Ballybofey, Lifford, Donegal Town, Ballyshannon. The lesser routes radiated westward from each of those points to a ring of western market towns: Killybegs, Ardara, Glenties, Dungloe, Dunfanaghy. The minibuses came from these outposts, drawing most of their passengers from the "townsfolk," but including, as we saw, several from "in through," to use the Killybegs locution for the western glens. To the east, another, similarly structured flow drew from the more populous and generally more sophisticated diocese of Derry. Prayer groups, not coincidentally, were organized in the towns — but probably in few if any of the smaller communities beyond. Thus the monthly Healing Mass functioned like a heart, drawing — in its monthly pulsation — from its hinterland body, by means of a minibus circulatory system. Although the total numbers of individuals involved was not great — in the hundreds for the whole diocese of Raphoe — most religious movements start modestly.

Their theology, however, at first led them back to the sacraments of the church; the Healing Mass, whatever its innovations, had both priest and Eucharist at its center. Yet the charismatic renewal movement was and is viewed by the clergy in Donegal, as elsewhere, with some unease. In the words of one bishop, "I don't like charismatics: it begins with charism and ends with schismatics." Prophetic words as it turned out. The bishop of Raphoe appointed a priest as "spiritual advisor" to the prayer groups, whose task it is to periodically attend local meetings and make sure they are not straying too far from orthodoxy. Even if they do not, however, the fact that they have religious experiences — to the extent of access to the Holy Spirit — under their own steam is threatening enough. The open competition for authority within each meeting is probably as threatening to the diocesan clergy as it is attractive to women, both lay and religious, who can, like Margaret, take leadership roles, especially in the face of continued Church opposition to their ordination. Finally, the network of national and international association that links local charismatic groups to one another represents a nascent institution potentially outside the control of at least the diocesan clergy.

This fact combined with an overall weakening of the once monolithic authority of the diocesan clergy and the normal, devotional structure does allow for the possibility of new configurations of power. Other arms of the Church may, however, be the ultimate benefactors. Such religious orders as the Jesuits who are involved in the promotion of Charismatic Renewals, are also introducing Cursillo, Search weekends, and other religious occasions promoting an alternative field of religious experience characterized by a novel discourse and psychodynamic. The fact that the Killybegs prayer groups members also found such occasions attractive indicates the ability of the Church to, once again, channel the burst of charismatic energy, and even the new therapeutic egocentric discourse, into clerically controlled contexts. The bishop, in turn, tries — as diocesan clergy did when missions were introduced in the area a hundred years earlier — to capitalize on the emotional engagement of those "alternative" occasions by maintaining ulti-mate control of such things as Search weekends.

There is of course another possibility, the one actually played out in the case of the Killybegs prayer group. In that case the subversive potential is realized, and the logic of the experience as well as the particular proclivities of a few individuals led to the formation, not of an alternative diocese, but of a new sect altogether. But that group is very much alone. The surround-ing social world, if suffering from some of the dislocations that come with shifting economic and social realities, is nothing like a mass of isolated individuals needing not only cures and healing but an alternative social reality. Thus the group will probably not expand in membership much less become the mother of daughter prayer groups with similar agenda. The Pentecostal reformation of Killybegs will not likely be repeated.

9. Conclusions

Occasions of faith. From holy well turas to charismatic prayer meeting, the range of Catholic religious experience, even in the narrow geographic scope of this corner of Ireland, is wide.

What, however, is religion? Power and meaning; a powerful organization of meaning, and a meaningful organization of power. That organization is an act — or a series of acts — by people; it is a process, not a thing. Or, as William Cantwell Smith argues, an adjective, a quality. The adjective "religious," in this sense, describes an idiom of thought, speech, and action through which individuals, groups, and even whole nations make themselves. In the process of making themselves, they make religion. That is to say, religion exists only in historical, material contexts — in particular formations, which in turn may take the form they do because of the religious idiom at work. But each time a new religious form takes shape it does so with pre-existing materials — language, objects, places, notions. One cannot find the beginning.

The holy wells can still be found in the landscape. They have meaning for the folklorist, for the antiquarian, for the priest, and for the folks of Rinnakilla who need a cure. In each case, that meaning is constituted in the use of the well: one person photographs it and notes its location; another goes around it saying "Our Fathers" and "Hail Marys." The meaning of the visit to the well also takes shape in relation to other occasions, before and after, and of course in relation to a more general cultural field (which, in part, is articulated through the visit to the well). The visit to the holy well expresses and reproduces a relation to the land, and to other people, that has to do with reciprocity. It should not be imagined, however, that this ethos and the well that empowers it are necessarily egalitarian and only communal. A holy well that now operates only in a local communal field may well have played a very different historical role, aiding in the establishment of a regime that used notions of reciprocal kin obligation and sacred earth in a hierarchical way, in the service of a chiefdom.

That political potential was not altogether lost in the modern era, for the appropriation of wells as emblems of a very "real" notion of sacred geography was part of the Irish nationalist strategy. If holy wells per se no longer figure prominently in that mythology, the sacred landscape certainly still does. Whether the well finds a place in one sacred landscape or another — that of the countrywoman seeking a cure, or that of the nationalist seeking a nation — the meaning of the well and the landscape it punctuates is also established in opposition. In both idioms that opposition is to *na gall*, "the foreigners." They desecrate wells and they colonize the land of Ireland.

Finally, however, all these meanings are dependent on discourse, and narratives in particular may play a crucial role. An interpretive community — people who not only use the well but know and contribute to the discourse of wells — together generate what I have called a field of religious experience. But that field may have more general import; it may amount to a "cultural field" that involves a general sensibility and comportment in which religion can be distinguished and separated out only artificially.

The relation of a way of being religious to a general cultural field and a class formation is clear again in the case study of Thomas C. McGinley — his life and his work. His story also evinces the crucial role of discourse and narrative. Though his book, *The Cliff Scenery of South-Western Donegal*, can probably not be described as a "religious" work, it uses a religious idiom in combination with other idioms — scientific and nationalist. This combination, which was hardly unique to McGinley, had consequences for all three idioms — each affected, infected, the others. But that was not something that did or could happen only in the text. McGinley and others like him were busy creating a social and cultural world out of their own circumstances. That involved reworking a geography, in which the text plays a part. And that textual play was possible only in the context of more substantial restructuring of the geography — the rise of the street town, the building of roads — a redefinition of domesticity and the household. The institutional Church was certainly at the forefront of these developments, as many have pointed out, but so also were landlords and their agents. The parish priest may well have been, as Tom Inglis argues, a model of civility. But he was only a part of the interpretive community which was in the process of forming and defining itself and which included teachers and doctors. Their civil religion took shape in the townscape, but also within the changing domestic space, where Victorian parlors and the act of reading entailed a discipline of the body as significant in its own way as the penitential exercises self-inflicted in devotional occasions. Both Church and class inscribed themselves on the body, one might say, but on the same body and so perhaps with undistinguished effect. Just as the verbal idioms are mixed and interactive in McGinley's discourse, so too perhaps with the shaping of the body.

The case of the evicted priest provides a vew of another dimension of the formation of local religion. Here both interpretive community and meaning are defined through confrontation. The priest and the agent each constitutes himself — defines the parameters of his status, role, and identity — vis-à-vis the other. The case reveals at least three different interpretive communities defining both themselves and the meaning of the event. The landlord and agent write letters, to each other and to the newspapers. Father Magroarty writes letters — amounting to tracts — to the newspapers as well, addressing not only the aggrieved peasantry but people like McGinley. If McGinley used a religious idiom to empower and authorize nationalism, then Magroarty used nationalist allusion and metaphor in the reciprocal service of religion — or at least of his own position as a priest. But that position — the power and authority of parish priest — is absolutely central to defining a kind of religiosity and a social world: *na bunadh an pharoiste*, "the people of the parish." Those people, in turn, even if pulled closer to their priest by his trials and further subjugated by his heroic status, appropriate him in their own discourse, their own stories, in which they too figure as heroes of resistance. Thus the priest is made to play a part in sustaining the world — what we called a folk or cthonic field of religious experience — which the very same cleric was no doubt undermining.

That process of appropriation goes further and is yet more obvious in the stories of drunken priests. The telling of these narratives and, of course, the actual visits to these priests, can be understood as based in "traditional" understandings of shamanic power, and as responses to historical experience of the power of the institutional Church and the foreigner colonizer. Though beginning with a representative of the Church, the stories relocate these actors in the sacred landscape — through which they wander again, like the ancient local saints. The visit to the drunken priest takes its place along side the visit to the well as an occasion that reinvigorates the cthonic field. So too the stories, the particular power and secrecy of which remind us that narration — from the local point of view — may be self-consciously understood as, in and of itself, a substantial, literally creative and transforming act. Stories produce the world they describe.

Efficacious speech — combined with control of the body — appears again in the mission. The Redemptorists performed religion as a renarration of life history. This sort of retelling of one's biography is perhaps always a central feature of what we call conversion. The new crisis recasts the plot. Once again, the context of the occasion is critical to its affect on the interpretive community: the audience. This is especially so now that the mission is regular: an expected biannual event. Is the mission encountered mainly as yet another, though particularly intensive, Church-centered devotional activity? Or is it part of a quest for therapy, along with visits to wells, drunken priests, and even prayer groups? Ironically, the power of the occasion and its efficacy in performing institutional goals may finally depend on the space it leaves for a range of interpretations.

The quest for a cure has, of course, always been a prime individual motivator—propelling the seeker from one occasion to another. This is understood by religious regimes, which generally seek to harness that motivation, appropriate the power of the cure or the expectation of a cure, in the service of their own institutional goals. Organized pilgrimage—whether to wells, graves, relics, or apparitions—has always tapped this current. The individual quest for a cure can also turn into a more general quest for therapy, for a reconstructed self. Such a self is, however, discovered and created in the company of others. The social world of the pilgrims—and even more dramatically the prayer group—is a necessary part of the therapeutic conversion experience. At the same time it is the result of that process. The prayer group is an interpretive community that trains the individual—through both bodily and verbal release—to reform herself, and the prayer group as a social entity is the consequence of that reformation process. Moreover, that sort of community of affliction, as strange as it may seem, is not altogether new to the scene. The practice of women within "religion" has long had this possibility. The social aspect of a woman's bus trip to Knock, Lourdes, or the Healing Mass is not evidence of the occasion's lack of religious intent. Rather it is a crucial aspect of the religious experience; it is another example of the formation of social worlds through religious action. But those worlds, if they remain in motion, are transient by definition. They come to rest in occasions like the prayer meeting. What larger world, however, does the prayer meeting fit into? What greater social system sustains the community where women come not just for cures but to write their own texts? Angus, Michael, and John—I noticed—often read from the Bible during the meetings. Margaret read from her notebook— her own thoughts and the received words of Christ, the testament according to Margaret.

The other core members of the prayer group, as we saw, were drawn back into the institutional structure of the Church through special lay devotional occasions like Cursillo. This use of lay organizations to capture the special charisma, enthusiasm, or psychodynamic of novel religious experience has been an important strategy since the Blue Army marched from Fatima. But in other respects, movements like Cursillo are part of an older dialectic in which new devotional forms, from the rosary to the missions to apparitions, are either introduced or promoted (having originated as folk events) by the religious orders. The secular, diocesan clergy — depending on their strength — either attack or institutionalize and routinize the charisma, making what was special an ordinary and repetitive feature of mundane religious life.

The religious dynamic explored here, while having a particular local configuration, is also present — indeed crucially important — on the national level as well. In Ireland, as a whole, the importance of lay Catholic groups in the political arena has increased as the legitimacy of direct political action by the clergy has diminished (though by no means vanished). Opus Dei, another organization of Spanish origin, is reputedly very important in Ireland, as it draws on its membership from the upper classes of society. More visible in the public arena is the group Family Solidarity, which has been at the center of the anti-abortion and anti-divorce campaigns. Even though these groups are acting in the political arena, they have by no means abandoned their specifically religious dimension. Opus Dei now has their saint, Escriva, as well as their daily Mass and other devotional requirements. In fact, their strong concentration on self-discipline and the achievement of a completely Catholic life, along with the structure of their organization — which includes a direct representative to the Vatican — is reminiscent of a religious order like the Jesuits. Among the various lay Catholic lobbying groups the increasing use of Marian imagery is striking. In particular, the Catholic wing of the worldwide Right to Life movement has appropriated the image of Our Lady of Guadeloupe, the Mexican Madonna whose pilgrimage draws over twelve million a year. The Irish women and men who carry her image into the streets, the "protectress of the unborn" as they now fashion her, seem unaware of her life in Latin America.

These religious movements on the social front, whether favored or opposed, have succeeded in defining the discourse of the conflict. As the Irish wrestle with their relationship to the new Europe, the national identity is very much at issue. While Ireland was imagined as a community — to use Benedict Anderson's apt phrase — in and through a religious idiom, the question is whether a new Ireland will do that again. *Na gaill*, the foreigners, are once again implicated in self-definition by opposition. The Irish are still on the periphery, but most seek further integration into the European Community. Will that mean an end of a distinctive Irishness?

Those who seek to define Ireland over against that Europe often find the Church an essential element in the opposition. New narratives are being composed that use a religious idiom to define Ireland and Irishness, and in the process, by virtue of the events chosen and meanings imputed, these same narratives define Catholicism. In the short space of one year, 1992, the entire nation was caught up in a series of moral crises that may not have enjoyed such a self-defining capacity in any other land. First there was the "X" case. A fourteen-year-old girl was allegedly (the charge was later substantiated) raped by her friend's father and taken by her parents to England for an abortion. In Ireland, abortion is not only illegal in nearly all cases but, as of 1983, unconstitutional. At the same time, an estimated four to five thousand Irish women seek abortions in England every year. The girl's plight was brought to the attention of police by the parents — she was a rape victim — and then reported to the attorney general, who felt duty bound to act on the illegal quest for abortion, which had not yet been performed. The parents were told to bring their child back to Ireland and, to everyone's amazement, they did. Had the order been ignored, most observers feel, the punishment would have been slight at most. But the parents' compliance generated a huge national crisis, played out in letter columns, phone calls, speeches, radio, and television talk shows. The case was given the fastest hearing possible by the Irish supreme court, who, in the end, interpreted the constitutional ban's clause allowing abortion when the life of the mother was at stake to cover the case in question, since the girl had spoken of suicide. That decision, which satisfied few on either end of the abortion question, generated continuing debate. The national contention over this case was not only about the morality of abortion and the definition of life and death — as it would be in the United States — but also about the definition of Ireland. The nation was seen, by both left and right, to be moving into the modern, secular world in a general cultural sense, and in a specific political sense in terms of the European Community. Throughout the X case, "Europe" was evoked by both sides — either as a model of "Enlightenment" to which Ireland should aspire, and in the face of which should be ashamed by her backwardness, or as the latest embodiment of soulless secularism; a megastate that will in the end never really tolerate the persistence of a distinctive moral, national entity on its periphery. The European Community was but the latest Empire ready to swallow up Ireland as a nation. Thus did the

X crisis define the national debate on the Maastricht Referendum, a few months later, in which the people were called upon to ratify the new European treaty that moved its member states closer to political and fiscal unity.

In the end, the vote went heavily for Maastricht, the hope of millions in economic aid evidently overriding fears of moral pollution or destruction of identity for two thirds of the voters. Then, a few months later, it was revealed that the very popular and active bishop of Galway, Eamonn Casey, was the father of a seventeen-year-old boy by an American mother (his distant cousin) and that he had misappropriated diocesan funds to pay for the child's education in a manner that some might call blackmail. Once again the nation was riven, and printed page and airwaves were filled with recrimination and approbation: was the event evidence of the ultimately corrupt and hypocritical nature of the Church, or the simple human fallibility of a great bishop led astray by the "American bitch," as she was figured by many?

Each case linked the definition of Ireland as a political, cultural, and moral entity to the position of the Catholic Church and religion as praxis. If the Church was thus seen to be protecting the boundaries of Ireland, or circumscribing them, then so too were they engaged with the circumscription of the woman's body, from within and without. The X case was linked directly to Maastricht by the fact that the girl not only sought an abortion but moved freely from one part of Europe to another. The control of women's bodies is, again, a familiar issue to Americans, but what is different in this case is its role in nationalist discourse: the borders of the woman were the borders of Ireland.

In the Irish context each of these events could be understood and narrated as occasions of faith, and opportunities to define Catholicism and Irishness in terms of one another. But the resulting stories choose from among possible Catholicisms and possible Irelands.

Notes

Preface

1. In that regard, it is interesting to note that in the Irish language the relevant local term is not *religiun*, which is rarely used, but rather *creidimh*, "belief."

Chapter One

2. The "rosary," here as everywhere in the Catholic world, refers to both a series of prayers and a string of beads with a crucifix on it with which one counts off the prayers. The rosary is divided into fifteen decades, representing three sets of five "mysteries" — events in the life of Mary. Each decade begins with an "Our Father" prayer followed by ten "Hail Marys" and finishing with a "Gloria Patri." Introduced by the Carmelite order in the thirteenth century, the rosary — as artifact and personal liturgy — is at the very core of Marian devotion. These matters are more fully discussed in subsequent chapters.

3. Such misapprehension arises from the standard interaction of tourist and local, here and elsewhere in the world. The tourist comments on the beauty of a scene, and the local counters with a bitter observation about the difficulties represented by such "scenery" to farmer or herder. Perhaps the "othering" goes both ways. The local retort may have more to do with asserting a relationship to the land and a distance from the — sometimes resented — outsider than a lack of aesthetic appreciation. Not that this local aesthetic has been unaffected by external perceptions and categories, but perhaps the simplest way to put it is that the local necessarily has a great many ways of relating to the land and landscape, while the visitor generally has only one or two, his or her categories varying over the years from "howling wilderness" to "improvable waste" to "sublime and picturesque landscape."

4. There is a long and controversial history of the application of the concept "stem family" in Ireland. See Taylor (1980a) and especially Gibbon and Curtin (1978).

5. A very thorough study of the Irish experience in Butte, Montana can be found in Emmons (1989).

6. There is an extensive historical geography literature on the *clachan* as a unit of settlement; see in particular Evans (1939, 1942, 1964) and Buchanan (1970).

7. The historical and contemporary character of the salmon fishery in Teelin is the subject of several articles (Taylor 1980a, 1981, 1987).

8. There are many references in Celtic Irish literature to the custom of fostering, wherein a chiefly family would have a son raised by another family of similar rank, thus forming an alliance perhaps even more important than that through marriage.

9. At that time only men went in. One night I remember a woman, an immigrant returned for a short visit, came to the bar to see friends and relations. She stood in the doorway for a half-hour or so, never stepping into the room. Instead, one or two men at a time would walk over to her for a short chat and then return to the bar.

10. Arensberg (1959: 125–45) had described this sort of gathering almost fifty years earlier in Clare, but I was soon to hear another anthropologist who had worked in this part of Donegal tell a professional audience that such gatherings were long since gone.

11. Although the parish is certainly a meaningful unit in certain contexts — like football matches and general identity — the everyday social picture is more complicated. The presence of another "village" with its own church, pubs, and shops on the other side of the parish created another social center. Furthermore, Carrick's location on the eastern edge of the parish also meant that its church, pubs, and shops drew as well from the western section of the parish of Kilcar.

12. In Teelin, and other coastal settlements, fishing — so important in the generation of communal ties — was also the linchpin for colonialism and the entry of the region into a world market economy. In the 1770s, the famous agronomist and traveler, Arthur Young (1892) got as far west along the coast as Killybegs, where he noted a flourishing herring trade. The landlord had financed a large vessel, which sat in Killybegs harbor, receiving, salting, and barreling the catch of the small fleets of a number of coastal communities — Teelin, with its relatively good harbor, being the most prominent among them. The merchant ships took the local catch to the growing market in the Caribbean, and the coastal people of southwest Donegal were now part of the world economy. But they were on the periphery of this trade, and the cottage industry of fishing resisted the next stage of industrialization. Fishermen remained peasant-fishermen, and when the international herring trade collapsed, locals continued to fish on a small scale, selling their product locally (see Taylor 1980a, 1980b).

These fish-traders, sailors, and carters, were the source of a local Catholic merchant class, whose development was very much aided by landlords like Thomas Connolly, who, from the late 1820s through the early 1840s, thoroughly transformed the local cultural landscape and social structure. The first decent road was brought through the parish of Glencolumcille, and the village of Carrick was created. Connolly offered "free" (meaning no entry fee) tenancies for established merchants. In the same period, as we shall read in the following chapters, other profound changes were introduced at the instigation of government agencies.

13. Conrad Arensberg and Solon Kimball (1968) have very little to say on the subject, an omission that could only be intentional at a time when the institutional Church was at the absolute apogee of its political power as well as cultural authority. More recent ethnographic accounts, when they do take up the subject (as in Messenger 1969 and Scheper-Hughes 1979) deal only with psychological and particularly sexual repression.

14. The indispensable guide through the thicket of Church political history, with particular attention to the powerful impact of Paul Cardinal Cullen, is Emmet Larkin's (see 1980) series of monographs. Of more theoretical interest is the same author's seminal article (1972) on the "devotional revolution" that changed the face of Irish Catholicism. Certainly the most thorough and insightful social historical account is Sean Connolly's (1982) of pre-famine rural Catholicism. Most sociologists of Catholicism have been concerned with quantitative measures, such as frequency of Mass attendance, but a few have attempted to bring sociological theory to bear on the historical terrain. The most theoretically ambitious of these is Tom Inglis (1987), whose application of Foucault and Elias in some way parallels the present study.

15. The anthropological study of European Catholicism has much developed over the past twenty years, following the general turns in anthropological theory and foci. Joyce Reigelhaupt's (1973) call for attention to local religious forms in Europe has certainly been answered. Indeed it had already begun with William Christian's (1972) look at local religion in Spain, which presented a very detailed account of the nature of local communal practice and the way it is understood. Most of the analyses of this period focused on the "community," and interpreted religious practice in terms of its functional role in maintaining or reproducing that world. In explaining how it was that religion performed this role, anthropologists naturally turned to the tradition of symbolic analysis rooted in the Année Sociologique and flowering in the works of Mary Douglas and especially Victor Turner. This approach threw much light on the differences between "folk" or "popular" and "orthodox" religion and the contest between them (see Badone 1990), but has much further to go in exploring the actual interaction among these forms.

16. In fact Geertz's analyses are far more complex and assume a far more contingent notion of culture than the famous metaphor suggests.

17. See Taylor (1990b).

18. See especially Chartier (1987). I was unaware of Chartier's writing on this theme when I developed the notion of "fields of religious experience."

Chapter Two

19. The word "station," in Irish *statiun*, is used in at least three related contexts — stations of the cross, the stations of a turas, and a Mass held by the priest in the home of a parishioner.

20. See Harbison (1991) and Price (1941).

21. See Lochlann McGill (1992).

22. See Harbison (1991: 33ff.).

23. This story is reminiscent of Bede's account of Saint Augustine among the heathen Saxons. It seems far more likely that the well renarrated above was venerated by the pagans for curing rather than causing disease.

24. And more so from the continental perspective: the Augustinians successfully promoted the notion of a penitential pilgrimage for the author of great sins. The account of Sir Henry of Saltrey was popular all over Europe. Few could make

such a journey, but the narrative probably did serve to promote a notion of the heroic wanderer who by moving west across the landscape arrives in the Other World.

25. Even in other Irish pilgrimage sites, where the built environment played a role, there is a difference from the continent. Early Christian and medieval Irish iconography is starkly powerful, but one wonders whether pictorial representation was as central in the construction and direction of experience as, for example, in France during the same period, where the Cluniac regime spread from the ninth century on through establishing the famous pilgrim's route to Santiago de Compostello in northern Spain. Along that route the pilgrim's experience was shaped through a series of encounters with the awesome severity of large scale Romanesque architecture — such as the basilica at Vézelay: on whose massive tympanum a gigantic Christ presided over a Last Judgment, and dozens of fiends and demons yanked souls on every column's capital. While there are much smaller and more restrained Irish versions of this — such as the frieze on the Church at Ardmore in Waterford for example, in Ireland the natural properties of the site — the charismatic landscape — seem to survive, retaining a stronger rôle in shaping the pilgrim's experience of the power of the place.

Cluny illustrates Weber's argument concerning the transition from magical-curing to ethical domination, and supports Ariès concerning the last judgment and Le Goff on purgatory. The shaping of mentalité in this formation is based on both architecture and the discipline of the body. Cluny's second baptism is a rite of passage — emphasizing a certain kind of liminality here — the kind that leads to rebirth or conversion, a major aim of the directors of pilgrimage from then on. The connection to the Christ cult, which would appeal to Freud, is a final link in the chain of psychological/religious/political domination. The physical reality of sin is retrospectively experienced in the travails of pilgrimage. This is perhaps the clearest case of how a regime can be consciously constructed by an order, who use pilgrimage, architecture, devotions, and doctrines to create a field of religious experience.

26. The Observantine Reform and the development of the Third Order Regular Franciscans proved very successful in Ireland, particularly in Connaught and west Ulster.

27. See *Annals of the Four Masters*.

28. Also see Hyde, *The Songs of Connacht*.

29. John Bossy (1985) has pointed out that this kin-based notion of sin and penance was probably prevalent at the time all over Europe. Ireland, particularly such strongly Gaelic zones as west Donegal, may have been particularly strong in this regard, however. First of all, corporate kin groups — clans and lineages — were still the important social components of the entire social system, and second, the relations and ethos of these kin groups also characterized the elite.

30. These matters are most extensively treated in Connolly 1982.

31. It is interesting to note the Sunday use of these stations, evidently in lieu of Mass.

32. There is an extensive literature on this settlement and landholding form, see Chapter 1, note 2.

33. The "Outrage Papers" contain crime reports for the period, and while faction fights seem to have been typical in the north, and to some extent to the east of southwest Donegal, the region itself is not much represented. This might of course be a function of reportage—the absence of police in the area—but both Ewing and O'Donovan, who traveled through the entire region taking notes—make a point of observing the quiescence of the region.

34. Oddly mistranslated as "The Hard Road to the Klondike."

35. Schneider's account of European peasant animism as fundamentally concerned with reciprocity—"equity consciousness"—accords well with many strains of local Irish faith. Of the three critical areas she outlines as subject to reformers—the earth spirits, spirits of the dead, and manifestations of resentment and evil among the living—two are clearly important in Ireland, where they were still on reformers' agenda even in the twentieth century. Witchcraft was not so much a concern—possibly because of the lack of political potential for local witchcraft beliefs in the relevant centuries. In what I have called a "cthonic" field of religious experience attitudes toward the human and natural environment continue to be characterized by strongly marked themes of reciprocity. I would agree with Schneider that, first of all, contra (to a degree) Weber, "magic" does involve a critical ethical dimension (as Evans-Pritchard 1936 showed in his study of the Azande) and that the characterization of magic as manipulative versus ethical religion is to some extent simply reformist propoganda (not unlike that used by Protestants to characterize Catholics). It is also clear that, as Schneider argues, reformists sought to displace this ethic with another, more abstract and inclusive. But whether this was the essential ethical shift that favored capitalism—or that it even worked—is another matter. The changes promoted by various Church regimes clearly favored their own success and domination. The more traditional reading of the churches' efforts vis-à-vis the peasantry is the attack on community in favor of individualism—a project also clearly in the interest of capitalism.

My own view of the local or cthonic field of religious experience is that it is clearly concerned with both—the boundaries of community and reciprocity or equity consciousness. Moreover, I would argue that the physical geography is clearly critical to both notions. The corporate link of a particular group to a particular territory or piece of land with boundaries as well as a center clearly plays a crucial role in defining relations with spirits and the like. This is perhaps particularly obvious in Ireland, where the earth itself is less disenchanted than elsewhere in Europe.

36. Philip Dixon Hardy (1836), a virulent enemy of well devotions, describes the still wild "secular" activities surrounding such pilgrimages as that up Croagh Patrick. For a good beginning guide to the literature on holy wells see Patrick Logan (1980).

37. See Inglis (1987) for a thorough exploration of the applicability of Elias's notion of civilizing process to the subject at hand.

38. Énri Ó Muirgheasa reports Vigils in a 1936 article, "The Holy Wells of Donegal."

39. This observation is Harbison's, whose discussion of the turas (1991: 105–110) is well worth reading. An earlier descriptive archaeological treatment can be found in Price (1941).

40. There was a major moving statue apparition at Ballinspittle, Cork in 1985. The statue in question was in a Lourdes grotto outside the village.

Chapter Three

41. McGinley is in fact mentioned in a few local historical sources, including P.J. MacGill's *Ardara* (1974) and the especially detailed account of Pat Conaghan (1989).

42. The biology text was published by Collins in London "one of a series of about forty published to help educate the masses, all the rest originated from famous seats of learning, McGinley's from Croagh, one of the very few places which the Carrick people would regard as the back of beyond" (personal communication from Dr. Conal Cunningham).

43. Mary Daly (1979: 152) warns that the commissioners paid scant attention to the so-called hedge schools in their reports, so there may have been yet more informal paid education going on that went unreported in these inquiries.

44. One of these was in the townland of Strade, close by what is now the village of Glencolmcille, where a Protestant schoolmaster named William Buchanan ran a free school on a salary of £27 and an acre of ground. The school, valued at £60, was of stone and lime construction and attracted something between fifty-four and seventy-eight students, depending on whether one believes the Protestant or Roman Catholic return. For this school, like the far more modest one in Malinmore (where George Woods taught in a small thatched cabin for an annual salary just under £5) was "mixed." According to the Protestant return, the school at Strade offered instruction to twenty-six Protestants (all of the Established Church) and fifty-two Catholics (56 male, 22 female), and the Malin More school taught twenty-three Protestants and thirty-nine Catholics (33 male, 29 female). In the third school, however, located among the more culturally and religiously uniform people of Teelin, Andrew Heagerty, a Roman Catholic, was schoolmaster to fifty-five Roman Catholics (38 male, 17 female) in a rented cabin; his salary was £6 a year. The Strade school was the "parish school," supported by parish funds and presumably under the ultimate control of the Protestant minister in Glencolmcille, whose new church, we remember, was built in 1828.

45. The issue was a huge and devisive one, with the Catholic bishops taking strong stances for and against. The bishop of Raphoe was for, following the archbishop of Dublin in that line, while the famous Archbishop McHale of Tuam led the opposition. See Larkin (1980) for a full discussion of the issue.

46. See Katherine Grier's (1988) perceptive account of the relation of such decor and accoutrements to a class mentalité.

47. In other versions, which come from the Kilcar and Teelin side of Slieve League, the chapel built is the one located just east of the present site of Carrick. O hEochaidh notes — after his recording of the version I've given here — that, while the structure to the east of Carrick is likely an eighteenth-century structure, the one near Glen — Faranmacbride — is clearly a far earlier church. It is interesting that of the two local versions, McGinley gives the western one, with the chapel at Glen,

rather than the eastern one. This choice seems to lend credence to the view that McGinley came originally from Meanacross, rather than Killybegs. Certainly his most detailed stories come from the west as well.

48. I'm indebted to Tadhg Foley, of the University College Galway, for identifying the source of these verses for me and to both him and Sean Ryder, also of UCG, for many helpful discussions on the use of these poems by McGinley.

49. Harbison (1991) argues, I think persuasively, that round towers were more likely built to be emblematic guides to pilgrimage centers, for which they would have functioned better than as defenses against Vikings. There is, however, no doubt that the fact they have long been believed to have served that defensive function makes them an impressive and very evocative symbol of Church resistance.

50. Published by John Ward (Seaghain Mac a' Bhaird) and Company in Killybegs, in 1909. My view of these people and events owes much to conversations with Nolaig McGonagle of University College Galway.

Chapter Four

51. Though not the statistical norm according to current historical research (Niall Ó Cíosain, personal communication).

52. These documents are located in the Public Record Office of Northern Ireland, Belfast.

53. The 1871 landowners' list for Donegal shows Thomas Young Brooke of Lough Eske with over 15,000 thousand acres.

54. Charles McGlinchey (1985), for example, writing of life in Inishowen, Donegal, tells us that his father — circa the 1840s — owned a copy of the sermons and could recite several from memory.

55. These disputes could be violent. In 1783 Bishop Coyle reported that "the opposition of the Franciscans to him was nothing new. . . . As far back as twelve years ago he had been appointed by Bishop O'Reilly to induct a priest into a parish which had been taken over furtively by a Franciscan, but was prevented from doing so by two relations of the friar, who, armed with a gun, tried to kill him at a short distance from the altar. The Franciscans had no fixed house in the diocese of Raphoe; they had only two priests there, one of whom was in charge of a parish and the other ministered in another diocese" (Giblin 1980: 37-38).

56. For a structurally comparable case, consider the conflict between regular and secular clergy — also involving Franciscans — in Yugoslavia, culminating in the apparition at Medjugorje. Bax (1987b) discusses this case at length.

57. An early indication of the cooperation between state and Catholic Church in the civilizing offensive; see Inglis (1987).

58. Given those two doctrines — along with the authority of Rome — were precisely those that most distinguished Catholics from Church of Ireland Protestants, one wonders whether they were mainly intended to counter proselytizing.

59. The number of parochial clergymen and their ratio to Catholic population in 1800-1901 is shown in the table:

Catholic Clergy in the Diocese of Raphoe, 1800–1901

Year	Bishops	Parish priests	Curates	Total clergy	Number of Catholic for each parochial clergyman
1800	26	986	628	1,614	2,676
1835	27	993	1,166	2,159	2,991
1845	28	1,008	1,385	2,393	2,773
1851	29	1,014	1,354	2,368	2,214
1861	33	1,036	1,491	2,527	1,783
1871	32	1,080	1,733	2,813	1,476
1881	27	996	1,745	2,741	1,445
1891	32	1,015	1,821	2,836	1,251
1901	29	1,022	1,916	2,938	1,126

Source: Hoppen (1984: 171).

60. The diocesan correspondence sheds some small light on events in th period, particularly on the controversies and processes that were part of the experi ence of the region through those decades of the nineteenth century. More than tha however, the correspondence, and published works such as the *Catholic Director* are both the product and cause of a self-consciousness, of a regime whose member communicate with one another and begin to share—to some degree at least— mentalité and an agenda.

61. Cullen became archbishop of Ireland in 1850, and was later raised t cardinal. For an exhaustive account of his life and contribution to devotional chang and religious politics in Ireland see the work of Emmet Larkin (1980).

62. See Inglis (1987) for an extensive discussion of the role of priests in wha Norbert Elias called the "civilizing process." Control of the body—discipline— central to Elias' thesis, and it was certainly a concern of the Church.

63. It is interesting to note that Drummond—who worked well with th landlord and concentrated his efforts in education and the promotion of devotio was rewarded for his efforts far more than Magroarty, becoming parish priest of th much more important parish of Killybegs at the age of thirty-one.

64. Peter MacDevitt was not, so far as I can determine, a relation of Bisho James MacDevitt.

65. For example, there is a letter from Donegal Town to that effect.

66. Actually, the repairs included dividing what had been a "business house up into "boxes" (in the words of the former tenant, Patrick Gallagher) so th Magroarty could have two sub-tenants, who were evicted along with him.

67. The letter is signed by Neil Byrne, Biddy Doogan, Mary McCunnegai Phelim Doherty, Patrick O'Donnell, John McMonigle, and with Xes for Dani McCunnegan, John McCunnegan, John Byrne, Mary McBrearty.

The table shows the annual rent and landholdings of the signatees as of th Musgrave rent roll of 1868 (presumably showing Conolly's rents). Since the tow land of Upper Carrick (see Figure 10) comprised not only agricultural holdings b the shops of the village, some of the small quantities of land may reflect lots on which shops sat — for the nominal rent of 1 s. per year (see Chapter Three).

Annual Rent and Landholdings, 1868

Tenant	Yearly rent			Quantity of land		
	L	s	d	A	R	P
				(acres, roods, perches)		
Neil Byrne		1				27
Biddy Doogan	2	3	0			31
Mary McCunnegan	2	4	0	45	2	38
Phelim Doherty	3	1	0	15	0	18
Patrick O'Donnell	(listed with commonage rights only)					
Daniel McCunnegan	2	12		6	3	24
John McCunnegan	3	18		14	2	4
John McMonigle (Eleanor McM)	1	15		7	1	22
John Byrne	1	15	0	6	2	6
Mary McBrearty (Cornelius McB)	1	15	0	6	2	6

Source: Musgrave Estate Papers, Rent Roll 1868; Public Records Office, Belfast, Northern Ireland.

68. Though a schoolteacher, Máire Ni' Cunnegean was at the very local end of the spectrum — not the Thomas McGinley type we met in the last chapter. In fact she was as fascinated with my tape recorder as anyone who'd never seen one before might be.

69. There were two celebrated cases, one concerning a priest's defense of the tenantry at Glenveigh (see Vaughan 1983) and another concerning a priest's involvement in the murder of Lord Leitrim.

70. This is the same Peter MacDevitt who fought with Magroarty when they were curates in neighboring parishes.

71. In Irish, "tharraing se an ribín agus chuir sé thar a mhuineal é, agus tharraing sé amach a leabhar agus thosaigh sé a leitheoireacht."

72. The power of the priest is also associated — as it is in popular speech — with the "cloth" he wears. The metonym is taken seriously, as revealed in folk stories that tell of fairies gaining power or destroying a priest by snipping off a piece of his cassock. These stories reveal the appropriating capacity of the discourse, because such costumes only appeared in the nineteenth century, before which time priests wore the dress of the rural middle class.

73. The *Irish Catholic Directory* was an annual publication widely distributed through Ireland. In addition to presenting a compilation of data, such as the clerical composition of each diocese, each issue contained a day by day account of significant Catholic events for the year. While in some cases this amounted to a mere list, certain events merited actual narratives, particularly in the cases discussed here. Also included were the full texts of encyclicals and, most significantly for Ireland, the often lengthy and sometimes very political pastorals of the bishops and cardinals,

particularly the very powerful primate of Ireland, Cardinal Cullen (for a detailed account of whom, see the works of Emmet Larkin).

74. According to sociologist Samuel Clark (1979: 356), Irish political movements of the second half of the nineteenth century must be seen in the context of a general social transformation from communalism to associationalism. The evidence presented here suggests that such a shift did not mean the dissolution of local communities, but rather their redefinition at the hands of, and in response to, increasingly intrusive external social forces. The rural parish or great estate became an increasingly complex social field within whose bounds relations of class played as important a role as those of kin and territory.

75. This argument of Pêcheux is developed and analyzed in MacDonell (1986).

76. Cooperatives had by this time an honorable history in Donegal—the most famous case being that of Paddy the Cope Gallagher (whose descendant is still known by that sobriquet, and represents The Rosses region of Donegal in the national assembly (Dáil Éireann). See Patrick Gallagher (1979).

77. A report on these enterprises was issued by a group from the department of geography at Maynooth. For a thorough anthropological assessment of Father McDyer's activities in this arena, see Tucker (1984 and 1989).

78. The few non-Catholic students in attendance are allowed to miss these sessions.

Chapter Five

79. This story is one of twenty three "priest stories" collected in one notebook by folklorist Sean O hEochaidh from his natal community of Teelin in Donegal, Ireland. The notebook containing these Gaelic tales is dated 1945, but there are also dozens of other priest stories scattered through the more than seventy volumes of oral lore recorded by O hEochaidh in his nearly half-century (beginning in the early 1930s) of folklore collecting in the area.

Chapter Six

80. The ritual of the Stations (or Way) of the Cross has a fascinating and instructive history. The ritual is derived from pilgrimages to the Holy Land, in which the pilgrim literally followed the path of Christ on the way to Calvary. Although the first commemorative "stations" were erected at the church of San Stefano in Bologna in the fifth century, the idea of a whole series of shrines commemorating the events of the Passion did not become generally realized until the fifteenth century. The Franciscans in particular, who took over custody of "the holy places" in Palestine in 1342, promoted devotions to those places and to their own symbolic representations of the Way of the Cross throughout Europe. After the mid-eighteenth century, stations of the cross became the common feature of many parish churches and they remain so today. The history of the ritual thus presents an

interesting case study in its own right. The Passion is ritualized first at the actual locus of the events, and the pilgrim gains indulgences by empathetically following Christ's literal steps. Then the Franciscans, who "own" this powerful ritual place, recreate it at one symbolic remove in their own monasteries and churches, and at first only Franciscans themselves can gain the indulgences. Later, pilgrims seek out the icons rather than the original site. Eventually the stations arrive in every Catholic church, and the ritual becomes a commonplace event for every parishioner, for whom the powerful empathetic experience of the pilgrim may have become rather attenuated (cf. "Way of the Cross," in *The New Catholic Encyclopedia*, pp. 832–35).

81. In this contribution to the changes summarized in the phrase, "devotional revolution," the Redemptorists were following in the path of the few other mission orders who had preceded them in Ireland, such as the Jesuits, Vincentians, and Rosminians. The Rosminian Gentili, for example, brought the Forty Hours and the Devotions of May 29 to Dublin in 1849 (O'Donnell 1981).

82. It is also worth noting that if the form of the mission was novel in places like nineteenth-century Donegal, the "master sermon" was not. Charles McGlinchy (1985) of the then Irish speaking Inishowen peninsula in the north of the county, remembered his father (b. 1810) reciting from the sermons of Father Gallagher. These eighteenth-century Irish language sermons by a noted bishop of Raphoe (Donegal's diocese) were apparently available in printed editions through the ensuing century and well known to the literate peasantry of that diocese. The Redemptorist—whether they knew it or not—were following in that tradition, for unlike several local priests, they missionized in Irish, not in English, and were probably more powerfully heard as a result.

83. Elsewhere in Europe more attention has been paid to the Redemptorists and their missions, but the impact may have varied with local conditions. See, for example, Eugen Weber (1976: 365–67) and P. J. Hélias (1978) for some views of the French nineteenth and early twentieth century experiences. Christian (1972: 93–99) includes a helpful discussion of the history and role of the Spanish missions in what remains the most penetrating anthropological study of contemporary European Catholicism.

84. The National Folklore Archives contain a marvelously rich and still underused resource for the study of local religious belief, behavior, and discourse. Although only a few stories are catalogued under the specific heading of "missions," my evaluation of the general religious discourse on this and related topics is based on my own fieldwork and the more than one hundred and fifty stories I have so far read of the vast number collected from the area by folklorist Sean O hEochaidh since the 1930s.

85. The document this conference produced, which still stood as the model for missions in the 1980s, does not recommend the elimination of devotional symbolics, or even the basic sermon series that is the centerpiece of the mission. However, attention is paid to both altering significantly the nature of discourse and supplementing the formal interactions of sermons and teaching with the structured informality of other kinds of group interaction. The following passage would be as familiar to upwardly mobile, self-seeking Americans as it would be strange to survivors of any "poitín mission."

Let us just take one aspect of our world. We live in a very personalistic world. The person is sacred. We stress the inviolability of the person, his or her rights, preferences, uniqueness, dreams. . . . The stress on the individual can be a very revolutionary thing. . . . In the past the preacher was in the pulpit, the people in the pews. . . . They were passive. . . . Now today the people want to speak, express themselves, be themselves.

In the house meeting they speak, they express themselves, they teach. . . . It is an exercise of a personalistic age. . . . In the past you had the "powerful" sermon. The missioner had a thunderous voice. He thumped the pulpit. He laid it on the line. . . . The crowd ... was being dominated. . . . [People] want to be talked to, treated maturely as persons, approached with respect, quietly. (Donlon 1971: 43–45)

This amounts to a prescription for a radical shift in mission discourse and performance. The very "personalism" that might be, and certainly was, condemned by the Church as fundamentally unethical is here celebrated as an awakening. The language of psychologism is adopted as mission rhetoric, in which salvation is barely distingushable from self-actualization. Confession is still the central sacramental act, but the ideal format described is egalitarian and therapeutic — in the modern sense of the term. The new term is "the sacrament of reconciliation." One is reminded of psychological counseling sessions. This shift is presented as an accommodation to a changing social world; the old style fit older circumstances as the new one will fit today's. It is more than that, however, for the recommended change of discourse and performance represents a shift in the relation of the mission, as a special event, to the ordinary life-world of the congregation. The power of the mission was a function of its extraordinary character, of a language and performance that condemned and challenged. The rite of passage sought required a "ritual death" (Van Gennep 1960) which forcibly separated the participant from his or her former life. The "new mission" eschews the dynamics of opposition and seeks, instead, to present its demands as merely the most effective version of "the good" as it is defined in contemporary western secular discourse; it is the best therapy in town.

86. The various forms the Irish mission takes today show that self-conscious symbolic politics is still (or again, particularly since Vatican II) an important consideration. It is in this light that the "new mission" described in the 1971 conference manual should be understood. Like so much promulgated by the Church in those times, the "new mission" represented a reaction to a perceived crisis. The Redemptorists who compiled the manual evidently felt the need to adopt a new discourse and style suitable for a new society. As pointed out, the Church in general had been (and still is) seeking a new language more appropriate to the times. Or, perhaps, languages. As is especially evident at such critical historic junctures, the Church is not monolithic, and various segments within it have always competed for both political power and cultural authority. Discourse plays a vital role in this competition, and where the prevailing language has broken down an opportunity exists for groups within the Church to propose new ones through which the people may interpret changing experience. As in similarly volatile times centuries ago, such religious orders as the Jesuits and Redemptorists have again played a key role in

disseminating novel forms — in the present case, therapeutic rather than baroque. They may have a stake in disturbing the diocesan status quo, and they do have the time and the places to introduce people to new ways of being religious.

Even within the Irish Redemptorist order, the various houses in different parts of the country seem to have adopted different discourses and symbolic strategies adaptive to their respective niches. In areas like suburban Dublin, there is a relative weakness in diocesan clerical domination and, perhaps, a decline in the power of traditional religious discourse in the face of a social and cultural life increasingly disconnected from it. The parish, which remains the organizational unit of the diocesan structure, does not necessarily correspond to any actual social world. Such conditions make the adoption of a therapeutic idiom and attendant interactional forms (all typically imported from America by members of various orders visiting Ireland) a sensible strategy, not only for revitalizing the religious life of the people, but for augmenting the power of the orders who control these occasions. Interestingly, the Redemptorists in the small, conservative city of Limerick are continuing to draw tens of thousands to their nineteenth-century style "Forty Hours Devotion" every June. In Belfast, the Redemptorists have found another niche altogether, situated as they are in the heart of Catholic West Belfast where they have played a variety of mediatory rôles in the conflict there. Finally, we have the Redemptorists in such regions as southwest Donegal, where the parish continues to correspond to a real social unit still clearly dominated by the diocesan clergy. Here there is less opportunity or need for novel discourse; here an American style personalistic therapeutic language would find little reinforcement in other settings.

That is not to say the Donegal mission has not changed at all. As noted, the people certainly perceive a general softening, and the mission does seem far less concerned to criticize the character of local life than in former days. Rather, the emphasis is more on preserving that way of life in the face of the threatening forces of the modern world. Withall, however, the mission remains a piece of religious theater whose message of power is conveyed as much in the structure of the event as in the content of the sermons. Nor, it must be observed, do such religious occasions seem hopelessly out of step in a Catholic Church whose papacy has itself become something of a perpetual mission.

87. This inversion of order does seem more "modern," in the sense of presenting salvation as more than the absence of sin, rather like defining health as more than the absence of illness.

Chapter Seven

88. Knock is currently the subject of an intensive historical and sociological study being carried out by James Donnelly and Eugene Hynes, a paper by Donnelly speaks directly to the issue of the genesis and use of the apparition and pilgrimage in "regime building."

89. The distinction between speaking and silent apparitions is used by sociologist Michael Carroll (1986) to distinguish between "illusion" apparitions — that is, atmospheric phenomena that are witnessed by many individuals but do not involve

any mental aberrancy on the part of the witness and hence don't speak — and "hallu-cination" apparitions in which the experience of apparition is conjured up by one or a few "seers" and hence can go on to communicate.

90. James Donnelly (1992) explores this political context for the development of the Knock pilgrimage in a way consonant with my interpretation of the priest and agent episode in Chapter Five above.

91. My wife, who was raised in an Irish Catholic neighborhood and parochial school in New England, was a "Child of Mary" and remembers having to wear blue — Mary's color — to remind her of this special dedication. When her behavior did not conform to expectations, she was told, "Is that a way for a Child of Mary to act?"

92. See O'Dwyer (1988) for a useful account of Marian Devotion in Ireland, including folk traditions.

93. Guidebooks and other devotional literature describe the face and hands as being coated with a thin layer of wax. However thin, it is totally opaque and the face a good deal more beautiful (to my eyes) than Bernadette in life, much less in death. The practice of covering up such saintly "incorrupt" remains has been carried on elsewhere as the expectations and aesthetic of pilgrims has changed. Another exam-ple is Santa Lucia in Venice.

94. Marina Warner has an interesting description of Bernadette:

> At Nevers, where she died, Bernadette lies in a glass case. She is dressed in her nun's habit, and reclines on sumptuous lace pillows, with a rosary threaded through her clasped hands. Her expression is very serene. Her fingernails are painted and her face powdered and rouged. Yet it would have been far greater tribute to that brief, pain-wracked life to have been buried beyond the em-balmer's reach or inquisitive eyes. (Warner 1978: 102)

Chapter Eight

95. Fasting, I found there and at Medjugorje, was interpreted in the Lenten fashion simply to mean giving up something liked — like candy, for example — sweets being more a draw than alcohol for most of the women.

96. There was a nearly unvarying ritual followed:

> "Mary — now — give us a song"
> "I will not — I haven't any voice a'tall.a."
> "You're great."
> "I wouldn't remember the words."
> "Go ahead now — oblige the company."

That's the short version. Some would show more reluctance, need more urg-ing. But any so requested would usually perform. If it were a private party, a "big night" in someone's kitchen, everyone would nearly have to play, sing, or recite, no matter how poorly or well. All of which is to say that there is great familiarity not only with music but with the act of performing it.

97. There is also a tradition — traces of which seem less visible today — of "wise women," a standard European type whose power also derives from inherited status and acquired knowledge. There are local stories that pit such women against priests, and in this genre (as in another that brings fairies into opposition with clerics) the priest often loses the battle. It is interesting to note the priests' view of this sort of heterodoxy as dangerous — involving, as it does, a competitor.

98. For a very different prayer group in a different social context see B. Szuche-wycz (1989).

References

UNPUBLISHED DOCUMENTS

DUBLIN

State Paper Office
Outrage Papers 1825–1850
    Land Commission
    1921. Record 10032. Musgrave Estate
Trinity Library. University College Dublin Trinity
    Congested Districts Board. 1893. Baseline Reports
University College Dublin
    National Folklore Archives (NFA)
    O hEochaidh, Sean. 1945. Notebook of Priest Stories (in Irish)
Dublin Four Courts
    National School Applications 1831–
National Library of Ireland
    O'Donovan, John. 1838. Ordnance Survey Letters. Mss.
    Ewing, John. 1823. "Statistical Return for Glencolumbkille." Mss.
    Musgrave Estate Papers. Mss. Collection
    Lawrence Photograph Collection
    Ordnance Survey Townland Maps: 1836, 1903. County Donegal
Marianella House, Redemptorist Library
    Donlon, K. 1971. "Mission Seminar." Conference typescript
    Mission Notebooks

BELFAST

Public Record Office, Musgrave Estate Maps and Rolls

ARMAGH

Armagh Archdiocesan Archives. Bishop's House. Mss. Letters

RAPHOE

Raphoe Diocesan Archives, 1840 — 1909. Bishop's House

DERRY

Public Library. *Derry Journal* (microfilm)

OFFICIAL PUBLICATIONS

PARLIAMENTARY PAPERS (microfiche)

Census of Ireland, 1841–1891
Correspondence and Accounts Relating to Measures for the Relief of Suffering
    Arising from Scarcity in Ireland. 1836
Devon Commission: Inquiry into the Occupation of Land in Ireland. 1844
Griffith Valuation of Tenements. 1858
Papers Relating to the Relief of Distress and State of Unions, In Ireland. 1848
Poor Law: Inquiries into the State of the Poorer Classes in Ireland. 1834
Report of Inquiry into Famine Relief. 1847
Schools Reports: Commissioners of Irish Education. 1825, 1834, 1857–58

PUBLISHED SOURCES

Adomnan
    [1961]   *Adomnan's Life of Columba*. Ed. with translation and notes by
                  Alan Orr Anderson and Marjorie Ogilvie Anderson. London:
                  Thomas Nelson and Sons.
Althusser, Louis
    1971   "Ideology and Ideological State Apparatuses (Notes Towards
                  an Investigation)." In *Lenin and Philosophy and Other Essays*.
                  Trans. Ben Brewster. London: New Left Books.
Annals of the Four Masters.
    [1966]   *Annala Rioghachta Eireann*, Ed. with a translation by John
                  O'Donovan. Orig. Pub. 1854. New York: AMS, 1966.
Anonymous
    1933.   *Two Hundred Years with the Redemptorists: 1732–1932*. Dublin:
                  Sign of the Three Candles.
Archivium Hibernicum, or Irish Historical Records
    1915   Annual. Shannon: Irish University Press.

Arensberg, Conrad
    1959 [1936]   *The Irish Countryman: An Anthropological Study*. New York: Peter
                   Smith. Reprint 1988, Prospect Heights, IL: Waveland Press.
Arensberg, Conrad M. and Solon Kimball
    1968 [1940]   *Family and Community in Ireland*. 2nd ed. Cambridge, MA:
                   Harvard University Press.
Ariès, Philippe
    1981   *The Hour of Our Death*. Trans. Helen Weaver. New York: Alfred
                   Knopf.
Asad, Talal
    1983   "Anthropological Conceptions of Religion: Reflections on
                   Geertz." *Man* 18: 237–59.
Badone, Ellen
    1990   "Breton Folklore of Anticlericalism." In *Religious Orthodoxy and
                   Popular Faith in European Society*, ed. Ellen Badone. Princeton,
                   NJ: Princeton University Press.
Bakhtin, Mikhail
    1984 [1965]   *Rabelais and His World*. Trans. Helene Iswolsky. Orig. pub.
                   1965. Bloomington: Indiana University Press.
Ball, Anne
    1983   *Modern Saints: Their Lives and Faces*. Rockford, IL: Tan Books.
Bax, Mart
    1987a   "Religious Regimes and State Formation: Towards a Research
                   Perspective." *Anthropological Quarterly* 60, 1: 1–11.
    1987b   "Religious Regimes in Medjugorje." Paper presented at con-
                   ference in honor of Norbert Elias, Free University, Amster-
                   dam, June.
Bossy, John
    1970   "The Counter-Reformation and the People of Catholic Eu-
                   rope." *Past and Present* 47: 51–70.
    1985   *Christianity in the West, 1400–1700*. Oxford: Oxford University
                   Press.
Bourdieu, Pierre
    1977   *Outline of a Theory of Practice*. Trans. Richard Nice. Cambridge:
                   Cambridge University Press.
Brady, John
    1971   *The Church Under the Penal Code: A History of Irish Catholicism*,
                   vol. 4. ed. Patrick Corish. Dublin: Gill and Macmillan.
Bradshaw, Brendan
    1989   "The Wild and Woolly West: Early Irish Christianity and Latin
                   Orthodoxy." In Bradshaw, *The Churches, Ireland and the Irish*.
                   Oxford: Basil Blackwell.
Brandes, Stanley
    1980   *Metaphors of Masculinity: Sex and Status in Andalusian Folklore*.
                   Philadelphia: University of Pennsylvania Press.

Brettel, Caroline
  1990   "The Priest and His People: The Contractual Basis for Re-
          ligious Practice in Rural Portugal." In *Religious Orthodoxy and
          Popular Faith in European Society*, ed. Ellen Badone. Princeton,
          NJ: Princeton University Press.

Brown, Peter
  1981   *The Cult of the Saints: Its Rise and Function in Latin Christianity*.
          London: SCM Press.

Buchanan, R. H.
  1970   "Rural Settlement in Ireland." In *Irish Geographical Studies in
          Honour of E. Estyn Evans*, ed. Nicholas Stephens and Robin E.
          Glasscock. Belfast: Queen's University Press.

Buckley, Daniel CSSR
  1948   *The Miraculous Picture of the Mother of Succour*. Cork: Mercier
          Press.

Burke, Peter
  1978   *Popular Culture in Early Modern Europe*. New York: New York
          University Press.

Carroll, Michael P.
  1986   *The Cult of the Virgin Mary: Psychological Origins*. Princeton,
          NJ: Princeton University Press.

Chartier, Roger
  1987   "Texts, Printing, Readings" In *The New Cultural History: Essays*,
          ed. Lynn Hunt. Berkeley: University of California Press.

Christian, William A. Jr.
  1972   *Person and God in a Spanish Valley*. New York: Seminar Press.
  1981   *Local Religion in Sixteenth Century Spain*. Princeton, NJ: Prince-
          ton University Press.
  1984   "Religious Apparitions and the Cold War in Southern Europe.
          In *Religion, Power, and Protest in Local Communities: The North-
          ern Shore of the Mediterranean*, ed. Eric Wolf. Berlin and New
          York: Mouton.

Clark, Samuel
  1979   *Social Origins of the Irish Land War*. Princeton, NJ: Princeton
          University Press.

Conaghan, Charles
  1974   *History and Antiquities of Killybegs*. Ballyshannon, Ire.: The Do-
          negal Democrat.

Conaghan, Pat
  1989   *Bygones: New Horizons on the History of Killybegs*. Killybegs, Ire.:
          published by author.

Connolly, Sean
  1982   *Priest and People in Pre-Famine Ireland*. Dublin: Gill and Mac-
          millan.

Corish, Patrick
  1985   *The Irish Catholic Experience: A Historical Survey*. Dublin: Gill
          and Macmillan.

Coulson, John
   1957   *The Saints: A Concise Biographical Dictionary*. New York: Guild Press.

Cucchiari, Salvatore
   1988   " 'Adapted for Heaven': Culture and Conversion in Western Sicily." *American Ethnologist* 15: 417–41.

Cuimhne Coluimcille: Being a Record of the Celebration held at Gartan on the 9th of June, 1897: the 13th Centennial of St. Columba
   1898   Dublin: M. H. Gill.

Cullen, Louis
   1981   *The Emergence of Modern Ireland: 1600–1900*. Dublin: Gill and Macmillan; New York: Holmes and Meier

Cutileiro, Jose
   1971   *A Portuguese Rural Society*. Oxford: Clarendon Press.

Daly, Mary
   1979   "The Development of the National School System, 1831–40." In *Studies in Irish History*, ed. Arthur Cosgrove and Donal Mc-Cartney. Dublin: University College Dublin Press.

Donlevy, Andrew
   1848 [1742, 1822] *The Catechism: or, Christian Doctrine, by way of Question and Answer*. Dublin: T. Courtney.

Donnelly, James
   1992   "Knock Shrine." Paper presented to American Conference for Irish Studies, Galway.

Douglas, Mary
   1966   *Purity and Danger: An Analysis of Concepts of Taboo and Pollution*. New York: Praeger.

Dublin University Magazine
   1858   "The State of Donegal—Gweedore and Cloughaneely." 51, 306: 731–41.
   1860   "Wanderings in Ireland: Northwest." 56, 333: 259–67.

Dun, Finlay
   1881   *Landlords and Tenants in Ireland*. London: Longmans, Green.

Dunne, Tom, ed.
   1987   *The Writer as Witness: Literature as Historical Evidence*. Cork: Cork University Press.

Elias, Norbert
   1978, 1982 *The Civilizing Process*. 2 vols. trans. Edmund Jephcott. New York: Pantheon Books.

Emmons, David
   1989   *The Butte Irish: Class and Ethnicity in an American Mining Town*. Urbana: University of Illinois Press.

Evans, Emyr Estyn
   1939   "Some Survivals of the Irish Open Field System." *Geography* 24: 24–36.

1942   *Irish Heritage: The Landscape, the People, and Their Work*. Dundalk: Dundalgan Press.
1964   "Ireland and Atlantic Europe." *Geographische Zeitschrift* 52, 3.

Evans-Pritchard, E. E.
1965 [1936]   *Witchcraft, Oracles and Magic Among the Azande*. Oxford: Clarendon Press.

Feldman, Allen
1991   *Formations of Violence: The Narrative of the Body and Political Terror in Northern Ireland*. Chicago: University of Chicago Press.

Foucault, Michel
1972   *The Archaeology of Knowledge*. New York: Pantheon Press.
1980   *Knowledge/Power: Selected Interviews and Other Writings*. Ed. Colin Gordon. New York: Pantheon Press.

Gallagher, Bishop James
1819   *Seventeen Irish Sermons, In an Easy and Familiar Stile*. Dublin: W. Pickering.

Gallagher, Patrick (the Cope)
1979   *My Story*. Dungloe, Ire.: Templecrone Co-op Society.

Geertz, Clifford
1973   "Religion as a Cultural System." In Geertz, *The Interpretation of Cultures: Selected Essays*. New York: Basic Books.

Geisendorfer, James V.
1977   *Directory of Religious Organizations in the United States of America*. Wilmington, NC: McGrath.

Gibbon, Peter and Chris Curtin
1978   "The Stem Family in Ireland." *Comparative Studies in Society and History* 20,3: 429–53.

Giblin, Cathaldus, O.F.M.
1980   *The Diocese of Raphoe (1773–1805): Documents illustrating the History of the Diocese from the Congressi volumes in the Archives of the Congreg of Prop. Fide, Rome*. Killiney, Co. Dublin: Dún Mhuire.

Gilmore, David
1984   "Andalusian Anticlericalism: An Eroticized Rural Protest." *Anthropology* 8,1: 31–44.

Giraldus Cambrensis
[1905]   *The Historical Works of Giraldus Cambrensis*. Ed. Thomas Wright. London: George Bell & Sons. Reprint 1968 New York: AMS Press.

Glassie, Henry
1983   *Passing the Time in Ballymenone: Cultural History of an Irish Community*. Philadelphia: University of Pennsylvania Press.

Goldsmith, Oliver
1949   "The Deserted Village." In *The Complete Poetical Works of Oliver Goldsmith*. London, New York: Oxford University Press.

Graham, Jean M.
  1970   "South-West Donegal in the Seventeenth Century." *Irish Geography* 6, 2: 136–52.
Grier, Katherine C.
  1988   *Culture and Comfort: People, Parlors, and Upholstery 1850–1930.* Rochester, NY: Strong Museum.
Halbwachs, Maurice
  1992 [1952]   *On Collective Memory.* Ed., trans., and with an Introduction by Lewis A. Coser. Chicago: University of Chicago Press.
Harbison, Peter
  1991   *Pilgrimage in Ireland: The Monuments and the People.* Syracuse, NY: Syracuse University Press.
Hardy, Philip Dixon
  1840   *The Holy Wells of Ireland, Containing an Authentic Account of Those Various Places of Pilgrimage and Penance Which are Still Annually Visited by Thousands of the Roman Catholic Peasantry.* Dublin: Hardy and Walker.
Hélias, Pièrre-Jakez
  1978   *The Horse of Pride: Life in a Breton Village.* Trans. June Guicharnaud. New Haven, CT: Yale University Press.
Hoppen, K. Theodore
  1984   *Elections, Politics, and Society in Ireland, 1832–1885.* Oxford, UK: Clarendon Press.
Hosp, Edward
  1960.   "First Redemptorist Missions in Ireland." *Spicilegium Historicum* 7, 2: 453–85.
Hughes, Kathleen
  1960   "The Changing Theory and Practice of Irish Pilgrimage." *Journal of Ecclesiastical History* 11: 143–51.
Hunt, Lynn, ed.
  1987   *The New Cultural History: Essays.* Berkeley: University of California Press.
Hyde, Douglas
  1972 [1906]   *The Religious Songs of Connacht.* New York: Barnes and Noble.
Inglis, Tom
  1987   *Moral Monopoly: The Catholic Church in Modern Irish Society.* Dublin: Gill and Macmillan.
The Irish Catholic Directory, Almanac and Registry. Annual. Dublin: Burns, Oates.
Keenan, Desmond
  1983.   *The Catholic Church in Nineteenth-Century Ireland: A Sociological Study.* Dublin: Gill and Macmillan.
Kenny, Michael
  1960   "Patterns of Patronage in Spain." *Anthropological Quarterly* 33 (January): 14–23.

Lacey, Brian
    1983   *Archaeological Survey of County Donegal*. Lifford, Ire.: Donegal County Council.

The Landowners of Ireland: An Alphabetical List of the Owners of Estates of 500 Acres or 500 Valuation and Upwards in Ireland.
    1878   Dublin: Hodges, Foster, Figgis.

Larkin, Emmet
    1972   "The Devotional Revolution in Ireland, 1850–75." *American Historical Review*. 77, 3: 625–52.
    1980   *The Making of the Roman Catholic Church in Ireland, 1850–1860*. Chapel Hill: University of North Carolina Press.

Le Goff, Jacques
    1984   *The Birth of Purgatory*. Trans. Arthur Goldhammer. Chicago: University of Chicago Press.

Leslie, Shane
    1932   *Saint Patrick's Purgatory: A Record from History and Literature*. London: Burns Oates and Washbourne.

Liguori, Alfonso Maria de'
    1867   *The Mission Book: A Manual of Instruction and Prayers Adapted to Preserve the Fruits of the Mission*. New York: O'Shea.

Logan, Patrick
    1980   *The Holy Wells of Ireland*. London: Colin Smythe.

Mac a' Bhaird, Seaghain (John Ward)
    1904   *Epistles and Gospels for Sundays and Holidays*. Trans. into Irish by John C. Ward. Killybegs, Ire.: John Ward.
    1909   *Leabhar Filidheachta fä Choinne na Scoil*. Killybegs, Ire.: John Ward.

McCourt, Desmond
    1954   "Infield and Outfield in Ireland." *Economic History Review* 7: 369–376.
    1955   "The Rundale System in Donegal: Its Distribution and Decline." *Donegal Annual* 5, 3: 47–60.
    1971   "The Dynamic Quality of Irish Rural Settlement." In *Man and His Environment: Essays Presented to Emyr Estyn Evans*, ed. R. H. Buchanan, Emyrs Jones, and Desmond McCourt. New York: Barnes and Noble.

MacDevitt, Rev. James
    1866   *The Donegal Highlands*. London: A. Murray.

MacDevitt, Rev. John
    1880   *The Most Reverend James MacDevitt, D.D. Bishop of Raphoe. A Memoir*. Dublin: M.H. Gill and Son.

MacDonell, Diane
    1986   *Theories of Discourse: An Introduction*. Oxford: Basil Blackwell.

McDyer, Canon James
    1982   *Father McDyer of Glencolumbkille: An Autobiography*. Dingle: Brandon Press.

MacGabhann, Mici
  1959   *Rotha Mór an tSaoil*. Baile Átha Cliath: Foilseachain Naisunta
              Tta.
McGill, Lochlann
  1992   *In Conall's Footsteps*. Dingle: Brandon Press.
McGill, Patrick J.
  1974   *History of the Parish of Ardara*. Ballyshannon: Donegal Demo-
              crat.
  1975   "Five Donegal Historians of Last Century." *Donegal Annual* 14,
              1: 53–65.
McGinley, Thomas Colin [Kinnfaela]
  1867   *The Cliff Scenery of South-Western Donegal*. Derry: Derry Journal.
McGlinchey, Charles
  1985   *The Last of the Name*. Edited and with an Introduction by Brian
              Friel. Belfast and Dover, NH: Blackstaff Press.
McGuire, Canon Edward
  1920   *History of the Diocese of Raphoe*. Dublin: Browne and Nolan.
McGuire, Meredith
  1982   *Pentecostal Catholics: Power, Charisma, and Order in a Religious
              Movement*. Philadelphia: Temple University Press.
McKenna, Lambert, SJ
  1931   *Philip Bocht O hUiginn*. Dublin: Talbot Press.
Marx, Karl
  1886   *Capital*. Trans. S. Moore. New York: Humboldt.
Messenger, John
  1969   *Inis Beag: Isle of Irland*. New York: Holt, Rinehart, and Win-
              ston.
Mooney, Canice OFM
  1952   *Devotional Writings of the Irish Franciscans, 1224–1950*. Killiney:
              Four Masters Press.
Moore, Thomas
  1979 [1929] *The Poetical Works of Thomas Moore*. New York: AMS Press
              (reprint of Oxford University Press ed.).
Mould, Daphne
  1957   *Irish Pilgrimage*. New York: Devin-Adair.
The New Catholic Encyclopedia
  1967–79   New York: McGraw-Hill.
Nolan, Mary Lee
  1983   "Irish Pilgrimage: The Different Tradition." *Annals of the Asso-
              ciation of American Geographers* 73, 3: 421–38.
O'Donnell, P.
  1978   "Foundation in Limmerick." *Search* 2: 9–18.
  1981   "Before the Redemptorists." *Search* 12: 28–38.
O'Dwyer, Peter, O. Carm
  1988   *Mary: A History of Devotion in Ireland*. Dublin: Four Courts
              Press.

Ó hÉalai, Pádraig
    1974–1976   "Moral Values in Irish Religious Tales." *Béaloideas* 42–44: 176–212.
    1977   "Cumhacht an tSagairt sa Bhéaloideas." *Léachtaí Cholm Cille* 8: 109–31.
Ó hEochaidh, Seán
    1955   *Sean-Chainnt Theilinn*. Bhaile Átha Cliath: Institiúid Árd-Léighinn Bhaile Átha Cliath.
Ó hÓgáin, Dáithí
    1982   *An File: Staidéar ar Osnádúrthacht na Filíochta sa Traidisiún Gaelach*. Baile Átha Cliath: Oifig an tSoláthair.
Ó Muirgheasa, Énri
    1936   "The Holy Wells of Donegal." *Béaloideas* 6, 2: 143–62.
O'Shea, James
    1983   *Priest, Politics and Society in Post-Famine Ireland*. Dublin: Wolfhound Press.
Ó Tuathaigh, Gearóid
    1972   *Ireland Before the Famine*. Dublin: Gill and Macmillan.
Otway, Caesar
    1839 [1827]   *Sketches in Ireland: Descriptive of Interesting Portions of the Counties of Donegal, Cork, and Kerry*. Dublin: Wm. Curry, Jun.
Pêcheux, Michel
    1983   "Ideology: Fortress or Paradoxical Space." In *Rethinking Ideology: A Marxist Debate*, ed. Sakari Hanninen and Leena Paldán. New York: International General.
Pococke, R.
    1891 [1752]   *Pococke's Tour in Ireland in 1752*. Dublin: Hodges, Figgis.
Price, Liam
    1941   "Glencolumbkille, County Donegal, and its Early Christian Cross-slabs." *Journal of the Royal Society of Antiquaries of Ireland* 71: 71–88.
Proudfoot, V.B.
    1959   "Clachans in Ireland." *Gwerin* 2, 3: 110–22.
Reigelhaupt, Joyce
    1973   "Festas and Padres: The Organization of Religious Action in a Portuguese Parish." *American Anthropologist* 75: 835–52.
    1984   "Popular Anti-Clericalism and Religiosity in Pre-1974 Portugal." In *Religion, Power and Protest in Local Communities: The North Shore of the Mediterranean*, ed. Eric R. Wolf. New York: Mouton.
Scheper-Hughes, Nancy
    1979   *Saints, Scholars, and Schizophrenics: Mental Illness in Rural Ireland*. Berkeley: University of California Press.
Schneider, Jane
    1990   "Spirits and the Spirit of Capitalism." In *Religious Orthodoxy and Popular Faith in European Society*, ed. Ellen Badone. Princeton, NJ: Princeton University Press.

Shanklin, Eugenia
    1985   *Donegal's Changing Traditions*. New York: Gordon and Breach.

Silverman, Sydel
    1965   "Patronage and Community-Nation Relations in Central Italy." *Ethnology* 4, 2: 172–89.
    1975   *Three Bells of Civilization: The Life of an Italian Hill Town*. New York: Columbia University Press.

Simmel, Georg
    1950   "The Stranger." In *The Sociology of Georg Simmel*, trans. and ed. Kurt Wolff. Glencoe, IL: Free Press.

Simms, J.G.
    1971   "The Ulster Plantation in County Donegal." *Donegal Annual* 10, 1: 3–14.

Smith, Wilfred Cantwell
    1963   *The Meaning and End of Religion*. New York: Macmillan.

Stebbing, George
    1924   *The Redemptorists*. London: Burns, Oates and Washburn.

Stephens, Rev. James
    1872   *Illustrated Handbook of the Scenery and Antiquities Southwest Donegal*. Killybegs, Ire.: McGlashan and Gill.

Szuchewycz, B.
    1989   " 'The Growth is in the Silence': The Meanings of Silence in the Irish Catholic Charismatic Movement." In *Ireland from Below: Social Change and Local Communities*, ed. Chris Curtin and Thomas N. Wilson. Galway: Galway University Press.

Taylor, Lawrence J.
    1980a   "Colonialism and Community Structure in the West of Ireland." *Ethnohistory* 27, 2: 169–81.
    1980b   "The Merchant in Peripheral Ireland: A Case from Donegal." *Anthropology* 4, 2: 63–76.
    1981   "Man the Fisher: Fishing and Community in a Rural Irish Settlement. *American Ethnologist* 8, 4: 774–88.
    1985   "The Priest and the Agent: Social Drama and Class Consciousness in the West of Ireland." *Comparative Studies in Society and History* 27, 4: 696–712.
    1987   "The River Would Run Red with Blood: Commons and Community in Donegal." In *The Question of the Commons: The Culture and Ecology of Communal Resources*, ed. Bonnie McCay and James Acheson. Tucson: University of Arizona Press.
    1989a   "The Mission: An Anthropological View of an Irish Religious Occasion." In *Ireland From Below: Social Change and Local Communities*, ed. Chris Curtin and Tom Wilson. Galway: Galway University Press.
    1989b   "Bas i nEirinn: The Cultural Construction of Death in Ireland." *Anthropological Quarterly* 62, 4: 175–87.
    1990a   "Stories of Power, Powerful Stories: the Drunken Priest in Donegal" In *Religious Orthodoxy and Popular Faith in European*

Society, ed. Ellen Badone. Princeton, NJ: Princeton University Press.

1990b   "The Healing Mass: Regimes and Fields of Religious Experience in Ireland." *Archives des Sciences Sociales des Religions* 71: 93–111.

1992a   "The Languages of Belief: Nineteenth Century Religious Discourse in Southwest Donegal." In *Approaching the Past: Historical Anthropology Through Irish Case Studies*, ed. Marilyn Silverman and P. H. Gulliver. New York: Columbia University Press.

1992b   "The Irish." In *Encyclopedia of World Cultures: Volume IV: Europe*, ed. Linda Bennett. Boston: G. K. Hall.

1993   "Peter's Pense: Catholic Discourse and Nationalism in Nineteenth Century Ireland." *Journal of the History of European Ideas* 16, 1–3: 103–7.

Thompson, Stith
1955–1958   *Motif Index of Folk Literature*. Bloomington: Indiana University Press.

Tucker, Vincent
1984   *Community Development Through Co-operatives: A Case Study of Glencolumbkille in the Northwest of Ireland*. Ph.D Thesis, Washington University.

1989   "State and Community: A Case Study of Glencolumbkille." In *Ireland from Below: Social Change and Local Communities*, ed. Chris Curtin and Thomas N. Wilson. Galway: University of Galway Press.

Turner, Victor
1968   *The Drums of Affliction*. Oxford: Clarendon Press.
1969   *The Ritual Process: Structure and Anti-Structure*. Chicago: Aldine.
1982   "Social Dramas and Stories about Them." In Turner *From Ritual to Theatre: The Human Seriousness of Play*. New York: Performing Arts Journal Publications.

Turner, Victor and Edith Turner
1978   *Image and Pilgrimage in Christian Culture*. New York: Columbia University Press.

Van Gennep, Arnold
1960   *The Rites of Passage*. Trans. Monika B. Vizedom and Gabrielle L. Caffee. Chicago: University of Chicago Press.

Vaughan, William
1983   *Sin, Sheep and Scotsmen: John George Adair and the Derryveagh Evictions, 1861*. Belfast: Appletree Press.

Verrips, Kitty.
1987   "Noblemen, Farmers and Labourers: A Civilizing Offensive in a Dutch Village." *Netherlands Journal of Sociology* 23, 1: 3–16.

Warner, Marina
1983 [1976]   *Alone of All Her Sex: The Myth and the Cult of the Virgin Mary*. New York: Vintage Books.

Weber, Eugen
    1976   *Peasants into Frenchmen: The Modernization of Rural France, 1870–1914*. Stanford, CA: Stanford University Press.
Weber, Max
    1963   *The Sociology of Religion*. New York: Beacon Press.
    1968   *Economy and Society*. Ed. G. Roth and C. Wittich. New York: Bedminster Press.
Wolf, Eric R.
    1956   "Aspects of Group Relations in a Complex Society: Mexico." *American Anthropologist* 58, 6: 1065–78.
    1966   *Peasants*. Englewood Cliffs, NJ: Prentice-Hall.
Young, Arthur
    1892   *Young's Tour in Ireland (1777–1779)*. Ed. A. W. Hutton. London: George Bell and Sons.

Index

This book has been set in Linotron Galliard. Galliard was designed for Mergenthaler in 1978 by Matthew Carter. Galliard retains many of the features of a sixteenth-century typeface cut by Robert Granjon but has some modifications that give it a more contemporary look.

Printed on acid-free paper.